CAMBRIDGE STUDIES IN
INTERNATIONAL RELATIONS: 1

SOVIET POLICY TOWARDS JAPAN

T0382539

CAMBRIDGE STUDIES IN INTERNATIONAL RELATIONS

Editorial Board

Cambridge Studies in International Relations is a joint initiative of Cambridge University Press and the British International Studies Association (BISA). The series will include a wide range of material, from undergraduate textbooks and surveys to research-based monographs and collaborative volumes. The central aim of the series will be to publish quite simply the best new scholarship in International Studies from throughout the world, including both Europe and North America.

SOVIET POLICY TOWARDS JAPAN

An analysis of trends in the 1970s and 1980s

MYLES L. C. ROBERTSON

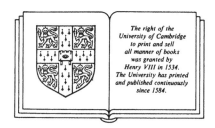

The right of the
University of Cambridge
to print and sell
all manner of books
was granted by
Henry VIII in 1534.
The University has printed
and published continuously
since 1584.

CAMBRIDGE UNIVERSITY PRESS

Cambridge

New York   New Rochelle   Melbourne   Sydney

CAMBRIDGE UNIVERSITY PRESS
Cambridge, New York, Melbourne, Madrid, Cape Town, Singapore,
São Paulo, Delhi, Dubai, Tokyo

Cambridge University Press
The Edinburgh Building, Cambridge CB2 8RU, UK

Published in the United States of America by Cambridge University Press, New York

www.cambridge.org
Information on this title: www.cambridge.org/9780521125932

First published 1988
This digitally printed version 2009

A catalogue record for this publication is available from the British Library

Library of Congress Cataloguing in Publication data
Robertson, Myles L. C. (Myles Leonard Caie), 1958–
Soviet policy towards Japan: an analysis of trends in the
1970s and 1980s / by Myles L. C. Robertson.
    p.   cm. – (Cambridge studies in international relations: 1)
Bibliography:
Includes index.
ISBN 0 521 35131 6
1. Soviet Union – Foreign relations – Japan.
2. Japan – Foreign relations – Soviet Union.
3. Soviet Union – Foreign relations – 1975–
4. Japan – Foreign relations – 1945–
I. Title   II. Series
DK67.5.J3R63   1988
327.47052 – dc 19   87-33835   CIP

ISBN 978-0-521-35131-7 Hardback
ISBN 978-0-521-12593-2 Paperback

CONTENTS

TABLES

PREFACE

The principal prompting behind this research was a belief – subsequently verified in many places – that, given what we might assume to be their importance, Soviet–Japanese relations do not seem to rate an accordingly high coverage in either Western or Soviet international affairs literature. An associated belief which prompted investigation was that what comment did exist, with few exceptions, seemed to be of a 'broad brush' nature. Moreover, many Western sources seemed to be inclined to present much the same story whether it concerned economics, the regional military situation, or overall political relations. This observation on its own was a worthy reason to inspire a closer examination of the available facts.[1]

A further shortcoming of the available literature was a lack of a comprehensive evaluation of the Soviet standpoint *vis-à-vis* Japan. Neither Soviet day-to-day contact with the Japanese nor the significance of Japan to the Soviets were detailed.[2] Consequently the work herein examines from a Soviet viewpoint the period in relations with Japan from the early 1970s to 1987, with an emphasis on the latter 1970s to 1985.

As we have alluded to above, one of our original considerations had been that most comment on Soviet–Japanese relations was of a general nature. In particular this had taken the form of a repetition of emphasis on specific incidents – the China treaty, 1977 fishery negotiations, the northern island dispute – followed by an outline of general Soviet policy principles *vis-à-vis* north east Asia.[3]

In the case of economic relations, the emphasis had been placed on repetition of the scale of contracts between the two nations with no attempt to place them in a comparative context. Noticeably absent from Western and Japanese studies was any attempt to place Japan in an ideological context as seen by the Soviets. This point has been verified by the work herein whereby the only references to the ideological influences which might be behind Soviet relations with Japan which this author has come across amounted to a handful of paragraphs scattered in a number of articles or chapters. The largest part of this work concentrates upon Soviet ideological concerns and Japan, and in doing so, hopes to begin to rectify the deficiency which exists in this area.

Concerning ideology the questions to which it was hoped to find answers were, for example: what has been the general Soviet ideological approach to relations with the West in the 1970s and 1980s and how and where does Japan fit in to those images? What is the ideological-based image that the Soviets have of Japan itself? What, if any, are the influences – and in what areas – that ideology has had on Soviet policy towards Japan?

A more general question posed was to what extent the Soviets 'understand' Japan, the Japanese and the Japanese governmental systems. Though in part a rather abstract concern, an attempt has been made to supply an estimation of this.

The approach taken in this work has been to analyse Soviet policy towards Japan in terms of delineating trends of that policy and the intention is not to become overly concerned with deriving policy from attention to the course of major incidents in relations with Japan. This, as argued above, is a criticism levelled at other work in this area, i.e. that too much attention and significance has been given to events (especially the economic) at the expense of the wider questions. We hope that this has been rectified in the work presented without swinging to the other extreme and neglecting detail when appropriate.

The approach taken in our investigation has been to divide the analysis into four major sections: Soviet ideology and Japan, Soviet–Japanese economic relations, the Soviet military and Japan, and Soviet policy towards Japan. A short introductory section outlines some important traditional and historical influences relevant to understanding Soviet approaches to Japan. There is also a small appendix on Soviet–Japanese fishing.

It is recognised that such a compartmentalisation is artificial. However for purposes of manageability it has merits in that it allows for trends in particular fields of Soviet–Japanese relations to be highlighted in order that they can be drawn together to produce a final analysis. One further point must be made at the outset concerning the chosen compartmentalised approach. It should be emphasised that this is a study of *Soviet* policy and processes; the external rhetoric, actions, national styles of other non-Soviet players have been considered only in the context of their influence on the Soviet position or on Soviet action. This study is not concerned with assessing the rationales, merits or weaknesses of Japanese policy or any other state's policy *per se* but only with the Soviet Union. Any study set in north east Asia must involve not only the Soviets but Japan, China and the United States. It was believed that the great danger, therefore, was to wander into expositions of other nations' strategies which were not entirely relevant to the issues which we wish to illustrate by aspects of our work. Given that the Soviet concern here is with Japan, when necessary certain aspects of the Japanese policy process or of Japan itself or of Japanese national traits have been set-out at length.

The short introduction outlines traditional and historical themes which can be seen to run through Russian and Soviet policies towards Japan. It is necessary to draw these out and point to their relevance as factors which should be seen as important elements in influencing policy, not least as in themselves they are not necessarily obvious influences due to their mainly abstract nature.

The first chapter consists of an examination of the influences of ideology on Soviet policy and is broken down into an analysis of Soviet ideological views of Japan at three levels, the global, the regional (Pacific) and of Japan as a social–political structure. Soviet ideological comment on the question of Japanese remilitarisation is also outlined. The salience of ideology to Soviet policy formulation throughout the 1970s is also detailed by explaining that within the Soviet Union during these years a debate, with ramifications for internal politics and external affairs, took place over how the changes which were being forced on Soviet society by the 'scientific and technical revolution' and the trends of modernisation could be incorporated into the body of Marxist–Leninist ideology. Aspects of this debate impinged upon the conduct of trading relations with the capitalist nations as the limits of contact with capitalism were questioned. As one of the major planks of Soviet relations with Japan concerns trade relations, this had direct relevance for our study.

Chapter 2 focuses on the issues of Soviet–Japanese trade. In the initial section the basic framework of the trading arrangements between the two nations is set-out; the trade contracts, the concentration of trade on energy-related materials and the development of Siberia, the role of coastal trading, and the significance of trade overall as seen by both parties. The second section of this chapter involves a closer examination of these trading arrangements and concludes by disputing the conventional wisdom. The overall value of Soviet trade with Japan is put in context by comparison with Soviet trade with other leading Western nations. The influences of the debate within the Soviet leadership over the extent and necessity of trade contact with the capitalist nations (part of the wider debate over ideological orthodoxy) are speculated upon and an impact on contact with Japan estimated.

The aim of these investigations into the trade relationship was to gauge what importance was attached to the scale of trade by both parties and to estimate how the structure of trade had changed (if at all) throughout the time-frame of the study. It was also hoped to assess how the trading relationship has been influenced by political factors and to decide if the two nations assigned trade the same importance as a factor in overall relations.

Chapter 3 deals with the Soviet military and Japan. Militarily, the Soviet presence in north east Asia has been growing in qualitative terms through the 1970s. The problems created for Japan as a result of this growth of military strength as well as the possible uses to which it could be put by the Soviets in any future war in the Far East are examined in this chapter. Initially the military situation which confronts Soviet planners in the Far East and Pacific has been estimated and subsequently possible operational plans for Soviet forces in the region in the event of war are suggested. From these an evaluation is made regarding the question of how powerful – or otherwise – Soviet forces in the region are. There is also an examination of the strengths and weaknesses of the Japanese Self Defence Forces (JSDF); this has been done with the intention of putting the 'threat' from Japan as the Soviets see it into a material context. Certain specific scenarios involving a Soviet war with Japan – the oft-cited 'blockade' and amphibious invasion – are also analysed in depth. This chapter concludes with an assessment of the political uses of Soviet military power against Japan and specifically of the thesis that the Soviets are pursuing a policy of deliberate military coercion *vis-à-vis* Japan.

The fourth chapter of the work seeks to provide an overview of the important trends in Soviet–Japanese relations. It is subdivided into Soviet views of the Japan–China, and Japan–United States relationships. A significant component of this chapter attempts to answer the question of to what degree the Soviets 'understand' Japanese politics and policy processes and indeed to what extent both parties understand each others' national 'styles'. Elements of this latter consideration are illuminated by the study of relevant 'styles' as manifested in negotiations.

The work concludes with some final comments which seek to draw together the main trends illustrated by the research and suggests how, if at all, they can be seen to represent what can be termed a Soviet 'policy' on Japan.

A small appendix considers matters arising from Soviet–Japanese fishing; specifically it seeks to examine the argument that the Japanese fishing industry has suffered due to exclusion from fishing grounds by the Soviets.

ACKNOWLEDGEMENTS

My largest debt of gratitude is to Geoffrey Jukes of the Department of International Relations at the Australian National University and to Paul Dibb, currently Director, Joint Intelligence Organisation, Canberra, Australia. Both provided valuable guidance.

Numerous interviews were conducted in Moscow at Soviet research institutes – the Institute of World Economy and International Relations, the Institute of the United States and Canada, the Institute of Oriental Studies and the Institute of the Far East. In all some fourteen Soviet academics participated in conversations with the author on the subject of Soviet–Japanese relations and Soviet views of Japan. The contribution made by these conversations to my views on the subject have undoubtedly made the final product far better than it otherwise would have been.

Special thanks are due to three individuals. Professor Hiroshi Kimura of the Slavic Research Centre, Hokkaido University, for his help which facilitated my study at the Centre. I am also indebted to J. A. A. Stockwin, Director of the Nissan Institute of Japanese Studies at Oxford, who granted me interviews and access to the Institute library, and who also corrected my more misinformed representations of Japanese politics. Lastly, the contents have benefited substantially from an exchange of views with Mr Malcolm Mackintosh of the Cabinet Office, London.

Officials of the Japan–Soviet trade association in Tokyo were kind enough to grant me interviews and provide me with material which otherwise I should not have been able to obtain.

In the United States, thanks are due to the Russian Centre at Columbia University, New York, for allowing me to utilise their library resources and to V. Petrov of the Sino-Soviet Institute, George Washington University for devoting some of his time to discussing Soviet–Japanese matters with me. I also conducted interviews with officials in the Pentagon responsible for Pacific security affairs and I am indebted to them for clarifying some specific points.

My final thanks are due to Rick Agnew of the Strategic and Defence Studies Centre at the Australian National University for bringing to my attention from time to time pieces of material relevant to my research.

NOTE ON TRANSLATION
AND TRANSLITERATION

The system of transliteration utilised in this work is that of the Library of Congress, United States. Other systems used in works cited have been retained as in the originals. Unless otherwise indicated all translations from Russian are the responsibility of the author.

INTRODUCTION

HISTORICAL FACTORS AND SOVIET POLICY

This study considers Soviet relations with Japan over a specific and limited period. There is, however, a broader context of ideas, themes and problems in Russian and Soviet policies towards Japan which have proven of a recurrent nature. Some of these are creatures of the twentieth century, but others have a lineage stretching back into the nineteenth century or even earlier; and, as we shall see, they crop up again and again as basic building blocks of Russian and Soviet policies. Those that are most directly relevant are discussed in greater detail in the analysis, but the existence of all of them has to be borne in mind as necessary background to the study. Their absolute or relative importance in particular situations cannot always be precisely assessed, but their absence can never be assumed.

Russian expansion into Asia, though punctuated by periods of relative inactivity, has itself been a constant of history since the seventeenth century. Until the late nineteenth century, such expansion mostly took the form of physical acquisition by military means, but by the end of the 1880s emphasis had come to be placed on economic penetration. Jelavich, in an historical study of Russian foreign policy argues that by the 1890s

> The inauguration of an active policy in the East was largely due to the actions of the influential and able minister of finance, Witte, who thought of the question largely in terms of economic gain. Throughout his career in office, he advocated Russian expansion in Asia, but he favoured a policy of gradual economic penetration. He thus came into conflict with those who wished to pursue the same goals quickly and by military means.[1]

Soviet leaders as Marxists are quick to proclaim the salience of the economic, but equally they can clearly be seen to have placed singular emphasis on the military in their dealings with Japan. Thus while the

1

economic–military dichotomy continues, the balance, for the present, has swung in favour of the primacy of the military.

A more obvious and long term constant which has dominated Russian and Soviet thinking and action has been the struggle to exclude outside powers from East Asia and to limit Japanese alignment with any of these outside powers. Russian and Soviet policy has been a catalogue of competition against these foreign entanglements in the region. The legacy of these experiences for the Soviets has been a hard and fast perception of continual interference by outsiders in a region where they view themselves as having a paramount legitimate interest.

In pursuing these related aims the Russians and Soviets have had their successes and failures. The evidence lies in the chequered history of, for example, the 1896 Russian–Japanese condominium over Korea; the Russian and later Soviet moves to arrive at a *modus vivendi* with Japan over Mongolia and China in which, implicitly, the presence of non-regional powers would be minimised, or from the Soviet viewpoint, preferably reduced to zero; the proposed bi-lateral treaty of goodneighbourliness of 1978.

A question related to the idea of limiting Japanese alignment with outside powers concerns the extent to which the Russians and Soviets have perceived Japan as a 'tool' of other powers. The evidence indicates that it is a matter of debate within Soviet policy circles,[2] but it has clearly been a dominant theme in the Russian and Soviet world views from before the 1902 Japan–British partnership, through to Japanese post-war co-operation with the United States. Two comments, separated by fifty years, made by a Soviet ambassador to Japan and by a prominent Soviet military commentator illustrate its abiding relevance.

> It's the Americans; foreign (American) circles want to set Japan and the Soviet Union at loggerheads.[3]

> In preparing for war against Russia, Japan received help from the USA and Britain. In 1902 Japan concluded an alliance with Britain. The USA, striving for mastery of the Pacific, was interested in pressing its influence over Japan and Russia. They lent Japan 500 million dollars specially for war supplies.[4]

A more speculative influence that has coloured both Russian and Soviet approaches has been that Russian expansion in the East has never won the real support of large sections of the Russian public. Nor has the Russian public shown great interest in Japan.[5] In a similar vein the present-day Soviet leadership's plans for the Eastern regions of the

2

country have constantly been beset by the lack of any large scale enthusiasm on the part of the Soviet population to settle in the Eastern regions on a permanent basis. Both Soviet and Russian governments devoted significant attention to overcoming this lack of support, but its absence has had implications in a wider external dimension: Tsarist governments were, and Soviet governments have been, compelled by whatever means to emphasise and reinforce their claim to be a legitimate participator in Asian affairs (lest others perceive Russian ambivalence) and have felt the need to dispel any idea that it is *they* who are somehow the 'interfering outsider'.

A further carry-over from Tsarist policies in the East to contemporary Soviet policies is the problem associated with the economic development of Siberia and the Far East. The Western, and indeed Russian, image of Siberia as a 'treasure house' of resources is an accurate one; however there are major problems associated with the cost of developing these resources. In the short term, or in the case of specific projects, the return on investment may have deemed these projects to be worthwhile but the hard fact for the Tsarist and Soviet governments has been that taken long term over the whole gamut of investment, the development of Transbaikal and the Far East has been, and was, a *burden* on their respective economies.[6]

Before turning to examine the last of the major long term historical trends – the legacy of experience – there are two more recent, but still 'historical', principally Soviet, experiences which have a background influence on Soviet policy formulations. After the United States had supplanted Britain, by the 1920s, as the dominant power in the Western Pacific and set about establishing a network of alliances, the Soviets – more forcibly than had ever been apparent to Tsarist governments – saw themselves as confronted by a barrier stretching across the Pacific rim from the Aleutians to New Zealand. Soviet perception of this can be seen as early as 1925 in a commentary in *Izvestiia* (27 January) which makes the point that in signing the Peking convention with Japan 'the USSR had forged an effective weapon to break the iron ring designed for the Pacific area by the Washington Conference'. We turn to the impact of this perception later in the concluding part of the study.

A recent survey of some Soviet writings on the Soviet intervention in the Far East in the closing stages of the war concludes that the writings 'illuminate Soviet perceptions of a turning point in East Asian history. They also underline the inseparability of the historiography of World War II and contemporary international affairs, notably the USSR's relations with the United States, China, Japan, North Korea and Vietnam.'[7] Despite Soviet umbrage caused by their not receiving the credit they think they deserve for intervening in the Pacific war, for our study of Japanese policy the important point is the *political* significance of historical Soviet actions; 'As a result of the capitulation of Japan, the peoples of China, Korea, and the other countries of South and South East Asia were able to create the favourable conditions for the successful gaining of freedom and independence.'[8]

The Soviet role in liberating Asian nations not only from Japanese but also from Western oppression is a central issue which the Soviets seek to propagate in their current efforts to mobilise opinion against the neo-imperialism of Japan and the United States, as the Soviets proclaim themselves not merely liberator but now guardian and guarantor of that liberation.

Lastly in outlining any major historical influences, which have made a notable contribution to Soviet views on Japan, we must try to come to terms with the most abstract: what are we to make of the general impact of Russian experiences – of all sorts – of Japan and of similar early Soviet experiences, on contemporary Soviet policies?

Russian contacts with Japan date back to the eighteenth century and took on various forms, initially trade, cultural and then of course more of a political complexion. Those contacts were limited. Japan became a military 'problem' by 1900 but after 1905 not again until 1918 and then remained so for another twenty-seven years. While Soviet contact with Japan increased, paradoxically the rigours of Stalinist orthodoxy limited any potential benefits and in some ways was detrimental to achieving a better understanding of the Japanese. This whole experience can be symbolised by the fall and rise (by the mid 1960s) of *Vostokovedenie* within the Soviet Union. The Tsarist Russian public had, as we have said, no enthusiasm or attraction for Siberian settlement, nor was Japan a subject of great interest. For the Soviet public the former is certainly still true, and, it is tempting to argue that the latter still remains true also. But for the present purposes it is the impact on, or speculation of, policymakers that is of importance. These impacts cannot be quantified; however there is sufficient evidence in the literature to note their existence as part of the context in which particular policy decisions are made.

1 SOVIET IDEOLOGY AND JAPAN

THE SOVIET IDEOLOGICAL VIEW OF JAPAN

Introduction

It is the intention of this section to examine the ideological context of Soviet relations with Japan. The main Soviet conceptions with regard to relations with Japan will be set out and an attempt will then be made to suggest some implication for Soviet policy with these ideological premises as a background. In the context of appraising Soviet relations with Japan it is helpful to identify two related aspects of ideology. First, ideology serves to legitimate not merely the foreign policy of the Soviet Union but also, by embodying elements of traditional, and historico-cultural beliefs, a Soviet presence in Asia as a whole and in particular north east Asia, an area with which Russia has had a long tradition of association. The second aspect of ideology is the concept most readily identifiable with the term itself, i.e. its Marxist–Leninist component which centres on the political and philosophical interpretations of relations within the world.

We can characterise 'ideology' as being of three parts: general philosophical assumptions, doctrinal elements that govern a political course at a given time, and 'action programmes' which are tied to particular circumstances. The last category is in practice the most pragmatic – but we should note that all of the preceding are subject to revision by Party theorists. This observation notwithstanding, during the time-frame in which this study is based nothing resembling a consensus on the question of ideology (its nature, its role or its place in Soviet policy) emerged in the West. Debate was, and is, still polarised between the old dichotomies of interpreting ideology as functioning as the 'real source' of Soviet action or as a 'verbal smokescreen'.[1] Agreement has not been reached even with regard to the nature of ideology itself, let alone its purpose. The conduct of this somewhat artificial debate in Western policy circles during these (Brezhnev) years by and large obscured the fact that what has been referred to as an 'ideological retooling' took place within the Soviet ideological arena. It was a retooling that held ramifications for both Soviet domestic and foreign polices. It paralleled and reflected the ascent of the Soviet Union to a perceived status of coequal with the United States. It is against this backcloth of ideological refurbishing that we should view Soviet relations with Japan during this period.

The art of politics for a Marxist–Leninist encompasses the idea of compromise; this view is probably no different from that held by a non Marxist–Leninist. Successful politics involves mastering the technique of managing the day-to-day antagonisms of conflicting orders. Compromise in politics in this sense is a tactical expedient and should not be seen as choice of course in itself for a Marxist–Leninist. On this question of compromise we should recognise the distinction made in dealing with it between politics and ideology. Politics embodies the idea of compromise, ideology does not. L. I. Brezhnev made this point quite clear:

> Naturally, in the course of co-operation between states with different socio-economic systems and different ideas, the peculiarities stemming from class distinctions cannot be removed. Evidently it would be an illusion to think that change may occur in the general approach of each country to problems which it views and resolves in its own way on the basis of its system and international ties. The relaxation of international tension is far from calling-off the battle of ideas. This is an objective phenomenon.[2]

The main approach of a Marxist–Leninist to international relations is one concerned with power and its measurement – be it political, social, economic or military. From this viewpoint the period of *razriadka* (*détente*) has been presented by the Soviets as an 'objective' situation forced upon the capitalist bloc through the West's reluctant recognition of Soviet power. Reflecting on the gains of the early 1970s Brezhnev made this point obvious: 'The transition from the Cold War and the explosive confrontation of two worlds to the easing of tension was connected above all with the changes in the alignment of forces in the world arena.' But while stressing that a turning point had been reached he also warned of over-optimism, 'The Communists are by no means predicting the "automatic collapse" of capitalism. It still has considerable reserves. However, events of recent years confirm with new force that it is a society without a future.'[3] Since before the revolution the concept of operations which has been utilised by the Soviets in their analyses of power relationships (global, regional and domestic) has been referred to as *sootnoshenie sil* or 'correlation of

6

forces'. As a concept it is altogether different (as the Soviets constantly emphasise) from those utilised in the West. Soviet commentators refer to these Western versions as a variant of the traditional 'power' or 'balance of power' concepts. G. Shakhnazarov, one of the foremost Soviet commentators on ideological matters and international politics argues that 'In the overwhelming majority of works published in the West the aforementioned "power" concept continues to hold complete sway and an attempt is made to attribute changes in the world situation to the transition from a bipolar world (USSR–USA) to a tripolar one (USSR–USA–China), or to a five polar one (including Western Europe and Japan).' While not denying that this idea can prove useful for 'limited tasks' in international relations, Shakhnazarov argues that 'what matters is that it cannot be used to solve global tasks. This calls for a fundamentally new, scientific construction and methods of evaluation.'[4] According to Soviet estimation, although nation states still continue to operate on the international scene, an adequate estimate of the correlation of forces and especially of the tendencies in international affairs can only be made by employing a 'systems' approach instead of a 'power' one.

Having outlined what the Soviets claim the 'correlation of forces' is *not*, let us outline what the Soviets believe it is:

> This correlation is indispensable both for the elaboration of long term foreign policy strategy and for the state's practical activity in international affairs ... Naturally the existence of a large number of factors influencing the general situation complicates the analysis and estimation of the general correlation of forces on a world scale. Nevertheless, Marxist–Leninist science has accumulated considerable experience in analysing and comparing the economic, military and political potentials of different states ... this makes it possible to give an objective estimation of the general balance of forces in the present world and to determine in time the basic tendencies in international relations, as well as foresee the prospects of their development ... Contrary to the concepts of bourgeois politologists, Marxist–Leninist theory proceeds from the fact that the category of the correlation of forces in the world cannot and should not be reduced to the correlation of states' military potentials, and that in the ultimate end this correlation is nothing but *the correlation of class forces in the worldwide system of international relations*. In effect classes interact not only within social systems of individual countries but also outside their framework. The social systems of different countries come out as the components of the world system of international relations. These relations are maintained in the form of economic, political, legal, diplomatic, military, cultural, ideological and other contacts between nations and classes through their political bodies

> ... As a rule various states, parties and political forces do not act in the world scene individually but unite into definite groups, systems of states, or political, economic or military coalitions based on common class or state interests. Hence, the foreign policy potential of a state depends not only on its own forces and internal resources, but to a considerable extent, on such external factors as the existence of reliable socio-political allies among other states, national contingents of congenial classes, mass international movements and other political forces active on the world scene ... Thus, the correlation of forces in the world implies not only the correlation of forces between individual states, but first and foremost, the correlation of contemporary class forces, namely the international working class and the bourgeoisie, the forces of socialism and capitalism, the forces of progress and those of reaction.[5]

The major factors influencing the international situation are, according to the Soviets, those forces actively influencing the international situation at a particular moment; the class nature of those forces and the ways in which they act; their potential for development, or their ability to reach their final goals and solve their immediate tasks; the form of their organisation – national, international, state, public, etc.; the mechanism of their interaction.[6] Thus, by the early 1970s, so the Soviets argued, the alignment of forces had swung – if not overwhelmingly in their favour – at least to a degree whereby the Soviet Union could legitimately be regarded as a global power. The most obvious symbols of this new alignment were the Strategic Arms Limitation Talks (SALT I) agreement (a recognition of Soviet strategic power) and the signing of the 'Basic Principles of Relations between the USA and the USSR' in 1972 (a recognition of overall Soviet equality with the United States). Such new found and long-strived-for acceptance was proclaimed via a more assertive ideological stance based on the greater confidence of a *de facto* overall Soviet strength, with particular emphasis on the military component as the most tangible and visible evidence of that strength.

The Soviets place most emphasis on the military component of their superpower status. Thus while Soviet spokesmen proclaim peaceful coexistence as being a multi-faceted process, it is the military aspects of the process which are in practice most heavily stressed. In theory the 'correlation of forces' can be in one's favour even if the military situation is not, and the Soviets claim that military factors only receive such attention because they are visible expressions of strength. Other factors, as detailed in the Sergiyev quotation, they are at pains to point out, still retain their importance.

Brezhnev's 'Peace Programme', as it has become known, of the late

1960s and early 1970s was designed to ensure Soviet security by combining two approaches: one at the national level and the other at the international level. As concepts these two approaches were given the labels of 'self-guaranteed peace' and 'peace' respectively. Despite the gains made on an international level, the maintenance of security for the Soviets was clearly interpreted by them as dependent on their ability to guarantee their security through unilateral means by holding a militarily strong position relative to the enemies which they saw arrayed against them.

'Détente' in this context is really 'military détente', for it was in this sector that the Soviets believed their political gains to be most vulnerable to Western advances in arms programmes, which they could only hope to match by forgoing the development of other sectors of the Soviet state, principally the economy. Furthermore it was assumed that without some sort of perceived equality in the military sphere any political moves would lack the necessary credibility.

V. Nekrasov made this point on the centrality of the military equation in an article in the Party theoretical journal *Kommunist*:

> Today the sharpest confrontation between the forces of social progress and reaction takes place precisely on the matter of war and peace ... however the specific nature of the present time in international relations is the need to surmount the opposition of aggressive and reactionary circles, extremely galvanised of late, to the positive changes in global politics. A most acute struggle is being waged on problems of detente in the military field and of supporting political detente with its achievements.[7]

Vasili Kulish, a Soviet writer on the political uses of force in international relations, similarly stated that in the present day when political processes have advanced further than military processes, 'questions of military detente assume exceptional importance'.[8]

Sergiyev sums-up the stress that the Soviets put on the military aspect of the correlation of forces. He distinguishes the Western approach to world politics from that of the socialist camp: the West functions as a *'military–political'* bloc whereas the socialist community is one of 'economic, political and cultural co-operation ... *complemented* by their military co-operation and mutual assistance'. However prior to that he states quite clearly that 'The military strength of a state is by all means a decisive element of its position in the world.'[9] Sergiyev's stance, as we have outlined it, is confused. In this he mirrors the overall Soviet position which seeks to solve the dilemma by fudging the issue. Regardless of the evidence in many Soviet statements which allude to the importance of non-military factors, it is recognised that the primary legitimation of Soviet superpower status lies with a perception of its military power. That notwithstanding the non-military factors which Sergiyev considers, economic strength, strength and solidarity of progressive forces, diplomatic links, and particularly the relationship of class forces, were all deemed by the Soviets to be areas where they had gained ground by the middle of the 1970s.

There is a consensus amongst Soviet ideologists with regard to these concepts outlined above. The concepts as such represent either 'core values' or basic judgements regarding the changes in the international situation. These are the basic building blocks for Soviet ideology.

This then is the ideological background against which we must examine how the Soviet Union conducted its relations with Japan in the 1970s and into the 1980s. How then do the Soviets view their relations with Japan in an ideological context? Where does Japan fit into the Soviet world view? For purposes of evaluation we can utilise three levels of investigation, which are in practice inter-related: first, an appraisal of Japan as a member of the capitalist bloc; second, an interpretation of Japan's relations with regional countries of the Pacific; and third, Soviet comment on Japan as a nation state – its social structure, its domestic forces and overall political stability.[10]

Japan as a member of the capitalist bloc

Prominent in the Soviet vocabulary for describing the world of the 1970s was, and is, the concept of 'centres of power'. The emergence of these new *loci* of power carried with it the implicit recognition that the world had become truly multipolar and the emergence of this multipolarity is characterised by Soviet ideologists as a function of exacerbated interimperialist contradictions. As is illustrated by a comment by G. Trofimenko, 'The multipolarity concept is primarily a recognition by US theoreticians of the limited nature of US imperialism's potential in the modern world ... it embraces a recognition of new "centres of power" in the capitalist world (such as the EEC and Japan); a realisation of the well-known lack of convergence between the interests of the US and the policies and interests of many of its chief capitalist allies'.[11]

It is to state the obvious that Japan is viewed as one of these new centres of power, but implicit in the Soviet view is that because of its potential in certain more dynamic aspects of modern development, Japan (like the EEC) has a fractious relationship with other leading capitalist states; thus in its relations with other capitalist states it is depicted not merely as a centre of power but as a *rival* centre of power. As the Soviets see it, though the scientific and technical revolution has caused a broadening of the ties of international economic co-operation, it also in tandem has caused a deepening of interimperialist contradictions such that 'in examining the internationalisation of economic life, no "liberalisation" of international economic ties can weaken the nationalistic character of state monopoly capitalism; neither can such measures diminish the desire of the monopolies of each industrialised capitalist country to strengthen its ability to compete at the expense of others'.[12] This theme of the irreconcilable nature of the leading capitalist economies runs as a leitmotif throughout Soviet commentaries on Japan. The moves toward economic integration in the West, the Soviets argue, presuppose a mutual interest which they (the Soviets) most emphatically deny exists.

M. Maksimova, in the second part of two articles on the subject of 'Capitalist Integration and World development', argues that while the later years of the 1970s have led to 'a strengthening between each of the capitalist states in their mutual dependence on each others' development of their own industry and markets, and science and technology and in the world currency markets' these years have also produced a 'deepening of economic and social contradictions' which have led the capitalist powers to undertake greater measures of economic and political collaboration such as the 'numerous attempts at reform of international currency regulation, an upgrading of the activities of the OECD, the creation of an international energy agency under the auspices of the United States etc'. But, she continues, 'these principal levers of state monopoly regulation lie in the hands of national governments. The economic and political development of the capitalist states has been separated into the economically strong (US, FRG, Japan) and the economically weak, thus preserving interimperialist contradictions. All of these serve as serious barriers on the path to overcoming the acute contradictions of contemporary capitalism – the contradictions between the growth rates of mutually dependent capitalist states and between the necessity in international politics to co-ordinate economic politics and the imposition of state monopoly limits on the regulation of economic life.'[13]

In the wider realm of capitalist development in the 1970s Japan is portrayed as having evolved from acting as a side-lines participant in international economic decision-making at the turn of the 1970s to acting as a central force in the mainstream of that decision-making by

11

the end of the 1970s. The decade of the seventies is persistently appraised by Soviet theorists as having been one of 'structural crisis' for the Western economies in which 'even Japan suffered more than the United States and a number of other capitalist states'.[14] However Soviet commentators suggest that because of the dynamism of the Japanese economy and its 'unscrupulous' methods of competition, Japan's technological momentum has been maintained at the expense of other (by implication, capitalist) nations' rates of recovery.

The central issue of friction between Japan and her fellow capitalist nations is the question of international trading and competition. Throughout the 1970s this has been of particular worry for the European nations, as one Soviet economist argues in a section of an article entitled *Trade Piracy*:

> most of all (the sources of worry) has been the chronic imbalances of trade in favour of Japan throughout the 1970s. If in 1970 the net balance in favour of Japan was 905 million dollars, by 1979 it had risen to 6.3 billion, and by 1980 to a further 11 billion dollars. Then there is also the range of Japanese exports which have spread to encompass the main centres of (European) industrial production. They have enveloped the heart of the shipbuilding industry, the iron and steel industry, home electronics, photographic goods, tape recorders, televisions, bicycles and car production.[15]

Given the scale of these statistics, Aliev concludes that underlying relations between Japan and Western Europe is a very sharp current of antagonism, the results of which have up until now been in favour of Japan.

The trading competition has also afflicted relations with the United States and spilled-over into international money markets where the competition with the United States has been especially severe, according to Soviet writers. The Japanese attempts to establish the Yen as a recognised international currency despite resistance from the United States has been successful by the turn of the 1980s in that Tokyo is now recognised as 'a financial centre of international significance'.[16]

Outside the parallel tracks of co-operation and competition with the main centres of imperialism, Soviet analysts have also commented – though far less frequently – on Japanese involvement in other regions of the globe, notably in South East Asia and Africa. The increasing involvement of both the Japanese government and Japanese business in the markets of the developing nations is characterised by Soviet writers as an entirely natural progression, inevitable due to increased activity by Japan in foreign policy circles and due to the fact that these nations, as trading partners, account for an estimated 60% of Japanese long-term private investment, 45–50% of Japanese commodity exports and more than 50% of Japanese imports.[17]

In line with a Leninist interpretation of colonial relations, Soviet theorists have been quick to argue that Japan has only ostensibly participated in the aid programme to developing nations and that it would be 'political immaturity' to believe otherwise as 'any honest researcher cannot but subscribe to the words of prominent Japanese scholar, T. Ozawa, that the purpose of the Japanese government's traditional approach to aid . . . is to create favourable conditions for the export of commodities and for direct investments'.[18] The donor countries, the Soviets point out, are extremely critical of both the relative size of the Japanese aid contributions and the hard terms of the loan arrangements. The Soviets claim that as a result of exploitative Japanese policies, the developing nations have exhibited a lack of faith in Japanese assertions of 'unselfishness' for Japanese aid is widely seen as being 'insufficient, wrongly motivated, poorly administered, too selective and out of step with that of other donors'.[19]

For the most part the picture drawn by Soviet analysts of the Japanese role in Africa is similar, one of classic textbook neo-colonialism. In her book, *Iaponiia i Afrika*, I. V. Volkova accuses the Japanese, in their dealings in Africa, of exploiting cheap labour and using African nations as a cheap source of capital investment and resources, as well as using them as new markets for cheap Japanese goods. She also asserts that the Japanese have been collaborating extensively with the racist South African government, giving it important aid which has facilitated the development of its nuclear industry.[20]

Japan and the Pacific

Theoretical calculations of the global correlation of forces are fraught with difficulties, as the Soviets themselves admit. One of these difficulties is that theorists are dealing with abstract concepts on a wide scale. However at a regional level the abstract becomes more manageable. A more careful balance sheet of the disposition of powers, effectiveness of military forces, influence of political variables and actual accumulation of information are all much easier to accomplish. Therefore the regional correlation of forces tends to possess more likely operational meaning for the formulation of Soviet foreign policy actions than the wide sweep of the global assessment.

Looking at the north east Asian region the Soviet Union sees an area whose prevailing trend is one of stability, with no prospect for sudden or unexpected change. In this context the conditions are seen as propitious for the Soviet Union to establish itself further, albeit slowly, as an Asian political and military power, and indeed since the mid-1980s this Soviet drive has assumed a greater vigour. The United States has been seen as the principal opponent, although concern has also been frequently expressed over China. For its part Japan, due to its economic strength and associated political influence in the region and to a lesser extent its potential for military growth, is seen as the only East Asian power capable of hindering the Soviet Union in its quest for greater status within the area.

Japanese involvement in the Pacific–Asian region is an intensification of its wider global concerns, where Japanese influence has less potential for success than in regions closer to home. In conducting its relations with states in the region, the Soviets see Japan having the advantage of being an Asian industrial giant, thus giving it a foothold in both the camps of capitalism and the developing markets of Asia. One Soviet researcher sums up the position thus: 'Being a major capitalist state in Asia Japan has long been trying to act as a mediator between the developing and developed capitalist countries, posing as practically the sole protector of the former's interests.'[21]

Japanese initiatives in the region are seen to be both political and economic and unlike their effect at a global level both (rather than mainly the economic) have an impact. Both come together in the Japanese prompting of the 'Pacific community' idea, a favourite target of Soviet commentators. Yu. Bandura, one of the small group of Soviet Japanologists decries Japanese expansionism as the root of the ideas behind the new trading association and labels it as an attempt by the Japanese to dominate the Asian market at the expense of other main capitalist rivals. More to the point, Bandura, while admitting that the Soviet Union has not been excluded from participating in these plans, contends that the creation of the community would merely 'facilitate Japanese diplomacy against the Soviet Union and serve as a basis of this diplomacy'.[22] Accepting the Soviet definition of the purposes of the organisation (effectively to create a captive market for Japanese producers), it is not surprising to see the Soviets claim that the United States has constantly resisted all Japanese proposals on the issue and sought to squash the idea of a closed economic grouping. The American response to any military grouping (created as a by-product of the economic arrangements) has been far more favourable. Yet despite this repeated American pressure to nullify Japanese efforts, the Japanese have persisted as 'in this struggle the ruling classes of Japan have attached special significance and consequence to establishing a wide-ranging economic and political

14

bridgehead in the Asia–Pacific region', an aim 'long desired' by Japan.[23]

The imbalance of Japanese trade with the Association of South East Asian Nations (ASEAN) in favour of Japan is utilised as a telling factor in unmasking the true nature of Japanese concern for the region. Japan accounts for 27% of total ASEAN exports and 24% of imports, whereas the proportional figures for the Japanese trade balances are 9% and 12% respectively.[24] In response to ASEAN requests for a system of guaranteed exports receipts involving Japan, the Japanese have refused to agree to its establishment on the grounds of being committed to free trade principles and thus unable to participate in a bloc economy. To the Soviets this reply only serves to illustrate that 'at present the structure of Japan–ASEAN trade only accords with the Japanese monopolies' long-range interests of keeping the ASEAN countries as suppliers of valuable raw material'.[25]

As indicated earlier, although contradictions within the capitalist camp are held responsible for Japanese moves towards establishing more advantageous trade markets, by and large this is not the case when tendencies of Japanese militarism are discussed. While the subject of militarism has always been prominent in Soviet discussion of Japan, until the middle 1970s the emphasis of these discussions had clearly been on the precedents set by past Japanese aggression in China and South East Asia. Virulent attacks were carried out on the past record of Japanese military adventures and warnings extrapolated from this evidence, but these attacks were not very numerous. There is a discernible change in this situation both with regard to the substance of the comment and its frequency by the turn of the middle 1970s, when the attacks become more frequent as the Soviets slowly became increasingly aware of a real Japanese participation in Western inter-alliance war planning in the Pacific.[26]

Militaristic tendencies evident in Japanese circles are seen by the Soviets at the end of the 1970s as the product of wider factors closely linked to US military–strategic doctrines of foreign policy. As Moscow sees it, in the present day there exists in Japanese conduct a 'clear discrepancy between the officially proclaimed doctrine of adherence to peace and the steadily increasing military potential ... which is a salient feature of Japan's foreign policy ... and is especially dangerous because it has the all-round support and encouragement of the imperialist NATO powers'.[27]

The growth of Japanese influence and involvement abroad is the most visible consequence of a more assertive stance on the part of the Japanese ruling classes. Professor I. Latyshev has commented that

'The road that Japanese diplomacy has traversed in the last 18 years was marked by contradictions and discrepancies in treating such vital problems of contemporary political life as the easing of international tensions ensuring lasting peace in the Pacific area, developing business and friendly relations between all countries of the area, and even defending Japanese national interests and security etc.'[28] He continues, 'However lately in 1969–70 the symptoms of change have become more apparent. The main causes of the changes envisaged in Japanese foreign policy have been the rapid growth of the economic power of Japan.'[29]

This growth of economic power has been utilised both as the base for expansion and the rationale for expansion, in that the Japanese claim that they must take steps to protect their overseas markets in South East Asia. Soviet commentators use these statements to substantiate the Soviet accusation that Japan is merely out to establish a new 'South East Asia Co-Prosperity sphere'. The Soviet warnings by no means fall on unreceptive ears, as present-day South East Asia arguably still harbours bitter memories of the last Japanese occupation.

One of the approaches taken by the Soviets over the question of Japanese plans of expansion into areas of Asia is that the Japanese, specifically the 'revanchists', have failed to see that they cannot turn back the clock: in trying to re-establish a meaningful presence they are working against the flow of events and the forces of change. No less a person than K. Chernenko set out the Soviet position by declaring that

> In spite of what would appear to be the instructive experience of the ignominious collapse of such anti-communist alliances such as SEATO [South East Asian Treaty Organisation], and CENTO, [Central Treaty Organisation], attempts are again being made to knock together militarist axes and triangles like the Washington–Tokyo–Seoul bloc. We are against such geopolitics, against all kinds of 'spheres of influence' and 'zones of interest', against closed military groups in general and in the Pacific ocean in particular.[30]

Japanese participation in American strategy in the Far East has always been a theme emphasised in Soviet commentary. For example, an entry in the *Bolshaia Sovetskaia Entsiklopedia* asserts that 'In August 1964, Japan gave its consent for American atomic submarines to enter Japanese ports, in November 1967 it agreed to admit atomic aircraft carriers and other surface vessels.'[31] The point which the Soviets make concomitant on this is that they see Japanese 'consent' or 'agreement' as largely concessions forced from the Japanese government by great pressure from successive American administrations. It is the idea that the American ruling classes wish to hold Japan as an outpost of imperialism that most dominates Soviet thinking, though it has been acknowledged with increasing frequency (as the threat from Japanese militarism looms greater) that Japanese militarists are more inclined to pursue their own state goals with the increasing military influence at their disposal rather than merely serve the military goals of United States policy. But nevertheless it is still seen as clear that the overriding threat to peace in the Pacific stems from American ambition and global hegemonism.

The Japanese response, or rather non-response, to Soviet proposals for security arrangements in the Pacific and Asia, launched in 1969 and intermittently raised ever since, has been a target for ideological attack also. Soviet ideology of course stresses the fundamentally peaceful nature of Soviet policy in the region, with the principle of collective security as one of its main pillars. 'The collective defence of peace envisages above all the assertion of the principles of peaceful coexistence as a universally recognised standard of relations between countries with different social systems', writes I. Kovalenko one of the principal Soviet Japanologists (and a Deputy Head of the Department for Eastern Affairs in the International Department of the Central Committee).[32] The continual refusal of Japan to take-up Soviet initiatives has been put down to the intransigence of the revanchist military circles, and their 'playing up' to the dangerous plans of outside powers with ambitions in north east Asia. In the past this accusation has always been levelled at the United States but by the later 1970s an old fear seemed to be materialising and it prompted an intensification of Soviet ideological rhetoric. 'A special role in the camp of the enemies of peace is assigned to co-ordinated anti-Soviet hegemonistic policy.'[33] This very real fear of a coalition of powers, of which Japan is an important member, hemming-in the Soviet Union provided new grounds for the further ideological indictment of Japan.

Japan as a nation state

The growing interaction of Japan with other states is a reflection of changes brought about within those concepts which had guided earlier Japanese diplomacy and foreign policy. Like their Western counterparts, Soviet analysts distinguish the idea of diplomacy from that of foreign policy but accept that at times they can be virtually indistinguishable. For the Soviets diplomacy is, in general, merely a bourgeois means of conducting foreign policy. In a Soviet assessment, foreign policy, like diplomacy, can only ever reflect the interests of the ruling class of the state it purports to represent. In the case of Japan these class interests are symbolised in power by the 'ruling circles' which comprise the Liberal Democratic Party (LDP) (seen as the party of 'big business'), elements of the military hierarchy and business groups, particularly the Keiretsu.

As Soviet writer Kapchenko points out, 'from the Marxist–Leninist point of view, home and foreign polices are individually linked, for both are an expression, different in form, but identical in content, of the interests of the ruling class of a given state. Their social class basis is absolutely wrong to separate foreign policy from home policy and all the more so to oppose the two.'[34]

In the piece by Latyshev cited earlier, the author provides an overview of the changes in the course of Japanese foreign policy and argues that

> Paying attention to the problems of economic relations with indi-
> vidual countries and to regional problems Japan's government was
> up to now rather slow to formulate any broad long-term foreign
> policy goals. However, lately in 1969–70 the symptoms of changes in
> the strategy of Japanese foreign policy have become more and more
> apparent . . . the new foreign policy doctrines, put on the order of the
> day by the ruling circles of Japan signify in total a new stage in the
> development of Japanese foreign policy. This is the stage when the
> ruling classes of Japan are striving for establishing themselves in the
> world politics as a self-independent political force. The aspiration of
> Japanese diplomats for bolstering the role of Japan in international
> affairs is a result of the change in the balance of forces between Japan
> and the other capitalist countries. The new doctrines put forward by
> the ruling circles of Japan contain an unambiguous claim for the
> extension of economic, political and territorial spheres of influence.
> The modern foreign policy concepts of Japan, like Japanese slogans
> in the past, contain the idea of a revision of the system of inter-
> national economic ties, territorial borders, international agreements
> and diplomatic relations in the Pacific. That is why these concepts are
> fraught with the danger of international conflict.[35]

Who are these ruling circles? How do they participate in the policy process? One Soviet analyst, A. Makarov, has provided a sketch of the relevant groups as he sees them: his assessment is worth quoting at length as it provides an illuminating representative insight into how at least some Soviet observers view the situation in Japan.

> As it develops, Japanese state monopoly capital tends to exert an
> increasing impact on governmental policy. Yet, owing to postwar
> political, economic and social reforms (1945–52), the introduction of
> universal suffrage and the growing prestige of progressive forces,

above all the Communist and Socialist parties, the monopolies are unable to flaunt their political influence in a conspicuous way. Like other imperialist countries the Japanese monopolies' political domination is a *de facto* rather than *de jure* affair.'

(p. 83)

The organisations of businessmen and trade associations

exert a significant influence on the planning of government measures in the economy and other spheres. However it is the big four of the national business organisations known as the 'Zaikai' [literally 'financial circles'] that take a most active part in deciding on the key issues of national policy and maintain an energetic pressure on the whole system of state institutions ... unlike the other developed capitalist countries, hardly any of the Japanese financial and monopoly elite are appointed to high governmental posts ... despite the formal independence of politics established from financial and monopoly capital, and an insignificant monopoly representation in political institutions and the civil service, the monopoly financial elite is directly involved in policymaking.

(pp. 83–6)

Therefore,

by exerting pressure on the state machinery as the most important link in the political system, monopoly capital is seeking the best political and social conditions for itself. Through the mechanism of state regulation, it exerts a decisive influence on the shaping of the most important policies, such as general economic structure, economic planning, financial system, social security, education, militarisation etc. Moreover, in Japan, which depends on foreign trade for its survival, the monopolies are particularly concerned with external economic expansion.[36]

One of the major mechanisms for maintaining the link between government and business circles is the practice, or phenomenon of *amakudari*. Literally the term means a 'descent from the sky' (or heaven: *ama* – sky, *kudari* – going down) and refers to the practice of high level government officials taking early retirement (often in their early fifties) and transferring to high ranking posts in industry or private companies. Obviously this creates circumstances for strong ties between government, the civil service and private business. Critics of these arrangements also point to the possibilities for corruption which can arise from such a relationship. Mention of this practice has not been found in any of the Soviet writings consulted for this study. Given the importance of the connection between business and government in Soviet ideological views of Japanese policy-making, this omission should be pointed-out. Either the Soviets have little knowledge of *amakudari* or they are unwilling to comment upon it.[37]

The question of explaining the trading relationship between the Soviet Union and Japan is one which, despite much discussion in the West over the practical results of its implementation, Soviet ideologists have no trouble in confronting. The Japanese encouragement of trade is said to stem from continual attempts by Japanese business to thrust trade upon the Soviet Union. The Soviets are sure that the motive behind Japanese enthusiasm for trade is that they (and the West) view it as a means of subversion, and use it as a tool to nudge the Soviet Union away from an autarkic command economy to one governed by a philosophy of 'market socialism'.

To Soviet ideologues one aspect associated with trading relations is in fact the most insidious tool of all utilised by the West in its struggle against the Soviet Union on the political front: the argument that through trade contact nations 'converge' is a constant target of attack for Soviet writers. It has been labelled by ideologists as a 'reactionary utopia' in that it tries to unite that which cannot be united. It is claimed that capitalists (including in particular the Japanese) have three aims in mind when propagating the concept: to try to get Communists to accept the legality of bourgeois systems; to embellish capitalism by associating it in a merger with socialism; and to denigrate socialism, to ideologically disarm the socialist public and to lead them to believe in compromise. These comments by Soviet writers serve to put trade with Japan into its proper political context. As Brezhnev reminded us, there can be no compromise on questions of ideology. (Though this convergence thesis must be a controversial subject for the future once economic *perestroika* (restructuring) gets underway.)

The issues of the political mechanism of a given country are always the subject of close scrutiny by party theorists. Soviet Japanologists correspondingly focus their work on the most important questions which they see as being based around the class antagonisms within the Japanese polity. They further claim that an understanding of the developments within Japanese society cannot be obtained without a prior understanding of the class struggle within Japan.

The conduct of relations between labour and capital is the crucial centre of the class struggle. Soviet commentators are aware of the various influences of particular traditions in Japanese society which have delayed effective labour-group formation there – such as the patriarchal attitude reflected in the systems of life-time employment, the automatic pay rises based on age considerations, the specific organisation of trade unions, the deferential attitudes towards superiors and the problems caused by the relatively late emergence of capitalism in Japan. These traditions, combined with a lack of class consciousness (perhaps the most serious problem to be surmounted) and reinforced by intensive bourgeois propaganda which emphasises the value to Japan of its economic stability because this, almost alone, has enabled Japan to play a special role in the world, have brought about until recently stability in Japanese labour relations.

The stability, Soviet writers now argue, has all but evaporated. The turning point in the state of relations between labour and capital came around the late 1970s. Since then relations have been undergoing 'intensive modernisation', so much so that Japanese employers, although seeking peaceful relations, have 'been forced to discard the now economically ineffective systems of employment and payment' so that relations are now characterised by 'a fierce economic struggle of the proletariat and the relative immaturity of political demands': for the future the predictions are that 'conflicting relations between labour and capital can worsen even further and this will depend on the stand that the Japanese working class adopt . . . whether they will pursue the "coprosperity of the nation" or consistently defend their interests from positions of class strategy'.[38]

These changes have forced the hand of the Japanese ruling groups into trying by more overt means to counter the growing anti-monopoly trends. The medium by which they have principally tried to achieve this goal has been the use of bourgeois ideology: specifically the twin ideas of anti-communism and anti-Sovietism.

A leading Soviet commentator on internal (labour) politics, Professor B. Pospelov, suggests that in Japan the two themes have been intermingled into the form of a 'modernisation theory'. The nationalistic elements of the theory constitute its main support but take two forms: Pospelov argues that Japanese monopolies have constantly emphasised that it is unpatriotic to struggle against what the proletariat label as 'the monopoly yoke' since to do so would impede Japanese revival. He further contends that nationalism in the Japanese context holds the peculiar connotation of referring to a 'community' and 'community relations' – the ideas of which have been styled as a successful alternative to the Marxist vision of a communist society. He states that 'the notion of community was the central category of the philosophical and sociological concepts of the ideologues of the monopolist bourgeoisie in prewar Japan. It was widely used to disguise the exploiter essence of the Japanese bourgeois state and to emphasise the character of personal relations in the East.'[39] The point which Pospelov is seeking to make is that it is still utilised today in a similar fashion by the ruling bourgeoisie.

Yet another Soviet author echoes Pospelov's judgement about the use of the concept of 'Japanese uniqueness' and suggests that 'Japanese bourgeois propaganda is trying to create an impression that Japan occupies a special place in the modern world and is allegedly immune to the social and economic upheavals which affect the majority of advanced capitalist states.'[40]

In conclusion Pospelov argues the case that the modernisation theory 'attaches particular importance to the capitalist state, interpreting it as a supraclass mechanism reflecting the interests of allegedly the entire nation by directing social developments along the road of industrialisation. "Serving the fatherland through industry" is a common slogan in Japan.'[41]

Changes in the equilibrium of labour relations in Japan were due to several factors. As we have argued above, the Soviets considered the decade of the 1970s as years of destabilisation for the Western economies, and therefore the first and major consideration in explaining the tension in labour relations that we have to look at is the affliction which beset the Japanese economy. Yu. Kuznetsov, writing in the Party journal *Kommunist*, describes how 'the case of Japan illustrates clearly Lenin's theory of unequal economic development of capitalist states in the period of imperialism'.[42] The Japanese pace of development was so fast that it was hailed as an example of 'model growth', but 'progress was neither smooth nor without pain, nor did the Japanese escape the internal contradictions of capitalism', for growth was achieved at the expense of other things and as a result the level of development of Japan's social infrastructure fell behind, leaving many social problems in its wake.

In common with almost every other economic assessment of Japan by Soviet analysts, Kuznetsov stresses that 1974–5 was a turning point for Japan. 'The crisis of 1974–75, occurring at the same time as the worsening of the energy and other structural crises of capitalism, along with sharp increases in the price of oil and certain raw materials, signalled the end to the high rates of growth for the Japanese economy and created the need for its restructuring.'[43]

By the early 1980s the Japanese economy was still experiencing growth but not at its impressive earlier rates. This, as the Soviets saw it, pointed to the truth that not even Japan was immune to the 'incurable maladies of capitalism'. Growth rates of gross national product (GNP) and of industrial production declined steadily – they were only 3% and 0.3% respectively in 1982 – the lowest they had been for seven to eight years. The general malaise affecting the economy was summed-up by the Tokyo correspondent of *New Times* who said that, 'For the first time since the crisis of 1974–75, owing to the curtailment of export, the volume of trade decreased . . . a sharp crisis occurred in state finances. The deterioration of the economy was due primarily to the internal processes, and above all the growth of structural disproportions between the not inconsiderable production possibilities and limited personal consumption, between the material intensive and energy consuming industries and the newest industries connected with scientific and technical progress'.[44]

One of Lenin's dicta had been that a state can only be strong when its people are politically conscious. An understanding of the consciousness within each class of a state is a central feature of understanding in turn the international and internal politics of any given nation. In Japan the intensification of the class struggle has been ascribed by the Soviets to the economic crisis and to an increased development of class consciousness itself within the proletariat. Both these developments led to the heightening of the role of progressive forces which are active over a wide range of issues and at all levels in Japanese politics. The Soviets give their support in the main to the Japanese Communist Party (JCP), (also, but with less sense of public commitment, to the Socialist Party (JSP)). This support for the JCP has not been without its fluctuations or trials. As with many Marxist–Leninist movements the Soviets have been confronted in the past in dealings with Japan with the problem of how to deal with – if at all – splinter groups and factions. After the JCP break with the Soviet Union over the Partial Nuclear Test Ban treaty in 1963 the Soviets lent support to the Japanese Communist Party 'Voice of Japan' group. This support continued until the late 1960s–early 1970s.[45] JCP proposals for the creation of a united progressive front and of a coalition government were 'made real' by the crisis of 1974–5 and since. Reporting on the 15th Congress of the Party, L. Mlechin attributes the popularity of the JCP to 'its advocacy of a radical reorganisation of the economy, its demands to put an end to the rapid rise of the prices of necessaries, rents, power rates and fuel prices, and its opposition to capitalist 'rationalisation' which has resulted in mass lay-offs and unemployment'.[46] The impact of the Lockheed scandal of the mid-1970s and the continuing disclosure of political corruption has been seen to enhance the popularity of the JCP as it has always made clear that it has been 'sharply critical of corruption in the upper echelons of society'.

Particularly praiseworthy in Soviet eyes has been the JCP's stand against Chinese expansionism and interference (via Maoist groups) in

Japanese internal politics. The Maoists were a 'small but vociferous' grouping in Japanese politics, who slavishly followed pro-Chinese tactics notable for narrow-minded sectarianism, dogmatism and adventurism. (The pro-Chinese groups in Japanese politics are still a target of Soviet attacks but less so than in the 1970s, and of course it is uncertain whether they can still be labelled as 'Maoist'.) In its activities the JCP not only mobilises its forces against Peking's subversive activity in Japan, but in doing so also consistently exposes 'the hegemonistic ambitions of the Great Han chauvinists in the international arena – and their collusion with US imperialism on the basis of anti-Sovietism'.[47]

Soviet treatment of the Japanese Socialist Party is more mixed. Particular policies pursued by the Socialists are labelled as 'progressive' (the same heading applied to those of the JCP) but in general the Socialists have been accused of slipping 'further and further towards anti-communism and right-wing opportunism, refusing to act jointly with the JCP, which weakens the left-wing pressure on big monopoly capital and its party the LDP (Liberal Democratic Party). Opposition is formed not through consolidation of progressive forces, but through collaborationist policies and right wing reformist ideological views of the Komeito and the SDP (Democratic Social Party).'[48]

In contrast, Soviet evaluations of the ruling Liberal Democratic Party are far from uncertain in their verdicts. In an article reviewing the 1979 Academy of Sciences Yearbook on Japan, N. Vladimirov speaks for all Soviet ideologists when he refers to the LDP as the 'political headquarters of the national elite'. The LDP has always been attacked as the big business party which has maintained power by its unscrupulous manipulation of the factional divisions in the Japanese political system. The economy has 'stagnated as a result of policies, its search to resolve economic difficulties by more intensely exploiting the working masses and encroaching upon the living standards ... has naturally provoked widespread popular resentment'.[49]

V. Khlynov, resident in Japan for many years, and now analyst at the Institute of World Economy and International Relations (IMEMO), in his overview of Japan in the 1970s lauded the efforts of the progressive forces in Japan and saw the 1976–7 elections as having been a turning point in the fortunes of the LDP and its supporters. The Democratic Socialist Party and the Komeito he dismissed thus: while claiming to be a democratic party the DSP is 'in actual fact by manoeuvring between the democratic and conservative forces thereby creating grave difficulties in Japan's democratic camp. The DSP supports the ruling party on many major political issues and often makes alliances with it. In recent years this won it notoriety. The DSP is often called "the other LDP" ... the political goals of the Komeito are vague, contradictory, and eclectic ... the reforms it suggests do not affect the foundations of capitalism'.[50]

The concern voiced by the Soviets over the trend towards militarisation in Japan, evident in the increased frequency of reports in the Soviet press on Japanese military issues, concentrates on the implications for regional security but also seeks to show the internal forces which are prompting the growing Japanese revanchism.

The Soviet view of the internal situation *vis-à-vis* the militarisation question is fairly straightforward. Clearly it is the LDP and other 'self-seeking' right wing groups who are at the centre of Japanese revanchism. At the same time, the forces of opposition to the trends of revanchism are not insignificant. While the most vocal of these groups may be the 'progressive forces', the Soviets are aware that they (the progressive elements) are only the vanguard of a far wider politically significant movement in Japanese politics which embraces a wide spectrum of associated causes from women's rights to general pacifism.[51] The Soviets consider that the women's movement (women were by 1982 the majority of the Japanese workforce) through annual conferences such as the 'Mothers' Congress' has become an important factor in the security debate in Japan and, for example, stress that the JCP's struggle to improve the material and political position of women in Japanese society has been the most important field of the Party's social activity and a cause which the Party has 'consistently' worked for. Religious organisations which have never before participated in political campaigning are now reckoned to be doing so with significant impact. The latent peace movement is broadly based and the Soviets are well able to recognise it and its potential. As Kuznetsov made plain, 'The special characteristic of the anti-war movement at the present stage in Japan is the wide participation of new sectors of the population, and new social and political forces. Standing resolutely against the nuclear threat are members of the intelligentsia from various political persuasions – writers, artists, actors and lawyers'.[52]

The Soviet appraisal of the internal mechanics of Japanese society seems to have been conducted via the guidelines of classical Marxism–Leninism. It is an overall view of a slowly changing, but politically stable, society. The changes which have taken place are not necessarily for the better. The 'working class' has become progressively worse-off but has in the process achieved a greater sense of class solidarity. However, that in turn has provoked a reaction from the ruling elites who have cleverly propagandised politics with the scare of a Soviet threat. Even more reactionary moves have been taken by the rightist group which has been growing in strength. The course of remilitarisation which has been increasingly pursued is one of hidden consequences and therefore of great danger to the Soviet Union. These moves, symbolised by the recent suggestions to modify the Japanese constitution where concerned with defence matters, are ones which the Soviets are no longer confident the widely-based pacifist sentiments of the population can suppress.[53]

INTERPRETING THE SOVIET IDEOLOGICAL VIEW

In the preceding section we have tried by the use of quotations from Soviet sources to present the overall views and interpretations which they (the Soviets) have of Japan or of Japan's role in the world politics. The picture that we have gleaned is, as stated, an overall one. This approach was taken firstly for reasons of brevity – as some of the more pertinent points will be expanded at greater length – but also secondly as a mode of operation imposed by the available sources. Settling for an 'overall image' is always an unsatisfactory compromise ('the Soviets' are not monolithic in their viewpoints) but Soviet commentary on Japan (let alone any real analysis) is both superficial and repetitive; Soviet investigation of Japanese involvement with Latin America and Africa serves as a good illustration of that superficiality. Apart from an occasional reference in the Japan yearbooks produced by the USSR Academy of Sciences, this author has encountered only one article on Japanese involvement in Latin America, yet Japan has substantial investment in the region (approximately one-third of Japanese overseas aid or investment goes to Latin America).[54]

There may well be valid reasons why Soviet ability to comment on Japan is limited – bureaucratic resistance, lack of incentive for researchers to work in less important fields, lack of co-operation with other specialist bodies. (For example, in conversations with Soviet academics concerned with Japan the author was told that liaison took place with other institutes involved in work but, for example, the Institute of Latin America was never mentioned. The implication was that this co-operation was limited to the Oriental and Far Eastern institutes.) These of course are not research oriented problems confined to Soviet scholars; aspects of Western analysis of Japan can be found equally lacking. Nevertheless the end product is still an inhibiting factor in that when looking at Soviet ideology and Japan at the theoretical level we have to move to the particular by deduction from the general.

26

As we indicated in the opening paragraphs of the preceding section the years which our study encompasses constituted a time in which an ideological reformulation was taking place within the Soviet Union. This fact has two important consequences for our study: first, the process of reformulation served to heighten the salience of ideology and the importance of ideological directives both in the international arena and domestic politics; second, this correspondingly overemphasised the issue of ideological conformity as a factor in decision-making. It came to be used by Brezhnev as a tool (amongst others) to settle domestic rivalries and in the process temporarily increased the influence of Party theorists in policy matters. Our starting point then is with the ideological debate in the Soviet Union during the 1970s.

The consensus among political scientists who study the Soviet polity is that the problem which Soviet political structures faced during this decade was one of legitimacy.[55] Expressed simply it was a problem of how to resolve the crisis created by the conflict between assuring the continuing legitimation of the Soviet bureaucratic system and accommodating the inevitable changes associated with the 'objective' trends of modernisation.

Why should accommodating these changes pose a problem for the Soviet system? Marx had stipulated that as the intermediate body of the state advances towards communism the idea and practice of functional specialisation becomes outmoded and surpassed. The doing-away with functional specialisation constitutes a fundamental prerequisite of the attainment of communism – as such 'specialisation' is viewed as a prime source of repression for those who wield political power within a state. The problem which confronted the Soviet leadership was that as a direct result of a process of technological modernisation functional specialisation in the Soviet state (as in other similarly advanced states) was *increasing* and not decreasing as communist theory postulated. The answer which the Soviet leadership sought to adopt to the problems caused by modernisation was to redefine in ideological terms the effects of modernisation and resolve the leadership's dilemma, of how to assure legitimacy while accommodating change, by producing an ideological justification for increased specialisation.

Specifically the Soviets redefined the Marxist concept of the 'division of labour' within society and argued that as technological complexity increases with communism, although class antagonisms have been eliminated, the requirements of the era of advanced socialism necessitate high levels of organisation. Thus they turned the Marxist concept of 'division of labour' on its head, for he had postulated that specialisation (high levels of organisation) would be eroded as the state advanced towards communism. G. Marchuk, vice-president of the USSR Academy of Sciences supported the new idea thus:

> The scientific and technical revolution is based on skilled specialist cadres who can actively influence the development of the production process ... this formulates particular requirements concerning the training of specialists and the upgrading of their professional standards ... scientific and technical progress is the basis for intensive national economic development. The future of our economy lies in upgrading effectiveness. This is the way of ensuring its successful and dynamic development. The Party is steadfastly pursuing a line of acceleration of scientific and technical progress, improved planning and management, and intensified levels of organisation and order at workplace and management level.[56]

The technical revolution (the Soviet term is 'scientific and technical revolution', abbreviated to STR) is of course a world-wide phenomenon and thus to tackle an idea which had application to the capitalist as well as communist camps Party theorists made a careful distinction between the *content* and *consequences* of the STR. Under communist control it would serve as a 'means of transforming human productive forces of society'. Administered under capitalist ideology it would serve only to increase the alienation of the workforce and deepen the contradictions inherent in the capitalist system. (The Soviets glossed-over the more positive stimulus provided to capitalism by high technology.)

Accusing the advanced industrial countries of 'technological exploitation' was a common feature of Soviet ideological criticism applied to the state of Japanese industrial relations during the 1970s but had ceased to be used by the end of that decade as a major tool of criticism.[57] In the particular case of comment on Japan the decline in emphasis is less apparent by comparison with its use against Western industrial nations. Given the international dominance of Japan in certain fields of high technology and the corresponding degree of Japanese reliance on technology in industry, the effects of high technology on the structure of the Japanese economy and workforce were still a source of trenchant Soviet criticism. But even in this context Soviet writers attribute the labour unrest in Japan to the wider problems involved in a restructuring of the Japanese economy during the 1970s rather than to the idea of technological exploitation.[58]

For the most part discussion of science and technology in the Japanese case is centred around an examination of the level of technological dependence of the Japanese themselves or in comparison to

Western nations. An examination of Japanese scientific and technical policy by Zaitsev is good evidence of this approach. In his *MEMO* article he argues that 'by the mid-1970s Japan had reached the level of S and T development of the leading capitalist powers, thereby achieving a most important strategic goal of the postwar period'. Moreover, according to Zaitsev, Japan did not achieve this by 'borrowing' or 'copying foreign technology' but by building 'primarily on its own S and T potential . . . and the sound professional training of personnel'. Japanese attainment of a high technical level is only surpassed by the 'latent possibilities of S and T developments', which Zaitsev sees as being of paramount future importance for Japan. The transition to a new stage of Japanese development is already underway. (Though Zaitsev also points out that these changes are not without their problems, e.g. reallocation of finance by Japanese companies to fund huge R and D efforts is causing capital problems and channelling research into the most profitable areas at the expense of other areas of longer-term importance.)[59]

Soviet leaders and theorists put forward various approaches on how best to combine the scientific and technical revolution with the benefits of advanced socialism in order to speed-up the entry (at an unspecified date) of the Soviet people to the stage of communism. Thus while there was a divergence of view between Soviet leaders over the question of technology, its uses (and by implication the necessity of its importation, on whatever scale from abroad) and its relevance to Soviet goals, this divergence would best be characterised as a difference over 'means' rather than 'ends'. In consequence it would be a mistake to see these differences of opinion as indicating deep divisions in the Soviet leadership and their extent should not be exaggerated. As we can see with hindsight, depicting these differences as 'deep divisions' was the very mistake which the Western and the Japanese governments in fact made. Hoffman and Laird, two Western watchers of Soviet science policy conclude in one of their studies on differing approaches to technolgoy that, 'despite some differences in the views of Brezhnev and Kosygin and other top leaders these analyses (of how to utilise the technical revolution) have been characterised by an increasing attentiveness to the interconnections between ends and means and between domestic and international politics'.[60]

Bruce Parrott, in the major work in English concerning politics and technology in the USSR, while positing two significantly differing tendencies with regard to how the Soviet Union should approach the West on the co-operative aspects of technology transfer, still qualifies his assessment by recognising that 'in proposing to weigh this hypothesis against the historical evidence, I wish to emphasise that it posits only differing tendencies and not hard and fast divisions within the elite'.[61]

As indicated in the opening paragraphs the debate over ideology had impact upon this internal debate over technology and its place in the Soviet system. Although Brezhnev and Kosygin were as one in accepting that there were serious economic problems, Brezhnev was stressing a slightly different remedy, more soundly ideologically grounded than Kosygin's. Brezhnev was talking of the problem in terms of a political solution by calling for an administrative rationalisation without a significant devolution of power. He was thus maintaining his own credibility by being seen to be an advocate of 'principled solutions', i.e. ones in accord with ideological dictate. Kosygin was approaching the problem from more of a technical viewpoint and found himself more at odds with ideological principles.

The interaction of ideological imperatives thus, in a more overt manner than had perhaps been the case in the past with regard to trading matters, merely served to complicate the picture for the outside observer. The Japanese failed to see the distinction between ideology and official comment: official comment can be designed to set-out the government's policy and prospects, which involves an open discussion of differing views; it can be used to legitimise governmental policies, in which case problems are minimised; or it can be used in a domestic context to support particular policies or individuals and to attack others. While differences in the expression of official thought can have significant consequences for particular policies we must remember that the policies themselves are always framed within the limits of the ideologically acceptable, and thus policy will not become a substitute for ideology.

Soviet economic analysts had been quick to point-out that an embryonic world economy was forming, in which all states could participate and from which all could benefit, including the Soviet Union. As Brezhnev saw it the consequent Soviet move into the international market would help to alleviate the domestic needs of the Soviet economy, thus allowing him to pursue investment in other sectors of expenditure. As events unwound through the early 1970s Brezhnev became aware that these hopes could not be fulfilled to the degree anticipated and there ensued a triumph of the more traditionalist approach to foreign trade. Soviet trade with the Council of Mutual Economic Assistance (CMEA) nations was not governed strictly by this approach however. The limits of the traditional autarkic view of foreign trade were relaxed in dealings with CMEA nations. In this case a 'division of labour' principle seems to have applied to a limited extent, whereby the Soviets accepted that a significant percentage of certain products or resources needed by the Soviet Union could be produced by Eastern European nations. Eastern European production of locomotive engines, buses and certain categories of merchant shipping are good examples of some of these types of goods.

By the end of the 1974 Brezhnev's original hopes had been dashed and domestic investment for the 1976–80 period was severely retrenched in order to maintain the projected levels of military spending.[62]

In this instance the attainment of foreign policy goals had become directly linked to the internal domestic challenge. Japan, for its part, had observed the debate over foreign trade and drawn an erroneous conclusion. It assumed, along with the rest of the advanced industrial nations, that detente was not merely possible, but necessary for the Soviet Union. It either chose not, or was not able, to take sufficiently into account the ideological debate in the Soviet Union which was to have particular relevance for the trading relations between the two nations; it chose not to (or could not) see that the Soviets were making it plain that irresoluble antagonisms between the opposing systems would limit the levels of exchange and co-operation. Mikhail Suslov, in an attack on 'panickers, capitulationists and opportunists' in *Kommunist* underscored the class character of the line taken on the trade issue when he argued that compromise with Leninist principles was out of the question – 'The very deepest roots of both domestic and foreign policy of our state . . . are determined by the economic interests and the economic position of the dominant class of our state. These must not be lost from view for a minute, in order not to lose ourselves in the thickets and labyrinth of diplomatic contrivances.'[63]

This point has been empahsised once again by M. S. Gorbachev in a speech made in Dnepropetrovsk in June 1985:

> We are ready to compete with capitalism exclusively in peaceful, constructive activities. That is why we stand for the promotion of political dialogue and interaction with capitalist countries and for the extensive development of mutually beneficial trade, economic and scientific, technical and cultural contacts, and we are ready to develop these contacts on a stable and long-term basis. But these should be honest and truly mutually beneficial contacts without any discrimination. It is hopeless, for example, to use trade to intervene in our internal affairs. We do not need such trade, we can do without it.[64]

While still considering general concepts stemming from ideology which affected Soviet policy towards Japan we should bear in mind the overall influence upon policy of Soviet strategic views moulded round the idea of the correlation of forces.

L. I. Brezhnev's glowing assessment of the Soviet Union's world position, delivered at the 25th Party congress in February 1976, was as much about validating Brezhnev's own foreign policy line as providing an ideological vision. Consequently, his predictions of a restructuring of world politics and of a decisive swing in the correlation of forces were somewhat overstated. At the global level, interpreting the correlation of forces, although it involves assessing things which can be quantified (military strength, gross domestic product (GDP), trade volumes), is a difficult task not least as the ability to 'measure' events at this scale and level is made difficult by the lack of any acceptable scale of values or method of categorisation. Moreover it also involves an estimation of factors which cannot be measured or quantified, such as political influence. Any assessment of these factors depends to a large extent upon the 'feel' that Soviet leaders have for these issues. There exists a further obvious problem in relating the factors involved at the global and regional levels and in determining to what extent the regional contributes to the global and vice versa. Those forces, which can be related to events at a regional level, are easier to measure due to the decrease in scale and a similar decrease in the number of variables which have to be considered. The overall Soviet predictions of a restructuring of world politics were, as Soviet commentators themselves admit, based on the extension of Soviet power to a degree unprecedented in Soviet experience, even if not at all levels comparable with that of the United States.

As we indicated in our opening remarks to this chapter, Soviet theorists argue that the correlation of forces can be theoretically favourable even if one is militarily weaker than the opponent. However, although the Soviets stress that military power is only one of various factors which contribute to the overall equation, it is clearly the most important. Aspaturian states with regard to the military factor that:

> Although the resulting Soviet position does not represent outright falsehood, it amounts to a kind of 'cognitive deception'. Since a critical, if not always decisive, component of the 'correlation of forces' is the state of the military balance, the two are obviously interrelated, and whereas it is possible to achieve superiority in the 'correlation of forces' without at the same time enjoying military superiority, it is nevertheless true that the military component of the 'correlation of forces' is the most precise, measurable, and visible component in the calculation. Furthermore, changes in the military balance affect changes in the overall 'correlation of forces' more

immediately and reliably than changes in any other component, many of which are tangible and amorphous, thus making their calculation and exact weight elusive and subject to differing intuitive estimates and judgements rather than precise and unambiguous measurement.[65]

The argument, which the Soviets put forward, that the military factor is not a critical component of the overall calculation is clearly a self-serving rationale. Although the Soviets are at their strongest in the military field by comparison with their position in non-military factors, they are still overall the militarily weaker of the two super-powers.[66] Hence they seek to de-emphasise the importance of the military factor in the overall equation but stress their military strength in particular circumstances.

We are therefore confronted with a situation in which both the West and the Soviet Union, but for different reasons, sought to emphasise the new level of the 'Soviet military threat'; the real emphasis of the new threat was placed not so much upon the strategic nuclear capabilities of the Soviet Union as upon the lower regional or theatre level capabilities or projection abilities. In the overall context of policy with regard to Japan then, Soviet ideology sought to stress the change in regional circumstances brought on by this new military strength in north east Asia and in the process endowed the military factor in relations with a higher profile than the realities of the regional military balance would otherwise have warranted.

In consequence, the central issue of Soviet–Japanese relations came to be an obsession on the part of both nations with the military equation in north east Asia. For the Soviets it would prove to be counterproductive as the Japanese military build-up was in the main justified as a response to this changing military situation and a concern over Soviet capabilities. A regional reading of the correlation of forces with the emphasis on the military aspect may well have given the Soviets the impression that they were in a position of at least equality in some respects but at a disadvantage overall. Recognising this, the Soviets perceived a severe threat to their security emanating from American, Japanese and Chinese forces and, reacting accordingly, assigned a high priority to military balances within the region.

Initially then, we have tried to show some aspects of the wider impact of ideology on the conduct of Soviet relations with Japan. First, it impinged more than might usually be the case upon Soviet internal politicking, which in turn had repercussions for the trade debate and the eventual course of trade with Japan – as we shall discuss in the later section which deals with trade, the Japanese were to misread the signals coming from Moscow and consequently their enthusiasm for trade with the Soviets (which they mistakenly thought the Soviets shared) was misplaced and illusory. Second, it had important consequences for the military situation by overemphasising aspects of this question. These aspects have been singled out for comment above others as their influence on the conduct of relations with Japan was indirect. Due to their global nature the effect that they would have in a particular region or in cases of bi-lateral relations was unpredictable and would vary from case to case.

Japan and the global assessment

The Soviet assessment of 'centres of power' within the capitalist camp is superficially accurate. But some questions can be raised concerning it. The first concerns the problem of how within the Soviet idea can we interpret the division or equation of power between the different 'centres'? Only if we reduce the concept of 'centres of power' to a purely economic measure does it make sense to talk of Japan as any real centre of power in its own right in a *global* sense. Japanese economic power gives it, arguably, a great deal of political power regionally but it is more questionable how significant that is at a global level. This also applies to seeing Japan as a rival power centre in comparison to other members of a multipolar capitalist system.

There is a further problem in that implicit in the Soviet idea is an assumption that these are 'rival' centres of power which are divided over objectives and means of operation which bring them into friction with each other. The problem for the Soviets is that capitalist bloc interrelations do not seem to bear-out Soviet theory on how they should be interacting. The difficulty lies in determining the depth of these divisions and their significance for policy. The Soviets realise these difficulties in practice but their concept of a divisive capitalist camp does not pay enough service to them. Despite the ideological belief the Soviets are clearly unsure about the idea of division within the capitalist camp as a sound base on which to conduct policy; some Soviet ideologists have suggested that it would be unwise to overemphasise the depth of division and the extent to which it can be counted on as exploitable for the benefit of the Soviet Union while others have continued to stress the basic divisive nature of capitalism. The former grouping seems to have emerged as the dominant force, but the debate clearly continues recently bringing forth analyses to explain 'resurgent capitalism' and its significance as to whether it should deepen capitalist divisions.

M. Maksimova, in an article on the problems of European integration argues that 'American–Western European contradictions have never been sharper in the post-war period than today', but she goes on to add that, 'these two networks of capitalism are linked by a close network of capital, growing interdependence of economic development and alliance obligations'.[67] This would seem to be a more moderating, not to say more accurate, account and a counter to the more extreme voices, counselling against exaggerated perceptions of rivalry in the capitalist camp.

Maksimova's statement is indicative of a wider trend in Soviet thought which advocates caution over this question. Though couched in terms of an American–European comparison, the same could be said concerning Japanese relations with the Europeans or with the United States. In contrast to some commentaries which suggest a bitter fuelling of division between Japan and these other two capitalist centres during the 1970s (mostly to do with economic matters), Soviet writers are also aware that Japan had at the same time moved closer to them, particularly the Europeans, over some issues such as the co-ordination of energy policy and the dialogue with the Third World.[68]

On the available evidence it cannot be said that this ideological uncertainty has been reflected in the conduct of policy *vis-à-vis* Japan. The Soviets have consistently acted in a fashion which has presupposed that on substantial issues there is no hope for the foreseeable future of achieving a meaningful rupture in policy outlook between Japan and the United States or Europe. In questions of trade or trade competition with the Soviet Union, between the Japanese and the Europeans the issue has never been a source of division as Japan and Western Europe share a like approach to dealing with the Soviets; and the United States, grain deals excepted, is effectively not involved in trading at all with the Soviets. On matters of military security, the lessons which the Soviets would have gained from the comprehensive failure of their collective security proposals notwithstanding, they have similarly made no serious overt moves to encourage the severing of the military aspects of the Japanese–American alliance. This has been because they see this aim as unlikely to be attainable, and active pursuit of it likely to be counterproductive.

These assertions are made in the context of what have been referred to as 'substantial issues' or as 'serious moves'; it would be inaccurate to state that the Soviets have not played upon the obvious frictions between Japan and other leading states but the point to be made is that this provocation has taken place at a lesser level, over specific events, and not where the wide sweep of policy has been concerned. The Soviets would see this as the distinction between a dialectical approach to policy and an approach centred around what they would term 'petty politicking' (*melkoe politikantsvo*). To be sure, in the framework of Soviet–Japanese relations there are examples of this 'petty politicking' or attempts to divide Japanese opinion or policy from that of the United States. These range from Soviet interference in, or attempts to exacerbate, trade wrangles between Japan and the United States to, for example, the Soviet verbal support for the Japanese groups hostile to the F-16 deployments at Misawa airbase in order that the decision be reversed or at least modified.

There are yet other examples which we might consider which show that the Soviets have not tried to exploit divisions beyond limits. When the Chinese invaded Vietnam the Japanese government's response was far more condemnatory of China than that of the United States. Indeed the Soviets reportedly complimented the Japanese for taking such a stance during the crisis. The Soviets could well have attempted to widen this divide between Japan and the United States but made no such attempt. The divisions in the Western camp concerning sanctions over Afghanistan and Poland are another case in point. In both cases the Japanese government adopted a position far short of the measures advocated by the American government, and in some instances by European governments. In no instance did the Soviets try to use those differences for some other purpose or lead Japan to abandon or lessen sanctions by providing an incentive to do so, such as offers of new contracts or promises of a better agreement over fisheries.

To conclude on this point: the evidence of this study indicates that, though ideological dictate suggests that the Soviets should seek to promote and exploit the divisions between Japan and the United States and to a lesser extent the Europeans, in practice the Soviets have not consistently operated by this principle. They have indulged occasionally in what they would term 'petty politicking'; however they clearly feel that further action in the hope of fuelling serious discord between capitalist nations is unrealistic. Thus despite the ideological guidelines it does not follow, at least in the case of Japan, that the Soviet Union has either wished or been able to exploit the frictions between Japan and her allies beyond certain limits.

Japan and the Pacific

There are two areas in which the Japanese are involved, and on which the Soviets comment, which are global in scope but which have more relevance for the region closer to home for the Japanese. Specifically these are the questions of Japanese oil or energy dependence and Japanese aid to developing nations, particularly in South East Asia.

Oil dependence is a central concern of the Japanese in their global relations. The Soviets latched-on to this point as quickly as other observers after the 1973 oil crisis. By the end of 1974, Soviet references to capitalist countries had become subtly divided between those they viewed as 'oil dependent' and those not seen as such. In their economic assessments of Japan, Soviet writers interpret the structural reforms they see as having been undertaken in Japan during the 1970s as due in part to the effects of the oil crises, and argue that the crises exposed the underlying vulnerability of Japan. Some Soviet ideologues have gone so far as to suggest that it was this dependence (99.8%) in the main that prompted Japanese expansionism into foreign markets and the build-up of Japanese armed forces which were needed 'to protect interests abroad and Japanese supply lines'.[69]

In the actual conduct of Soviet–Japanese relations the issue of oil, and of energy in general, is one of no substance. The Soviets, despite trading agreements over the supply of natural gas from Siberia to Japan, are not a supplier of oil or fuel to Japan on any significant scale. Even though Soviet analysts have sought to contend – à la textbook Marxist economic analysis – that Japan has 'needed' the Soviet Union as a market for exports and as a source of trade (especially of fuels), the conduct of Soviet policy has been guided by a more realistic appraisal of the true circumstances. Figures for 1979 illustrate the situation vis-à-vis Japanese 'dependence' on the Soviet Union as a source of energy: imports from the Soviets as a percentage of total requirements constituted only 0.8%.

The argument that the Japanese have built-up their armed forces (in this case their naval forces) with the serious aim of protecting their interests or sea lanes of communication in areas as far away as South East Asia (as some writers imply) is not one which the Soviets have used to any lasting real effect except to score propaganda points. In these instances the propaganda value of these assertions is hard to estimate. The real thrust of the militarism argument in the context of day-to-day Soviet–Japanese relations has been the concomitant threat from militarism to the Soviet Union itself and not some ill-defined threat to far away places. It has been this threat to Soviet territory which has been attacked in ideological pronouncements and which has been one of the central problems reflected in the conduct of relations; we shall discuss this later.

The other area of concern which impinges upon Soviet estimates of Japan at both a global and regional level is the issue of Japanese overseas aid and its functions in the South East Asian region. The Asian economic journal, the *Oriental Economist* in its 1980–1 yearbook on Japan comments that despite the improvements in aid throughout the 1970s 'Japanese economic assistances are widely believed to be far from satisfactory'.[70] If we choose to look at the Japanese contribution to aid projects as a gross figure Japan emerges quite favourably; but measured as a percentage of GNP Japan emerges poorly compared to other members of the Organisation of Economic Cooperation and Development (OECD). The Soviets are very critical of both the scale and purposes of Japanese aid, as we illustrated in the first section of this chapter. In practice, when Soviet writers speak of Japanese overseas aid it is by inference Japanese aid to Asia (even more specifically, South East Asia) which is the subject of discussion. Japanese aid to Africa is occasionally mentioned, aid to Latin America and to the Middle East (which receives about 14% of total Japanese overseas aid) is mentioned only infrequently.

Having delineated the form of Soviet comment let us establish some facts on Japanese aid – a sizeable percentage of it goes to Latin America (some 30.2% in 1978), the majority of official government aid goes to Asia (60% in 1978) but as an overall percentage of the total (private plus governmental), contributions to Asia rank roughly on a par with those to Latin America. Africa holds third place on the ranking of recipients.[71] None of these points are effectively made by the Soviets. The non-discussion of Japanese involvement with the Middle East is a particularly striking omission, especially if we were to subscribe to the argument that the Soviets are very much informed on the Middle East oil and Japanese fuel dependency relationship. How can we explain these omissions? The Soviets are aware of the discrepancy between Japanese economic power and political influence, and as the Japanese are deemed to have no meaningful political influence in Latin America and the Middle East this might explain the lack of comment. It could equally be for other reasons, for example, a lack of Soviet expertise in the specific field of Japanese overseas aid and development funding (though a lack of expertise in itself indicates a low priority), a lack of knowledge on Latin America (it was hinted at the beginning of this section that co-operation between the Institute of Latin America and the 'oriental' institutes is perhaps not all it should be), or a problem of categorising both the Middle East and Latin America, since neither fits neatly under the heading of 'developing countries'; or a combination of the above.

The relevance to Soviet policy of Japanese involvement with the developing countries overlaps with a wider issue of Soviet ideological views of the Third World itself and with the idea of a 'world economy'; while not wishing to become involved in a long discussion of Soviet views of these, it would be worthwhile making some points pertinent to Japan.

Soviet analysts have pieced together a sophisticated appraisal of the factors relating to the changes in position of the developing states within the world system and of recognising that each developing state will inevitably pursue different approaches to its relations within the system. Karen Brutents (a First Deputy of the International Department of the Central Committee), in his otherwise ideologically traditionalist comment, conceded such a point; 'The emphasis on anti-imperialism and socially progressive policies differs from one country to the next. It depends on the degree of independence, government policies, socio-political complexion of the state ... Another point to note is that the development of non-discrimination (by the developing countries) in economic co-operation between socialist and capitalist states helps to establish normal and equitable economic relations throughout the world.'[72] What Brutents is implicitly admitting is that the Soviets have accepted the continued connection between developing states and the capitalist world – if only because it is inevitable and the Soviets can do nothing to change the circumstances.

The second factor to be considered is the emergence in Soviet ideological circles of the debate over the idea of a 'world economy', its functioning and its consequences. We have encountered the ramifications of this debate earlier in the Soviet theories of a divided Western camp. One of the reasons for a Soviet reluctance to exploit division beyond certain limits was the potentially adverse effects this would have on the world economy, and hence on the Soviet Union. Acting thus would imply Soviet support for the argument which asserts that if there exists a state of global interdependence there must be global problems from which no nation is secure. The Soviet advancement of the interdependence argument signalled that the process of development for the Third World lay *within* the capitalist world economic system. Brezhnev himself made this clear,

> A broad international division of labour is the only basis for keeping pace with the times and being abreast of requirements and potentialities of the scientific and technical revolution. This, I should say, is axiomatic today. Hence, the need for a mutually beneficial long-term

and large scale economic co-operation, both bilateral and unilateral ... of course this applies not only to Europe, but also to all continents, to the entire system of present day economic relations.[73]

To emphasise this point, N. S. Patolichev, Minister of Foreign Trade, at a meeting of the fourth United Nations Commission on Trade and Development (UNCTAD) in Nairobi in 1976 stated that while the Soviet Union was against 'all manifestations of inequality, diktat and exploitation in international economic relations', the Less-Developed Country (LDC) plans for new stabilisation measures for commodity prices should be at 'levels which, first, are economically sound, remunerative, and fair for producers and consumers alike' and continued to say that the Soviet Union was aware 'of the intention of the developing countries to consolidate efforts in protecting their interests on world markets ... we assume, however, that implementation of such activities will be made with due regard for the interests of both commodity producers and consumers'.[74]

There exists an obvious 'ideological unease' about the whole issue of Japanese relations with the developing world. In these circumstances of global interdependence (which the Soviets implicitly, and more recently explicitly, accept) and if, as Patolichev stated he expected that 'mutual consideration' should be the prevailing attitude to the conduct of economic relations between the developed and developing states, to what extent can we accept the Soviet criticism of Japan's relations with the South East Asian states and LDC states as neo-colonialist, as a serious influence on the actual conduct of their policy towards Japan?

In their own relations with the states in South East Asia the Soviets have used the ploy of an 'exploitative' Japanese presence as a means of making propaganda gains – but to what extent they have been successful is open to question. Other than for reasons of propaganda, the economic relationship between Japan and these states has not figured as a source of contention between the Soviets and the Japanese. Neither has the Soviet view of Japanese relations with these states been a source of friction between the Soviets and South East Asians.

It is more open to doubt, though, whether the same can be said of the political, and to a lesser degree of the military, implications of the Japanese relationship with the states of South East Asia. This brings us into contact with the Japanese ideas for a 'Pacific community' and with the militarism question.

The issue which the Soviets always regard with caution is what the Japanese might achieve by translating their economic power into military or political influence. The Pacific community project is a target for attack precisely because it implies gains for the Japanese in these very directions. As one Soviet spokesman sees it 'although mention is made all the time of one community, in reality it is hoped to kill two birds with one stone: to form a military–political alliance in the Asia–Pacific region headed by the United States to serve the interests of international reaction, and to create an exclusive economic grouping that would accord with the interests of Japanese imperialism'.[75]

The rhetoric in front of the ideological pronouncement has its basis in a real fear, and for that reason the Soviets have always considered Japanese attention to community proposals as important. The Soviet fear is not that an actual community will come about, (all commentators are sceptical that the practical problems can be surmounted), but rather that the mere idea of a Pacific grouping will act as a block to the growth of Soviet influence.

In interviews with Soviet commentators the author was told in no uncertain terms that actual creation of a Pacific community 'was doomed as nobody will follow Japan' and that 'while in principle a good idea, the practical problems make it a non-starter'. Yet the evidence suggests that the Soviets are concerned either that the Japanese will make some gain from it or that it will be used to fuel continual anti-Soviet feeling, even if nothing concrete ever comes from it. Even though comments made to the author at four Soviet research institutes were universally dismissive of the Pacific community idea, it was significant that lengthy comments were made at all and that staff in all four institutes wished to discuss it.

Attack or comment on the community proposals is a frequent feature of Soviet writings on Japan, second only to comment on the remilitarisation issue, and this of itself is significant as an indication of its concern to the Soviets. It seems that in this instance the concern expressed in ideological rhetoric has been reflected in policy, in an attitude of caution against any manifestations of a scheme which might provoke an unexpected development detrimental to Soviet interest in East Asia.

Soviet ideology and the remilitarisation of Japan

In part Soviet attacks on the Pacific community have been due to a belief on their part that the economic co-operation which forms the basis of the community has also the potential to form a framework for political, and perhaps military, co-operation.

With regard to the military situation in the East Asian region the Soviets have always stressed their capability to rebuff any aggressor and that they view the increase in their capabilities in the region as the most important factor in preventing hostilities and strengthening security. However they also make clear that in a region where the superpowers and other major powers intersect any unfavourable trend must be carefully watched as it can be potentially dangerous.

The two main influences on the military equation in the area – be it the perceived Soviet build-up or the claims of a Japanese build-up – are central to Soviet–Japanese relations. Furthermore, it is arguable that the issue has so dominated the analysis of relations between the two countries that Western observers tend to regard relations mostly as a military problem.

It would be useful to precede Soviet views of militarisation and Japanese defence capacity with a look at how the Soviets have interpreted the legal basis upon which that defence capacity is premised, i.e. Article 9 of the Japanese Constitution, which states that

> Aspiring sincerely to an international peace based on justice and order, the Japanese people forever renounce war as a sovereign right of the nation and the threat of use of force as means of settling international disputes.
>
> In order to accomplish the aim of the preceding paragraph, land, sea and air forces, as well as other war potential, will never be maintained. The right of belligerency of the state will not be recognised.

Soviet commentators have, from time to time, claimed that the existence of the Japanese Self Defence Force (JSDF) is a violation of Article 9. These references though are few and far between; the subject itself is usually given cursory passing mention in a wider context. For example, *Krasnaia Zvezda* in March 1978 commented that, 'the strength of the Japanese "self-defence forces", created in breach of the Constitution, now total ...'.[76] I. Latyshev suggested that 'despite the fact that Article 9 of the Japanese constitution prohibits the country from having any armed forces, Japan since 1954 has got an army of her own'.[77]

Despite Soviet claims since its inception that the Japanese Constitution is merely a device of the United States and of Japanese monopoly circles for justifying and achieving Japanese rearmament, equally, it has long implicitly been accepted that, regardless of semantic niceties, Japan would have armed forces of a sort, whatever they were called. The best evidence of this can be found in Soviet statements at the San Francisco conference of 1951 convened to ratify the US–UK–Japan (and hopefully, USSR) draft Peace treaty. The Soviet document, presented by Gromyko, which attacked the Western bias of the proposed treaty, also attacked it for not containing 'any guarantees against the re-establishment of Japanese militarism'. More to the point, Gromyko also submitted eight new articles for inclusion in any treaty. Two of these articles envisaged 'The strict limitation of the nature and size of Japanese defensive forces' and 'Restrictions on the nature of military training in Japan'.[78]

The Soviets clearly harboured no illusions that Article 9 of the Constitution would act as a bar to a sovereign nation possessing armed forces of some sort. They conceded in the above statement that they expected that there would be military training/activity in Japan – their concern was to try and limit it. This 'limitation' theme has been continually pushed by the Soviets; the Latyshev article mentioned above symbolises this – his point of departure for criticism relates not to the fact that Japanese armed forces exist but to the fact that they are *rapidly expanding* armed forces.[79]

We indicated in the first section that publicly the Soviets appear divided over whether to attribute the rising trend of militarisation in Japan to the Americans 'whose ruling classes wish to hold Japan as an outpost of capitalism' or to lay it at the door of the Japanese who have become more involved in pursuing their own goals by their own means. On balance the weight of opinion in the Soviet press seem to favour the former thesis.

V. P. Lukin, head of the section in the Institute of the United States and Canada which deals with American strategy in the Pacific, commented on this question that 'It would be oversimplistic to say that Japan is either a puppet or independent of the United States. The truth is in the middle somewhere. The strength of the links varies from topic to topic and situation to situation', but that 'in specific terms Japan is less independent from the United States than the other allies'. He added that over the question of military co-operation (in technology in particular) the first priority of the United States was to 'use' Japan.

Japanese military associations with China have received considerable attention in the Soviet press and were highlighted by the 1978 treaty coverage. However, even here where Soviet concerns are very real, there are strands of ideology which stress that the irresoluble contradictions between the Chinese and the Japanese will place limits on the extent of collaboration.

> China and Japan remain as before, two rivals in the struggle for domination in Asia which is likely to intensify as China's economic and military might increases and it exerts greater influence on the continent, and in particular in south east Asia. Each side considers the region to be its zone of influence and would be unlikely to make

concessions there ... although Peking hypocritically declares that it welcomes the build-up of Japanese military might it would take all the necessary steps to keep the armed forces of that country below a certain level, so that they do not become superior to the Chinese military machine.[80]

Western observers tend not to appreciate the substance of Soviet concern over trends in Japanese force development, especially as there is for the most part no Chinese criticism of Japanese expansion. But the situations for the Soviet Union and China are very different. To take one important difference as an example of how the Soviets would see the problem, let us compare the populations of the respective stretches of coastal territory facing Japan: that of the Soviet Far East (an area of 6,215,900 square kilometres) according to the Soviet 1979 census, totals only 6,819,000 persons. The Chinese coastal provinces of Liao-nung, Jilin and Heilongjiang have a combined population in excess of 90 million, further south the provinces of Jiangsu, Fujion and Zhejang have a population of over 126 million.[81]

In an interview with the author in late 1984, a Soviet academic suggested that the situation *vis-à-vis* Japanese militarisation had reached new degrees of seriousness 'not present five years ago'. He listed seven factors which he thought especially significant; the deployment of F-16s to Misawa airbase; the decision to fit Cruise missiles to American ships in the north west Pacific; the Japanese government's decision to co-operate more fully with the United States on matters of military technology; the plans for a '1000 mile zone' which he viewed as 'if not feasible today then tomorrow'; the *de facto* Japanese ability to blockade the straits around Japan to Soviet ship-ping; the realities of Japanese co-operation with Korea, the United States and NATO; and the general mood of anti-Sovietism in Japan.[82]

That which is observable in the conduct of Soviet policy both at an operational and strategic level with regard to Japan has reflected the fear over the course of militarism. Soviet attention to the issue has taken the form either of direct attacks on Japanese initiatives or indirect approaches designed to limit the possibilities of Japanese action. The best recent illustration of this two-sided approach has been the Soviet call for discussions on Confidence Building Measures (CBMs) in the Far East.

The original Soviet collective security proposals advanced in 1969 have long been accepted as a dead letter but in his speech at Taskhent on 25 March 1982 Brezhnev added new substance to the idea by expanding on a reference he had made a year earlier on 'discussing mutual fears' and making the offer more direct, 'our proposal on

CBMs in the Far East does not necessarily presuppose an immediate collective assembly of all that region's countries. It is fully possible to begin movement along the path on a bilateral basis – for example, between the Soviet Union and Japan. What is bad about that? Nothing!'[83]

In subsequent statements it became obvious that some sort of collective scheme was being floated but the real basis of Soviet hopes was two bi-lateral agreements involving Japan and China.[84] Officials from both the Soviet Union and Japan publicly stated that the lessons learned from the European experience of CBMs would be of use and the Japanese publicly endorsed the idea. However Tokyo subsequently changed its attitude, suggesting that the situation in East Asia was sufficiently different from Europe as to make the scheme impractical.

Andropov pursued the idea further and proposed that the Soviet Union hold talks with Japan over the deployment to the Far East of Soviet SS-20s.[85] It is noteworthy that commenting on this proposal, A. A. Gromyko specifically indicated that the missiles were being deployed to the Far Eastern theatre so openly because there was no agreement with Japan that could limit such a move.

As with the question of trade, over the issues of Japanese militarism it is fair to argue that there is a clear connection between the ideological rhetoric and the salience or centrality of the issue for the conduct of overall policy. High placed Soviet officials commenting publicly on Japan invariably seemed to include (and this is certainly the case by the late 1970s) a reference to Japanese revanchism in their speeches and perhaps this, as much as any other indicator, is a guide to the issue's importance for the Soviets.

Japanese internal politics

We stated in our opening section that any Soviet ideological evaluation of a state political system begins with an analysis of class interests. Other factors, which in a non-Marxist–Leninist estimate might be deemed of significance, such as 'values', are only seen to play a role in the sense that class interests are viewed as constituting the ultimate in values. Other variables which might be of importance in determining the political mould of a state are seen as merely a means to an end for the ruling class of the state.

The Soviet analyses of the role the Japanese ruling classes have in policy-making unanimously stress the decisive influence of the big business groups. They maintain this influence either through the necessity to secure overseas markets or through their capacity as the main weapons manufacturers – as one Soviet writer expressed it, 'one out of every seven companies registered on the Tokyo stock exchange works for war'.

This is not to say that there is not friction between business and government, or between both and the Prime Minister. That this does occur is aptly demonstrated by the attacks on Prime Minister Miki over the Lockheed scandal. Commenting on why Miki had to shelve some of his plans to reorganise aspects of LDP policy, I. Kovalenko considered that

> Finding himself at the helm of government but having practically no major faction to back him, Miki is forced to reckon with the Party bosses and big business. His 'welfare policy' – the fight against inflation and economic recession, restriction of the growth of commodity prices, promulgation of anti-monopoly laws, and a promise to reorganise the electoral system and follow a policy of dialogue with the Opposition – has been shelved. Premier Miki has been forced to admit that 'there are limits to the LDP concessions to the Opposition'. He has been reminded that he must adhere to the traditional conservative policy and faithfully serve big business. [86]

Yet the Soviets saw the Lockheed affair as Miki's chance to fight back against those elements who opposed him. Miki used the information that the Lockheed corporation had been bribing members of the Japanese government and business community, including former Prime Minister Tanaka, as a means of organising support (both parliamentary and public) behind him.

Concerning the alignment of progressive forces in Japan, the Soviet view recognises the potential for the pacifist groups to limit the expansion of 'undesirable trends', due to both the scale and broad base of these groups' support. Indeed they recognise that the wide, national feeling of pacifism which exists in Japan sets the general limit for militarism. However the placing of the JCP in the forefront of the action against these 'undesirable trends' is an ideological decision not without its political complications. We have already seen how Tamghinsky has dismissed the JSP as 'slipping further right' and how he accused it of refusing to co-operate with the JCP; in contrast to his attack on the JSP he subsequently lauded the efforts of the JCP.

In turn, in contrast to Tamghinsky's assessment consider opinions voiced by Kovalenko on the same subject

> It must be pointed out that in the first place, in spite of the serious difficulties between the JCP and the JSP there is much in common in the provisions of their programmes which creates a basis for develop-

ing broader co-operation. The bulk of the JSP members are against US imperialism and Japanese monopoly capital, fights against the revival of militarism and demands all US troops be withdrawn from Japanese territory ... nevertheless the JCP and other progressive forces have failed to draw up a broad programme of united action against imperialism and reaction in defence of the vital interests of the people.[87]

Implicit in this statement by Kovalenko is a criticism of JCP policy and at the same time a more optimistic appraisal of the merits of JSP policy. This puts him at odds with Tamghinsky. Though, obviously for reasons of politics, Kovalenko fails to make his criticism more than implicit, the telling factor is that his article written in 1980 – except for detailing JCP success in the 1979 elections – makes no mention of JCP activity after 1975. The reason for this omission is that post-1975 JCP relations with the Communist Party of the Soviet Union (CPSU) became exceptionally acrimonious. The gulf had not been significantly narrowed by 1980, at the time when Kovalenko was writing, nor has it been ameliorated since.

To take the above points (salience of big business groups, divisions in Japanese politics, role of the JCP) can we say that these have had any role in Soviet policy? Have the Soviets sought to exploit these divisions or sought to influence the course of events in Japanese politics in their favour? Here, unfortunately we have to concede that we are dealing with imponderables – in most cases it is only the Soviets who can provide answers. There is evidence, from the Soviet defector Levchenko who was based at the Tokyo embassy, that there were by his estimate 200 Soviet agents in Japan (mostly defined under that unsatisfactory heading of 'agents of influence'). Levchenko's objective via them was

> to create a pro-Soviet lobby among prominent Japanese politicians (through penetration of the Liberal Democratic and Social Democratic parties) leading to closer economic and political ties between the Soviet Union and Japan and the creation of a political monopoly in the Japanese parliament. The Japanese government likewise was to be penetrated through the use of high ranking agents of influence, business leaders and mass media.[88]

Even if we assume that any grouping which could legitimately be labelled a 'pro-Soviet lobby' had emerged in Japanese politics it would be safe to say that, outside individual business deals where it was motivated as much by self-interest as Soviet interest, it has not been an effective 'pro-Soviet lobby'. If the Soviets have seriously tried to exploit divisions which they believe exist in Japanese politics then the results of their efforts are not evident. Despite Soviet support for the

JCP it is a party unlikely to achieve government or even coalition status and consequently the Soviets have never risked a permanent souring of relations with the LDP or the Socialists over Soviet connections with the JCP, or over the role of the JCP in Japanese politics. In several speeches, and during visits to Japan, the Soviets have made a point of courting the Socialists (JSP) but the results have been variable. Soviet moves at intervening in Japanese politics have not succeeded in changing the general climate of suspicion of them; at best what can be said is that the Soviets have influenced the outcomes of single events. It has been suggested that the Soviet 'agents' or lobby in Japan managed to get Belenko's Mig-25 returned faster than might otherwise have been the case.[89] The Japanese circumvention of American sanctions over Afghanistan might arguably be another case where the influences of a 'pro-Soviet lobby' within the business community might have played some role.

If there is one area where the Soviet ideological vision can be seen to have application to Soviet relations in an internal Japanese context, this could be the case of Soviet dealings with the large business groups in Japan. In their trade relations with the Japanese the Soviets have only dealt with the large groups of Japanese firms: this could (economically) be explained by the fact that only the large companies were capable of providing the goods, on the scale and at the price, that the Soviets wanted. We could speculate that (politically) given the ideological supposition that the big business groups were a main source of influence in Japanese policy-making, it makes sense to direct efforts at trade, or at creating a pro-Soviet lobby in Japan through those groups, perhaps at the expense of any gains that might have been forthcoming from trading with smaller companies.

The Soviet interpretation of the worsening condition of the working class in Japan is probably the closest to a textbook evaluation such as we would expect from a Marxist–Leninist standpoint. The evidence used to substantiate Soviet interpretations revolves around the figures showing the increasing number of unemployed, the greater frequency of industrial disputes and the rising trends in prices. Much as with the Soviet estimation of Japanese overseas development aid, the final picture depends on how we wish to compare the statistics. Compared to Japanese circumstances of earlier years, the 1970s were certainly not as dynamic. But this does not of itself make them 'bad' years; compared to other advanced industrial nations Japan fared particularly well overall. Japanese government figures for 1971–9 show a tripling of private consumption expenditure, an increase in real income by 2.4 times, and an increase in disposable income by 2.2

times. Statistics bear out the case that 1973–4 and 1975–6 were years in which unemployment rose exceptionally fast – from 730,000 in 1972 to 1,117,000 in 1979. This represents an increase of 53% but taken in the context of total population, a figure of 1,117,000 unemployed out of a population of 116 million was not disastrous.[90] (In the United Kingdom during the same time-frame unemployment rose to 2.5 times the Japanese level in a population only half the size of Japan's.) When compared to the performance of Western economies in the same period, the outstanding durability of the Japanese economy speaks for itself.

The real significance of the Soviet point on the increase in frequency of Japanese labour disputes is similarly open to qualification. The highpoint was 1974 when they numbered 10,462. The largest number of participants involved in disputes was recorded in 1976 at 17,178,000. But these years of the middle 1970s proved to be a turning point as both figures have since declined dramatically, with the actual number of participants striking being very much less than that involved in disputes (i.e. increasingly disputes have been settled without recourse to strike action).

R. Buckley, Professor of International Relations at the International University of Japan, is of the view that Japanese industrial relations have been less antagonistic than Western counterparts for two basic reasons: firstly, the rights which the unions secured, and secondly, the fact that 'some of the harsher medicine can be handed out to subcontracting firms and part-timers who are not unionised'.[91]

The positions of unions are secure. Most large corporations possess an enterprise union which is empowered to negotiate for everybody. In general, Buckley is of the view

> it should not be taken to imply that Unions in Japan are puppets of management ... Unions, thanks to the encouragement of SCAP's [Supreme Commander Allied Powers (Japan)] labour division, gained immense power during the occupation that neither the companies nor successive conservative governments have been in a position to alter substantially ... Unionisation is part of the fabric of larger Japanese companies ... the closed shop rules.[92]

In conversations with the author, V. Khlynov, now a resident analyst at IMEMO, posited that given their problems – the creeping collapse of the system that has served so well in the past – it was uncertain what would develop in Japan in the future. The rise of worker participation was one speculated option. Class distinction, he said, was very much a fact of life in Japan. Referring to frequent Japanese censuses Khlynov stated that although 90% of respondents had claimed to be 'middle class' there were many categories of 'middle class' and that the majority of respondents were in fact in the lower echelons of the 'middle class' bracket. Japanese workers were undoubtedly worse-off, but he was willing to speculate that perhaps the Japanese would work something out as 'they are a flexible people'.

The claims made by Khlynov with regard to this oft quoted '90%' are in a general sense probably true. This figure, which has been repeated in Japanese censuses over many years, is in dispute in the West also, as failing to represent the true distinctions which exist in Japanese society. Japan, its image apart, is still a nation of small businesses. The view of the economy as booming and successful is no more than one way of viewing a nation – there are always distinctions to be found beneath the surface. An example of this is given by Buckley who, commenting on the image of the Japanese worker, suggests that it tends to be drawn from our image of the large corporation whereas the reality for the larger number of workers employed in the smaller businesses can be very different:

> blue collar workers, those employed in subsidiary firms and the temporary staff get a rawer deal. These categories gain fewer benefits from their employer and are regarded as no more than adjuncts to the company for whom they work. Wages in smaller companies are lower, working conditions are less pleasant and safe, bonuses can be minimal and job security non-existent.[93]

Social circumstances of the Japanese present a mixed picture, with steady improvements being made in areas previously held to be deficient. While the stress in Japan has been placed on economic growth, little thought had been given to the social consequences of that growth, and the effects of that became transparent in the 1960s. Social welfare at a level commensurate with that in European nations was lacking throughout the 1960s and did not start to make inroads until well into the 1970s, but it has made great headway since. In some areas, such as health and education, the Japanese are world leaders.

The estimates, of which Khlynov's is a typical example, of the effects of the structural reformation of the Japanese economy in the 1970s and early 1980s and of the situation of the Japanese workforce are clearly at odds with the typical Western assessment of the Japanese economy. Even the British *New Left Review* wrote that while Japan has had problems from structural recession things are far from bad.

> Although the 1973–75 recession forced a slow down in Japan's growth it has still managed to stay ahead of its main competitors. Japan's GNP now surpasses that of the USSR, while its per capita GNP is roughly equal to that of the US (depending on fluctuating

exchange rates) and about 15 per cent higher than that of the EEC. Real GDP growth over the decade 1970–79 was 6 per cent per annum, nearly double the OECD average of 3.4 per cent and that of its chief competitor, West Germany (3.2 per cent). Furthermore, Japan is still much more agile than the other leading OECD countries at industrial reconversion and is also ahead in several areas of technology. In addition, Japan enjoyed for a time a very large current account surplus ($25 billion in 1978) that was greater than all of the OECD countries combined . . . Japan is, in general terms well positioned to take advantage of the next phase of economic development in East Asia.[94]

And even if somewhat overenthusiastic, Vogel still sums-up the general Western view of Japan when he writes that

> At present, in political and cultural influence and even in gross national product, Japan is not the number one power in the world . . . Yet in the effectiveness of its present-day institutions in coping with the current problems of the post-industrial era Japan is number one. Considering its limited space and natural resources and its crowding, Japan's achievements in economic productivity, educational standards, health, and control of crime are in a class by themselves.[95]

2 SOVIET–JAPANESE ECONOMIC RELATIONS

THE SOVIET–JAPANESE ECONOMIC RELATIONSHIP

It is our intention in this part of the work to review the question of Soviet–Japanese economic relations. Soviet leaders have constantly emphasised that good trade relations between countries form the basis for the further expansion of relations. In the particular case of relations with Japan, both sides have claimed satisfaction with the state of economic ties throughout the 1970s but have subsequently lamented the deterioration of those favourable conditions. During the decade of growing trade relations the general state of overall relations between the two nations was, by common agreement, far from satisfactory. Japanese commentators almost uniformly refer to past circumstances as 'bad'. Soviet counterparts tend overall to be less damning but still contend that during these years there was 'room for greater development' in the scope of association between Japan and the Soviet Union. In this situation of uneasy diplomatic accommodation we should not be surprised to find, as was claimed, trade continuing apace: the depoliticisation of trade is not uncommon in international affairs.

Soviet pronouncements apart, it is not inevitable that a good trading partnership equates with good relations. Certainly there is room to doubt the validity of the often hyperbolic claims made with regard to both the content and prospects of Soviet–Japanese economic association given the static nature of other facets of relations and the positively hostile content of the military aspects as evaluated by Western and Japanese commentators.

The mainframe of Soviet–Japanese economic relations involves the economic development of Siberia and the Soviet Far East. Siberia by the mid-1970s and more so by the turn of the 1980s was accounting for a very large share of the range of resources required by the Soviet economy. Western Siberia by the present day has become the primary energy producing region of the Soviet Union, producing more than half of the country's fuel requirements. Consequently, the development of the region was a first priority for the Soviet leadership. The presumed advantage for Japan in helping to develop Siberia lay in its proximity, and consequent cost advantage. Almost without exception Western economic observers characterise Soviet–Japanese trade structures as 'complementary' – reducing this to an equation of Japanese technology traded for Soviet mineral resources.

Trade collaboration began in the late 1950s. Spandaryan, the Soviet trade representative in Japan for many years, suggests that they have been 'developing dynamically since December 1957'.[1] Jain contends that this situation came about at that time due to a Soviet search for new markets to replace the Chinese, and so the Soviet approach to Japan changed from a denunciation of Japan as an appendage of the American economic system to one that stressed the complementary nature of the economies and the proximity of a 'natural trading partner'.[2]

The 'proximity' argument, as we shall term it, returns again and again as an explanation for Soviet–Japanese trade. Even in 1983, when trade levels were falling, a leading Japanese economist and Director of the Japan–USSR trade association could still write:

> Japan and the Soviet Union are two neighbouring countries. Despite their different socio-economic systems, the geographical proximity alone is conducive to the development of close economic and trade relations between them. Moreover, the structure of trade activities and the nature of trade commodities between the two continue to be mutually supplementary and beneficial ... This trading pattern, which will not change drastically through the 1980s basically fits the trade structures and economic needs of both countries.[3]

Although the existence of a trade agreement is not necessarily a prerequisite for trade, since 1966 trade between the two nations has been regulated by five year agreements, the first of which covered the period 1966–70. Until the middle 1970s the value of trade doubled almost every five years: in 1961–5, 1,300 million roubles; 1966–70, 2,600 million; 1971–6, 6,100 million roubles.[4] Although trading has been carried-out within the framework of these plans since the middle 1960s, the Soviets have continually lobbied for a long term trade agreement of ten to fifteen years' duration. The Japanese for their part have consistently refused, and so remain, according to Spandaryan, the only major developed capitalist country which has no long term economic co-operation agreement with the Soviet Union. It would be legitimate to ask why this should be so. We shall return to this question in the second part of this section.

The basic medium of Soviet–Japanese dealing has been trade via a 'compensation agreement', a system favoured by Brezhnev himself, and utilised in dealings with other Western nations. Under a compensation agreement the Western partner contracts to supply machinery or equipment to the Soviet Union on usually long-term deferred low-interest credit. The Soviets then repay the original loan plus interest in the form of finished goods or raw materials.

The commodities covered by these agreements can be principally classified as energy equipment and technology and lumber products, but include a wide range of products varying from petroleum industry heavy equipment, timber, chemicals, mineral ores and agricultural machinery at one end of the scale to clocks, radios, calculators, whale meat, handicrafts and 'products of Tibetan medicine' at the other. The Soviets export a more diverse range than they import, the balance (in terms of categories) being roughly 78–61 in their favour.[5] However these latter commodities (clocks, radios, handicrafts etc) constitute only a very small percentage of both volume and value of overall trade. The significant orientation of trade is towards energy, whether petroleum, gas or coal. Japan is the largest market for Soviet timber and coal exports and in 1979, for example, it is estimated that some 45% of total; Japanese exports to the Soviet Union were energy related. Among the many projects in which Japan is involved, the three most important are the exploitation of Yakutian natural gas, the extraction of South Yakutian coal and the Sakhalin offshore oil and gas project, and these will be briefly described.

For Yakutian natural gas the first contracts were signed in 1975 in a tripartite agreement between the Soviet Union, Japan and the United States. It was agreed then that production would not start until the end of exploration whereupon the gas discovered would be divided three ways at market prices. Japanese firms and the government advanced an initial $25 million. The plan for development also included the construction of a pipeline to the new port of Olga on the Pacific, and of new facilities at the port site. Initial estimates for overall development placed the cost at $3.4 thousand million. Completion of the project would have involved the construction of more than 1,700 miles of pipeline across a mountain range and otherwise rough terrain in appalling climatic conditions. (It is not unusual for the temperature in mid-winter in Yakutia to reach −60°C and lower). In order to minimise the problems the Soviets in 1978 suggested constructing a pipeline to Magadan but by 1980 had reverted back to the Olga location. The Japanese, not surprisingly, were rather hesitant about committing capital to such an undertaking and

54

the issue of who should bear the majority of the costs is still under negotiation.[6]

Known substantial reserves of coal in South Yakutia led to Japanese involvement in 1974 to provide $450 million in credit for its mining, which would be repaid in coal exports beginning in 1983, resulting in Japan receiving 85 million tons of coking coal by the year 2000. The Japanese loaned another $42.5 million to the project in 1980. The general agreement also allows for the provision of one million tons of coal from the Kuznetsk basin annually between 1979 and 1999. Involved in the Yakutian project has been the construction of the 400 kilometre 'little BAM' (Baikal – Amur Mainline) railroad which joins the coal fields at Neriungri with the new BAM line. A number of Japanese companies have been involved in the project, selling a variety of mining equipment; coal rotors, excavation machinery, transport vehicles and even electric locomotives. The full-scale development of the coal fields in Eastern Siberia is regarded as a priority by the Soviets and by 1982, 50% of all investment in the BAM zone had gone into the South Yakutia territorial production complex,[7] while the coking coal project has come to be regarded as the centre-piece of Japanese involvement in Siberia.[8]

Recent new Gorbachev initiatives on joint venture programmes may have played a part in speeding-up the agreement between the Soviets and a consortium of Japanese companies, in May 1987, to establish a major polyester production complex at Blagoveshchensk. It is planned to enter production in 1990–2 and is planned to increase total Soviet polyester production by at least 40%. The Japanese companies have invested $600 million.

The Sakhalin Oil Development Corporation (SODECO) is responsible for the exploration for oil off the continental shelf; begun in 1975 with $100 million of Japanese credit it serves as a good example of co-operation between the two nations. In return for their investment the Japanese will receive for a period of ten years 50% of the oil and gas discovered at a discount price. Oil has already been found north east of Sakhalin in the Sea of Okhotsk. The *Chaivo* field deposit has reserves estimated at 630 million barrels of crude oil, 140.5 thousand million cubic metres of gas and 142 thousand million barrels of condensate. Further exploratory drilling has been undertaken in the *Odoptu More* field and there are plans to explore in the Tatar Strait.

The Soviets have plans to build a special facility on Sakhalin to construct ice-resistant equipment for drilling.[9] But it is far from certain when the first deliveries will begin, as the construction of a transport infrastructure will require further substantial outlays of capital.

Both parties also signed a scientific–technical agreement in 1973 and the Soviets in particular pushed for a bi-lateral agreement on Atomic energy co-operation, which was eventually signed in 1977. Under the terms of the agreement both parties undertook to send survey teams to each others' countries and exchange researchers on power reactors. The Soviet Union would also like to sell enriched uranium to the Japanese in return for Japanese equipment to be used in Soviet nuclear power facilities.[10]

Given the scope of negotiations, trade agreements were often made through semi-official Japanese government agencies. These for the most part are the Keidanren (Federation of Economic Organisations), the Joint Soviet–Japanese Economic Committee (established 1965), Japanese Chamber of Commerce and Industry, Japan Export–Import Bank and the Japan Association for Trade with Socialist Countries. The Soviets have effectively dealt only with major Japanese corporations (by 1980 over twenty major Japanese firms had offices in Moscow); however, in recent years the Soviets have begun to propose smaller scale collaboration projects 'in which there are no compensation or financial problems and in which participation by medium and smaller businesses is feasible – for example, the production of aluminium from nephaline, lumber mills for making fuel (briquettes) from scrap lumber [sic], mobile facilities for processing scrap lumber into briquettes, and secondary raw material processing (e.g. the processing of cable scrap or used tirecord)'.[11]

The one exception to the pattern followed hitherto of trading with major corporations is to be found in coastal trading. This is regional or local trade conducted, in this case, basically between the Soviet Maritime province and the Japanese main island of Hokkaido. The Soviet trade organisation 'Dalintorg', based in Nakhodka, is the main agent on the Soviet side. The actual scale of trading is minimal; its total value rose from $66.35 million in 1977 to $122.91 in 1981. It encompasses small scale agreements for the trade in timber, small machine parts and consumer-oriented goods. The Japanese mostly import timber and petrol, oil and lubricants and (sea) foods; they export mainly clothes and textiles as well as a wide range of smaller products such as chemicals, paints, polyvinyl sheets, shoes and wire tyres.[12] In the opinion of one Soviet writer

> coastal trade is particularly significant in that it meets consumer demands. A part of the funds received from coastal trade is channelled to meet the needs of those local industries which produce for export ... coastal trade provides opportunities primarily for small enterprises which suffer the most from competition from the big

Table 1 *Japanese containerised shipments on the trans-Siberian, 1971–81*

Year	Total	Westbound	Eastbound
1971	2,314	1,823	491
1972	12,558	9,601	2,957
1973	28,289	18,959	9,330
1974	51,500	34,400	17,100
1975	62,600	50,100	12,500
1976	79,861	57,684	22,177
1977	–	–	–
1978	73,723	52,832	20,891
1979	81,669	56,216	25,453
1980	97,156	74,030	23,126
1981 Jan–Jul	63,563	51,113	12,450

Note: Transportation Freight Units (TFUs), 20-foot units
Dashes indicate information not available
Source: J. L. Scherer (ed.), *USSR Facts and Figures Annual* (Florida, Academic International Press, 1982, p. 327

firms. It is no exaggeration that many small businesses and co-operatives would be crushed by monopolies without the stable market for goods produced by coastal trade and this would mean unemployment and loss of substance for many working people.[13]

By 1976 this trade was being transacted involving over 100 small and medium sized Japanese companies and was the largest growth area in the sphere of economic relations.

Aside from Siberia's resource significance, the region is also of importance to Japan as the shortest transit route for goods to European markets. In order to encourage the Japanese to utilise this service the Soviets have constantly quoted lower transport rates than the alternative water route charges. The trans-Siberian container service (TSCS) is the world's longest land transport route. The Soviets and Japanese signed their first agreement on containerised traffic in 1970 but arrangements over the unloading and carrying were rather *ad hoc* and it was not until 1971 that an actual container freighter unloaded in a Soviet port. The new port of Vostochnii is the principal container centre in the Maritime province. Both partners operate specifically designed and built container ships and all the profits from the freight carriage are 'pooled and then divided in proportion to the time spent on the line by the ships of each side'.[14] Table 1 illustrates the volume of containerised freight traffic carried on the trans-Siberian. From the figures it can be seen that growth in this trade has been fairly constant throughout the 1970s, a slight decline in 1977–9, and a sharp increase

57

Table 2 *Comparison of Soviet trade with the Federal Republic of Germany, Finland and Japan*
(values in millions of roubles)

Year	Country	Total trade	Exports	Imports
1971	Federal Republic of Germany	666.6	254.7	411.9
	Finland	569.1	322.8	246.3
	Japan	733.6	377.4	356.2
1972	Federal Republic of Germany	827.3	255.9	571.4
	Finland	601.7	297.6	304.1
	Japan	815.6	381.7	433.9
1973	Federal Republic of Germany	1,210.2	453.8	756.4
	Finland	777.4	415.1	362.3
	Japan	994.4	622.0	372.4
1974	Federal Republic of Germany	2,208.7	834.5	1,374.2
	Finland	1,539.7	937.6	602.1
	Japan	1,683.2	905.7	777.5
1975	Federal Republic of Germany	3,008.8	1,069.2	1,939.6
	Finland	1,979.1	990.3	988.8
	Japan	2,120.5	748.4	1,372.1
1977	Federal Republic of Germany	2,967.3	1,222.7	1,744.6
	Finland	2,173.5	1,050.2	1,123.3
	Japan	2,297.8	853.4	1,444.4
1978	Federal Republic of Germany	3,304.2	1,362.6	1,941.6
	Finland	2,868.2	1,003.8	1,864.4
	Japan	2,319.8	736.1	1,583.7
1979	Federal Republic of Germany	4,246.6	2,005.9	2,240.7
	Finland	2,606.5	1,468.7	1,137.8
	Japan	2,597.9	944.4	1,653.5
1980	Federal Republic of Germany	5,780.0	2,859.4	2,920.6
	Finland	3,888.5	2,023.4	1,865.1
	Japan	2,722.8	950.2	1,772.6
1981	Federal Republic of Germany	6,009.3	3,387.9	2,621.4
	Finland	4,189.3	2,524.4	1,664.9
	Japan	3,029.5	816.8	2,212.7
1982	Federal Republic of Germany	6,629.7	3,796.6	2,833.1
	Finland	5,193.5	2,395.7	2,797.8
	Japan	3,682.4	756.6	2,925.8
1983	Federal Republic of Germany	7,022.0	3,772.8	3,249.2
	Finland	5,173.3	2,483.3	2,690.0
	Japan	3,004.0	828.5	2,175.5
1984	Federal Republic of Germany	6,826.7	3,649.2	3,177.5
	Finland	4,679.9	2,118.5	2,561.4
	Japan	2,894.3	840.0	2,054.3
1985	Federal Republic of Germany	7,086.0	3,992.0	3,094.0
	Finland	4,986.0	2,299.0	2,687.0
	Japan	3,215.0	928.0	2,287.0

Note: By 1982 both Italy and France had surpassed Japan in terms of the value of total trade. In 1982 their values stood at 4,086.1 and 3,558.6 million roubles respectively. By 1983 these had risen to 4,434.7 and 4,149.9 respectively. In 1985 their values stood at 3,793.5 and 3,778.4 respectively.
Source: *Vneshniaia Torgovlia SSSR* (Foreign Trade of the USSR), Moscow, Ministry of Foreign Trade)

Table 3 *Soviet trade with Japan as a percentage of total trade (millions of roubles)*

Year	Total trade	Japanese trade	% of total
1971	23,657.5	733.6	3.09
1972	26,037.4	815.6	3.13
1973	39,572.2	1,683.2	4.25
1976	56,755.0	2,120.5	3.73
1977	63,353.3	2,297.8	3.63
1978	70,224.1	2,319.8	3.30
1979	80,290.3	2,597.9	3.23
1980	94,010.0	2,722.8	2.89
1981	109,739.2	3,029.5	2.76
1982	119,576.1	3,682.4	2.66
1983	127,476.0	3,004.0	2.35
1984	139,759.0	2,894.3	2.07
1985	141,566.0	3,215.0	2.77

Source: Vneshniaia Torgovlia SSSR (Foreign Trade of the USSR), (Moscow, Ministry of Foreign Trade)

in 1982. But Tavrovsky has stated that this level declined sharply in 1983.[15] Japanese exports (Westbound) have always been at least two or three times the volume of imports carried by the line. Though seemingly impressive figures, we shall show that only a very small proportion of Japanese trade is carried by the trans-Siberian.

Japanese trade with the Soviets appears of immense value, but to gauge its true significance we should compare it to trade with major Western trading partners of the Soviets. Table 2 provides a comparison of total trade values between Japan, West Germany and Finland. Tables 3 and 4 provide further comparative information on Soviet–Japanese trade.

The main emphasis of Siberian development has been on energy (oil, coal, natural gas) extraction. By 1975 the Soviets were involved with five major Western nations in natural gas projects alone. By that date Japan (in consort with the United States) had supplied $50 million in credit for such projects – yet Italy had supplied $190 million, France $250 million and West Germany $1,500 million. At that stage it was estimated that by 1981–5 the value of their respective contracts would be worth $2,200, $1,462 and $5,700 million respectively.[16] In fact the values of the contracts have increased since, while the projected Japanese figure ($5,000 million) has not materialised due to delayed negotiations and changes of mind on the South Yakutia development.

Table 4 *Soviet Trade with Japan as a percentage of trade with capitalist bloc*

Year	Total trade %	Exports %	Imports %
1971	14.43	14.76	13.70
1972	13.88	15.64	12.61
1973	11.92	16.58	8.11
1974	13.57	14.47	12.66
1975	–	–	–
1976	11.36	9.56	12.67
1977	12.25	9.68	14.56
1978	11.79	8.46	14.43
1979	10.09	7.55	12.48
1980	8.62	5.99	11.27
1981	8.56	4.73	12.21
1982	9.75	4.01	15.48
1983	7.82	–	–
1984	6.95	3.93	10.49
1985	8.49	4.99	11.87

Note: Dashes indicate information not available
Source: *Vneshniaia Torgovlia SSSR* (Foreign Trade of the USSR), (Moscow, Ministry of Foreign Trade)

West German imports of natural gas, for example, are far in excess of Japanese figures; in 1980 these stood at 10,000 cubic metres or 18% of West German requirements and all imports of gas to Italy, Finland, Austria and France are estimated to rise dramatically by the 1990s in return for greater investment by these countries in Siberian development projects.[17]

There are two areas where Japanese trade involvement differs significantly from that of Western nations; one is the involvement in large scale forestry development (there are some Soviet–Finnish forestry projects), the other the sale of large quantities of steel pipe. Since the early 1970s Japan constantly supplied credit to forestry projects in Siberia, either for timber, wood pulp or chip and timber mill construction. Investment in these schemes can be substantial (but divided over long term) – the second forestry resources contract (July 1974) was worth $500 million, for the third (March 1981) which covered 1981–6, the Japanese agreed to loan $1,000 millions. The European nations are not involved at a scale comparable with Japan in these projects.

The Soviet Union ranked in 1981 as the third highest importer of Japanese steel (after the United States and China). This is due solely to the sale of large quantities of steel pipe by Japan to the Soviets. The export of these 'pipes, tubes and fittings' by Japan in 1975–9 reportedly constituted between 34 to 53% of all trade in these goods between the European nations, Japan and the United States and the CMEA nations (almost wholly to the Soviets).[18]

THE POLITICS OF SOVIET–JAPANESE TRADE

What is the Soviet view of foreign trade? The early Bolshevik leaders opted for the goal of economic self-sufficiency as necessary for the independence and protection of the new Soviet state. Serious dependence on any capitalist state was viewed as leaving the Soviets open to pressure and subversion. That basic line has not changed.

V. Gruzinov, a Soviet writer on foreign trade has the following to say on various aspects of trade:

> Foreign trade is trade between countries. Its specific features, the way it develops, and its role in the economy are determined by the mode of production, as is the case with any other branch of the economy . . . (in capitalist countries) foreign trade does not accord with the interests and needs of the nation. Maximum profit, not the needs of the economy, is its driving force . . . under socialism the role of foreign trade is quite different. It serves as a means for utilising the advantages of the international division of labour particularly the international socialist division of labour, in the interests of strengthening the socialist system. But this is not its only distinctive feature. It also stimulates the intensification of production and helps to improve its technical level . . . Throughout the entire existence of the Soviet state, foreign trade was and is an important factor in the growth of our country's economic potential. Its role in this respect has been guaranteed by the planned management of both the state monopoly of foreign trade and the related monopoly over foreign exchange, which on the one hand, have effectively protected socialist production from the chaos of the world capitalist market and, on the other hand, have enabled the state to concentrate its material resources on solving critical problems arising at different stages in the process of building socialism.[19]

A contrary view, which became prevalent in the West in the early 1970s, and is still current, can be typified by the writings of American economist, M. Goldman in a seminal article on the subject of Soviet economic autarky.

Goldman attacks the rhetoric of the Soviet position on autarky stating that in reality autarky no longer exists, and further, he argues that the continuous erosion of autarky is a process which the Soviets can do little to change. In the latter half of this paper Goldman asserts the validity of the argument associated with the assumption of the decline of autarky, i.e. that the West has been endowed with a politically effective trade weapon against the Soviets, as Soviet dependence on Western-provided goods can be used as 'leverage' to extract concessions.

> For decades their economists boasted that the Soviet Union with its insular economy was immune to capitalist recessions ... But ... whether they realise it or not, Soviet trade authorities are playing by the rules of the world trading system. They may have backed into such a position inadvertently, but there is clear evidence that the Soviets have had to alter their preferred way of conducting foreign economic affairs ... (Soviet officials) are involving the Soviet economy in an ever growing entanglement with the capitalist world.[20]

Goldman argues that this phenomenon has been encountered before in the 1920s and 1930s but that it was subsequently curtailed by Stalin. However, the phenomenon this time is 'qualitatively different'. Now the Soviets are particularly dependent on petroleum exports, and on the importation of the latest technology for the exploration, drilling and pumping associated with petroleum exploitation. The cost to the Soviets of severing the ties which they have with the West increases as this process continues, according to Goldman, and thus implicitly any severance becomes less likely.

As alluded to above, these comments represented a view prevalent in the West, but it was not a view confined to political commentators alone, as it was also propounded by Western governments – in varying degrees. Goldman is cited here merely as one of the most articulate spokesmen of this general group.

The most strident advocate of these theses was clearly the United States. American hopes were enshrined in the Soviet–American trade agreement of 1972 which made provision for the Soviets to place 'substantial orders in the United States for machinery, plant and equipment, agricultural products, industrial products and consumer goods' (Article 2, paragraph 4 of the agreement). This agreement was backed-up by further accords on trade, such as Nixon's ten year agreement on economic and technical co-operation. The United States then proceeded to try to extract concessions from the Soviets in the misguided belief that they could utilise trade (especially grain sales) as a secure lever with which to pressure the Soviets. The most blatant attempt came in 1974 when Congress, via the Jackson amendment, attempted to directly link the granting of Most Favoured Nation

(MFN) status in trading for the Soviet Union to gaining an increase in Jewish emigration from the Soviet Union. As a result of American pressure the Soviets abrogated the 1972 agreement and turned inwards to expanding the co-operation between CMEA members in 1975.

The West Germans, too, used trade with the Soviets for political concessions during the years of Ostpolitik. In direct dealing with the Soviets the Germans utilised it to establish firm relations, and in wider terms of Ostpolitik it was viewed as a way to encourage East European governments to 'demonstrate greater independence from Moscow and adopt more liberal policies towards their citizens'.[21] However, West German pressure was arguably used more subtly and with more discretion than American.

These arguments represent one major school of thought on Soviet trade. However there are other Western commentators whose analysis of Soviet foreign trade trends has been proved by events to be more correct. Trading with capitalist countries is organised separately from the other activities of the Soviet economy and also from dealings with the Socialist bloc and developing nations. In his work,[22] Turpin argues that in the 1970s Soviet foreign trading entered a qualitatively new stage, but he still holds to the belief that while the volume of trade may have increased the fundamental guidelines remained unchanged. In arguing this view he challenges the growing belief in the West which suggests that Soviet approaches to the nature and conduct of foreign trading changed through the 1970s as contacts with the West expanded.

The point to be made from this latter school of thinking is that those aspects of Soviet policies and actions which indicated a slackening of belief in an autarkic economy were overemphasised by Western and Japanese governments. Even though the signs that the Soviets had not changed policy were still there, Western governments chose, for whatever reasons to ignore them – or simply did not see them at all. It may have been that the Japanese government, encouraged by the warmer climate of overall relations between the two nations as well as the general circumstances of *détente*, perceived a weakening of the Soviet position on trade. If so, future events show that it was a misperception. Another writer on Soviet trade has suggested that understanding how the Soviets approach and direct trade is akin to understanding a 'black box'.[23] It is suggested that the Japanese, like other governments, failed to understand the workings of the 'black box'.

How can we characterise the essential policy guideline behind

Soviet trading with capitalist nations? In a survey of Soviet trade, Turpin sums up the main concerns as he sees them as oriented towards the primacy of maintaining the industrialisation drive and minimising trade with capitalists. On that basis foreign trade is conducted to obtain essential goods which are temporarily or permanently unavailable.[24]

This summation has been widely questioned by Western analysts but on the evidence available it would seem to describe accurately the premises behind Soviet trade policy. In summarising the essential points thus, Turpin shows that for the Soviet Union in conducting economic relations with the capitalist powers all that really needs to be considered is the question of imports, as an autarkic nation, so defined, is free to export at its discretion.

Turpin summarises the Soviet position as

> determined to avoid dependence on foreign and particularly Western sources of supply so far as possible, while remaining free to use the Western market for tactical and strategic advantage, but without accepting any obligation to participate responsibly in the operation, improvement or the maintenance of that market.
>
> (p. 11)

Foreign trade is used in this context to achieve the goals of the state. In the case of the Soviet Union, as Gruzinov pointed out, trade is not regulated by the State; it is the State itself which trades through subordinate agencies.[25] As part of the structure of a command economy which functions according to goals and targets, trade is also operated on that same principle, i.e. under a legal obligation to fulfil specific goals.

Due to increasing Soviet participation in the world economic process and the concomitant increase in Soviet trade revenues Western economists began, as we have indicated, to cast doubt upon the validity of the text-book stance *vis-à-vis* trade proclaimed by the Soviets. Was the Soviet Union still adhering to a policy of autarky or had it been abandoned?

Adopting an approach of mirror-imaging, the West chose to appraise three Soviet objectives of trade policy: they (the Soviets) would try to procure certain goods which were not produced in the country at all, which were produced but not in sufficient quantity; and which were produced, but more expensively than they could be acquired overseas. The desire for these goods, so Western economists calculated, would be particularly acute in the context of the imperative to develop Siberia.

As one more example of Western perception of a slackening of Soviet rigour let us consider Marshal Goldman's review of Soviet behaviour on the international oil market. He contended that by the early 1970s the Soviet Union was no longer regarded as a nuisance or a threat by the international oil companies. It was viewed as having oil for export 'at a time of growing market tightness. Instead of being treated as a pariah, by the early 1970s the Soviet Union was being treated more and more as a partner'.[26]

Western oil interests never considered whether the Soviets in fact wanted to be a partner. Goldman passes over a central matter of contention regarding Soviet trading practices, that of achieving a balance of imports against exports. 'For Soviet officials in charge of the task', writes Goldman, 'the great values of petroleum and raw materials make the job of balancing exports and imports simple'.[27] But Goldman is assuming points which are far from certain. It is a moot point whether such officials exist within the trade bureaucracy, not least as no such aim (balancing the books) appears in Soviet trade theory. Although a rough balance can be seen to exist in some cases of bi-lateral trade this is not the case overall. It is one thing to observe the phenomenon another to explain it successfully. Concerning the cases of a balance in trade figures the West can only speculate. It may well be the result of official policy decision, administrative convenience or simply coincidence. We do not know.

The evidence shows that despite Western belief to the contrary the Soviet Union has never been taken by the 'mercantilist credo', as Goldman terms it, of exporting for export's sake. In 1974, when the oil crisis had increased oil prices dramatically, Soviet earnings from oil sales doubled raising income to $23.26 thousand millions. Yet at a time when they were not suffering oil constraints and could have made a massive export killing, Soviet exports to the hard currency countries actually fell by roughly five million tons.

The illustration from Goldman contains all the classic Western erroneous interpretations of the Soviet position. He talks of Soviet authorities 'playing by the rules' – as if there were a set of objectively definable rules; of the Soviets being 'deeply entangled'; of Soviet 'dependence' and 'particular need'; of 'imposing restraints' on the Soviet Union. As events were to show the truth lay with the counter analysis provided by commentators like Turpin.

One qualification needs to be added. The Soviets have stretched the limits of autarky in their relationship with their fellow CMEA members in Eastern Europe to produce what amounts to a socialist division of labour. In practice throughout the 1970s the Soviet Union has given Eastern Europe preferential trade treatment in the form of trade subsidies, by exporting underpriced raw materials and energy resources to it in return for overpriced machinery and consumer goods. There are various reasons why the Soviets undertake to maintain these substantial subsidies. They all relate to the continued utility to the Soviets of maintaining the cohesion of the bloc, in some cases in the form of the Warsaw pact (military reasons), the propagation of Communist ideas (ideological reasons), and the maintenance in power of Communist governments which will support the Soviet Union internationally (political reasons).

There are also economic reasons. Soviet subsidies promote greater economic stability in Eastern Europe, and in return the Soviets receive a steady influx of technologically higher grade machinery than they can produce themselves in some cases. In some circumstances the Soviets have forgone a great deal of their own production capacity and effectively left the production of some goods to Eastern European industries. For example, much of Soviet railway stock is of East German or Czechoslovak make (East Germany supplies carriages and wagons, Czechoslovakia electric locomotives). Hungary supplies a significant percentage of the Soviet Union's buses, and a sizeable proportion of Soviet merchant ships and trawlers has been constructed in Polish or East German shipyards.[28]

Approaches to foreign trade and autarky remained unchanged during the Andropov and Chernenko years, though it is undeniable that undercurrents of criticism centred on economic stagnation became more vocal, attaining their prominence under Gorbachev. However, is it the case that *perestroika* has significantly modified the accepted views and practice of autarky? Gorbachev has reshaped the *mechanisms* of foreign trade[29] – reorganised the Ministry and the Committee for Foreign Economic Relations structures, devolved responsibility to individual foreign trade organisations, for example *Dalintorg*, placed emphasis on self-accountability and financial autonomy for those enterprises producing foreign trade commodities – but there is little evidence in public pronouncements (let alone implementation) of a change in state policy.

Gorbachev has given warnings on the use of trade as a political lever. Even among the most strident advocates of reform, the progressive economists, there are noticeable divisions of opinion on the pace and extent of reform (for example, compare statements by L. Abalkin or L. Loginov with those of T. Zaslavskaia or A. Aganbegyan). The views of the policymakers and bureaucrats are far more restrained – not to mention retrenched – by comparison. It has been reiterated in various official statements that the State will, despite the promotion of increased autonomy, maintain control over the production and import of 'strategic resources' i.e. coal, steel, oil, gas, precious minerals etc. In a widely publicised interview, V. M. Kamentsev, deputy Chairman of the USSR Council of Ministers and Chairman of the State Foreign Economic Commission had this to say:

> The main line pursued by the planned measures is, while maintaining and developing the principle of state monopoly in foreign economic activity, to persistently expand the rights and enhance the responsibilities of ministries... The USSR Ministry of Foreign Trade and the USSR State Committee for Foreign Economic Relations will monitor foreign trade operations for the purpose of ensuring statewide interests ... the USSR Ministry of Foreign Trade retains the functions of trading in the most important raw materials commodities and products of statewide importance.[30]

Thus, while ministries' rights may well be being 'enhanced' this is demonstrably a process implemented under close supervision and further, subject to predetermined limits.

The politics of Soviet foreign trade and the development of Siberia

Having outlined the organisation of the trade strtucture we must now place this within the wider context of Soviet economic needs and the 1970s debate over those needs. Many assessments of the Soviet economy depict it as an economy perpetually in crisis, bureaucratically overburdened and inefficient to a degree unbelievable in the industrialised countries. Yet the fact remains that despite all the predictions of calamity the Soviet economy has, until fairly recently, achieved constant growth. By devoting large sections of available economic resources to investment the ability of the Soviet Union continually to expand its production capacity has been assured, though at the expense of other sectors such as consumption.

Let us simplify the strategy choices which confronted Soviet planners by the early 1970s. We can characterise the means of Soviet growth as lying with two measures: the quantitative, involving more labour and more capital, and the qualitative, by improving the factors of production or production methods. The dominant Soviet approach before this date had been overwhelming reliance upon the first of these, and growth had been achieved by massive application of manpower and capital investment. The problem confronting Soviet planners by the early 1970s was that pursuïng such a strategy would

67

no longer suffice to achieve the desired goals especially since the demographically uneven distribution of the population located the labour pool in Central Asia, whereas the resources lay in the Eastern regions.

Consequently, to ensure continuing growth more emphasis than hitherto had to be laid upon improving the factors of production. The goals could be met from two sources, first, by the application of technology – including the importation of Western equipment – and second, by reforming the organisation and administration so as to improve the efficiency of economic sectors. The only questions left were ones of how far these reforms could go, and of where could the limits be set?

Since Japan features as one of the major Soviet trading partners for the importation of technology and specifically for the development of Siberia – the driving force of Soviet growth – these questions and debates over them are of direct relevance to the conduct of Soviet–Japanese trade.

For various motives and rationales it was the inclination of Western and Japanese traders to base their dealings with the Soviets on hopes of some sort of economic liberalisation based on a transfer of capitalist trading principles to Soviet managers, on a negative appraisal of the state of the Soviet economy, and on a belief that the 'economic modernisers' headed by Kosygin were sufficiently strong to prevail.

For example, Ogawa argues that 'noteworthy' developments in trade were triggered by 'the stagnation of the Soviet economy' which showed no sign of rapid recovery. Thus 'it is unlikely that the Soviet Union will take any action which will jeopardise detente with the developed capitalist countries'.[31] Hoffman and Laird contend that to the extent that Soviet economic and political development during the Brezhnev years was predicated on East–West co-operation and interdependent patterns of modernisation, 'the Soviet economic modernisers' influence was augmented', such that 'each of the critical trends in the Brezhnev period directly affected the role and significance of the policy group of Soviet economic modernisers'.[32] Belief in these outcomes fuelled an expectation of greater prospects and of more extensive contact.

In assessing the 'economic modernisers', Hoffman and Laird, both analysts of the impact of science and technology on the Soviet system, depict them as representing different strands of Soviet economic sectors. They see them as 'both advocates of modernisation (a tendency of development) and a subgroup within the economic elites (a set of interests within various organisations or parts of organisations)'.[33]

68

The origins of these groups are varied: from Gosplan, the academic institutes, those managers of the domestic economy who direct ministries, associations and factories, theorists of management, managerial rationalisers (specialists employed to plan and carry-out administrative changes), managers of foreign trade and analysts of the global economy. All to a greater or lesser degree have an interest in seeing some changes in various sectors of the economy.

An inaccurate appraisal of the motivation of these groups and of the extent of their influence by the Japanese led to misunderstanding of the goals at stake and over-optimism concerning what could be achieved. The debates within the Soviet leadership undeniably helped to fuel this misunderstanding by creating confusion and magnifying the significance of otherwise unimportant comment by members of the leadership or of the trade bureaucracy. It is a not uncommon phenomenon for policymakers to see only what they want to see or what they expect to see, and Japanese trade representatives were no exception.

The debate over economic relations with the West naturally involved specifically the area of trading and the questions of diversifying economic activities centred on four main issues: what kind of economic activities should be pursued? how extensive should they be? which countries and businesses are the most desirable partners? what changes are needed in the planning and management of foreign trade to facilitate this?

As these questions were being settled by the Soviet leadership, outsiders sought to portray the situation as a clash of rivals. This is the tendency displayed by Breslauer, for example, in discussing 'conservatism' and 'reformism' during the Brezhnev years. He defines 'reformist' policies as 'those which challenge core traditional values' and Brezhnev he depicts as having led since 1973 a 'political coalition on behalf of conservative domestic policies and reformist foreign policies. He has avoided economic decentralisation and slashes of the defense budget, but has sought to increase economic efficiency.'[34] Kosygin is pictured as very definitely 'the reformer'. 'Alexei Kosygin was not a vocal advocate of this approach ... Kosygin now re-embraced reformist causes in response to Brezhnev's conservatism, while simultaneously seeking to counter Brezhnev's efforts to parry responsibility for failure.' On matters of light industry the Kosygin 'dissent' was 'elaborate'. Overall, the breadth of the dissent of which Kosygin was the figurehead was 'striking'.[35] By his own definition Breslauer sees Kosygin as challenging in some way 'core values'. But in fact the opposite is the case. Kosygin owed his position to the fact that he *shared* these core values with Brezhnev and the other top leaders as well as the Party rank and file.

Mikhail Suslov at one point had appraised Brezhnev as 'the embodiment of collective reason and will'. It should be noted that Brezhnev's economic plans reflected to a large degree the views usually ascribed to Kosygin, and certainly given Kosygin's position as head of the Council of Ministers, policy could not have been developed without his co-operation. It would seem erroneous therefore to pursue Western arguments depicting a faction-fight between the two men or their offices too far. If we wish to portray, as a number of Western analysts seek to do, the main trend of internal politicking in the Brezhnev years as one of two ideas – either confrontational or consensual – then we should be careful to do so only with regard to certain specific issues. There was no overall opposition to Brezhnev *per se*, but its existence and strength at any time depended on particular policies advocated by him. Much the same can be said on the issue of support for Brezhnev.

If we define power over policy as the ability either to enforce one's priorities or the ability to prevent inclusion of serious compromises in one's programme, then in a broad sense Brezhnev's line prevailed via the second of these methods. By the eighth five year plan (1966–70) agriculture and defence had received huge investments but it was recognised that there could only be sustained growth through heavy investment in the industrial sector and in order to achieve that the necessary funds were diverted from other sectors such as chemicals, housing, and foreign investments. This new programme failed and was modified by 1970 and the following five year plan. Reduction of domestic investment in Siberian development was broached as a means of finding the necessary capital for investment in other domestic sectors. If Siberian developments were not to be slowed the shortfalls would presumably have to be made up from overseas sources.[36]

Soviet leaders at the same time had made public statements concerning the increasing Soviet participation in the international division of labour. Accepting this we might then expect, in order to make-up for needed investment, a rapid expansion of Soviet involvement in overseas marketing. However, from an internal bureaucratic viewpoint this was not necessarily the solution. In touching on this issue Volten concludes that, 'In sum, the Soviet leaders were not against trade, but against Brezhnev's unbridled enthusiasm; there were fears that it would result in too much interdependence and too much interference from both inside and outside the Soviet Union.'[37]

Couching the argument in these terms, as merely a backlash against Brezhnev, oversimplifies a complicated series of factors. If he can be accused of 'unbridled enthusiasm', numerous examples can also be cited of Brezhnev making clear that there were limits to what would be tolerated in the way of contact with the West.[38] In the same vein we can testify to the continual reaffirmation by Soviet leaders that contact with the West is a matter for convenience not necessity. For example, Brezhnev's reply to the editor of the *Asahi Shimbun*;

> I don't want to leave the readers of your newspaper with the impression that the Soviet Union could not develop the very rich resources of Siberia and the Far East on its own. It is quite obvious, and our country's entire history bears this out, that we have every opportunity to cope with this task. We make use of co-operation with other countries only to speed up the fulfillment of our plans to develop these regions.[39]

In his capacity as leader, and therefore chief spokesman, Brezhnev's remarks should have been noted, but the Japanese business community and government should have been more aware of the limitations placed upon, or the various motives behind, public comment by a Soviet leader.

No monocausal explanation of Soviet–Japanese misunderstandings does justice to Brezhnev and to the other leaders. The optimism with which Brezhnev regarded co-operative ventures had to be modified by the problems of conducting any large scale operations and long-term planning schemes, even those in which all parties have a genuine interest in their success. Some of these bureaucratic and planning hurdles will be discussed later. But what of those groups supposed to be opposing Brezhnev?

Kosygin – even if we accept that he personally favoured certain bureaucratic reorganisations which would enhance Soviet ability to import and utilise Western technology – was still head of the government/Council of Ministers *apparat* and as such responsible for reconciling the differing tendencies within the government economic machine. Thus in his role as head of government his ability to undertake controversial measures, regardless of his personal views, was constrained, more so as he was ultimately responsible to the Supreme Soviet which Brezhnev eventually headed.

The classic picture presented by Western analysts has been of Brezhnev the centraliser trying to hold the line against Kosygin and the other decentralisers and modernisers.[40] However the issues involved are more diverse than a mere contest over acceptance of a more liberal trade policy and reflect a complex interaction of political positions. For example, Suslov was willing to grant the validity of entering into negotiations over the arms race with the United States but was far more qualified in his support for the extension of economic ties. Both these positions were backed by Brezhnev, so Suslov was a Brezhnev 'supporter' over one issue but differed from him over the other. So it was with other Politburo members.

Both Brezhnev and Kosygin agreed that the Soviet Union faced economic problems, but by the early 1970s Brezhnev had come to stress a solution more related to manpower management reforms not involving devolution of power rather than an emphasis on expanding foreign trade as a remedy.

An important proviso should be recognised with regard to differences of opinion within the Soviet leadership, namely that advocacy of international policies often has as much to do with enhancing a leader's domestic prestige as with the conduct of successful foreign policy. In that light the conviction with which policies are advocated will fluctuate over time. For example, while it was useful for Brezhnev to pursue an increase of trade contacts in the short term, it was not so in the medium and long terms, because the policy had come to threaten domestic programmes he wished to advance. Thus while the shifting balance in leadership support perhaps facilitated some experimentation with foreign economic relations, its very nature constrained the duration and extent of experimentation. Behind that was the belief that the Soviet Union had solved past economic problems unaided, and could continue to do so in the future. The message to the West and to the Japanese should have been clear: the reasons for maintaining economic impetus were unchanged, and Western aid might have a contribution to make in solving economic tasks sooner, but it was otherwise dispensable.

The limits to trade: bureaucratic and organisational

The inertia and lack of co-ordination associated with large bureaucracies and large co-operative development projects had their part to play in hindering planning between the Japanese and Soviets in Siberia. They also functioned as a means of limiting trade expansion. The causes were magnified in the Soviet case by the particular requirements of a planned economy in which each ministry or department is held responsible for fulfilling specific targets.

As we have tried to show, the support at top leadership level for a technology import policy was kept within ideologically and politically acceptable bounds. Support for it fluctuated due to both international changes and domestic convenience. In these circumstances the tendency is for departments to continue to function as they have in the past, even while supposedly the object of reforming legislation. As mentioned earlier most Soviet ministries involved in projects in Siberia are domestically oriented and consequently place their internal responsibilities before their contribution to foreign-related projects. The reforms proposed in 1976 did little to alleviate unbalanced and uncoordinated approaches to development in the Siberian and Far Eastern regions. The same problems which had flowed from the independent approaches of parties involved (centred around the need to fulfil a system of planning indicators) continued to beset project development.

Ekonomicheskaia Gazeta protested in 1982 that 'ministerial niggardliness in relation to infrastructural investment has made the maintenance of a stable working population (in Siberia) all the more difficult'.[41] Continuing criticism of deficiencies in Siberian construction projects permeates the Soviet press. The overall responsibility for the construction of BAM[42] lies with the Ministry of Communications, with other ministries involved with specific tasks. With an 'overlord' responsible for the planning we would expect some sort of overall co-ordination. But this is not the case as Dyker once again points out in one example: 'At the end of 1978, for example, on the Tynda–Chara section of the line, earth moving teams had got 510 kilometers out of Tynda, the bridge-builders 386 and the general construction only 130.'[43] Two *Pravda* correspondents reporting on the projects at Vostochnii port in Wrangel Bay, detailed how only 60% of the available port capacity was being used and how long periods (months) had to be spent eliminating and correcting appalling mistakes made by design and development ministries.[44]

Gardner's comment on the processes of decision-making on Soviet foreign trade is worthy of note. He described the problems involved as akin to understanding the workings of a 'black box'. While we can delineate a structure of the organisations involved we cannot tell, for example, to what extent decisions are subject to political rather than economic influences. Much of the difference in emphasis between Brezhnev and Kosygin fluctuated around questions of bureaucratic inertia. As early as 1966 Kosygin had been suggesting reforms to counter departmentalism. The trend of pushing ahead with some sort of reform of the foreign trade structure began in 1976 with a decree from the Council of Ministers. However a follow-up decree of May 1978 was substantially a re-run of the 1976 decree, indicating that the earlier proposals had had little effect

The original idea had been to enhance the role of the foreign trade organisations *vis-à-vis* the Ministry of Foreign Trade. Paradoxically, as these organisations were essentially middle-level sections of the bureaucracy, strengthening their position was a centralising move which solidified branch monopolisation. These reforms can be seen as characteristic of the trend in approach to changes during the Brezhnev years whereby institutional adjustments were legitimised without actually altering the essentials of the planning, pricing and incentive structures.

Andropov's campaign against 'departmentalism' and atrophy has been continued with renewed vigour by Gorbachev. It remains for the future to show his degree of success. Initially reform has brought confusion and hesitancy, compounding institutional obstruction. Despite good intentions and increased motivation, over-bureaucratic procedures continue to defer the achievement of full potential.

The limits to trade: costing problems and technical difficulties

Despite the enthusiasm for development and for application of technology as the best means to fulfil development tasks both the implementation of Soviet–Japanese agreements and the general development of Siberia were significantly limited by Siberian conditions and by the abilities of the Soviet economy to absorb and utilise the technology at a pace acceptable to the Japanese.

As Dienes, one of the foremost Western commentators on the economic development of Siberia, argued in one of his articles, 'Despite the enormous impact of Siberian development on the whole USSR, previous enquiries into the economy and industrial structure of the trans-Urals provinces have had to be descriptive, intuitive and limited in nature.'[45] These would seem not to be a sound basis for judgement on policy for the region, and the lack of such a basis has been reflected in the problems that have occurred in costing projects and applying technologies in harsh and variable climatic conditions.

Because Siberia and the Maritime province constitute a vast area, they have very varied resource combinations and accessibility and hence divergent development prospects. Western Siberia has the strongest links to European Russia; it is the primary energy supplying region of the Soviet Union and priority in Soviet development funding and capital investment was allocated to it, particularly to the Tyumen oil–gas complex. In interviews with the author, Dienes commented that in 1980 for example, Soviet sources stated that Tyumen oblast' alone accounted for 18.3% of the net value of all Siberian construction work.[46]

The role of the more distant regions, east of Lake Baikal is somewhat different. Economically or geographically they do not form a less cohesive whole than Western Siberia. It is only in those zones which lie along the BAM and trans-Siberian railways that we can, in any sense talk of accessibility to the Pacific. On the north-east side, only the immediate coastal districts are developed and then only in certain areas. In both tonnage and value, the movement of goods to and from the Far East amounts to only a small fraction of that of West Siberia. In a paper unpublished at the time of writing, called 'Siberian Economic Development and Strategic Importance' Dienes argues that inshipment exceeds outshipment in volume by 2.5 times and in value by 1.8 times and that despite the region's extensive natural resources, Siberia east of the Yenisei 'is heavily subsidised'.

As on most large scale, long-duration projects, construction and development costs in Siberia spiralled enormously between planning and implementation. Costs at all levels increased, often dramatically, especially at the extraction end of a project. In a region where materials have to travel 5,800 kilometres on average to their destination – 6.7 times the average for the rest of the USSR – even shipping costs escalated dramatically. Projected costs for the Yakutian gas-complex project have risen from an initial $3.4 thousand million to $8 thousand million, according to a Japanese estimate.[47] Quoting Soviet economist Shinyar,[48] Dienes contends that investment in Siberia was even more wasteful than elsewhere in the Soviet Union, 'By 1975 the value of unfinished construction in Western and Eastern Siberia in fact *exceeded* total capital investment (in East Siberia alone) by 24%: in the country as a whole it reached "only" 75% of total investment in that year. Since 1975 . . . the literature implies no improvement in Siberia to date.'[49]

Overall the trans-Urals districts are net beneficiaries of the geographical redistribution of national income. The investment subsidies are often on scales unimaginable in the West. In Eastern Siberia and the Far East every administrative unit appears as a net recipient of income flow. This income 'exceeds 700 million roubles in 6 of the 12 provinces of these two regions'.[50]

It is not only the costing and construction problems associated with the major developments such as BAM or the Urengoi gas complex that were, and are still, bedevilling progress in Siberia. All the projects are short of workers, and the provision for facilities, housing or services for them lagged behind even more than the actual projects. This is because the priority of investment lies with the actual construction project rather than with necessary infrastructure for the labour force. Much the same can also be said regarding the attention given to the support infrastructure around project developments, roads being particularly susceptible to neglect.[51] Transportation outlays more than doubled the cost of goods produced in Yakut ASSR, for example.[52] The construction of sites for workers and of towns involves the use of special high pressure steam machines to melt the permafrost long enough for the supports to be sunk into the ground then refrozen. An alternative method is to scatter expensive coal across the ground and set it alight. Ice has to be broken up by special high-powered drills. Drilling for oil off Sakhalin Island can only be undertaken for four months of the year due to ice problems.

Low worker productivity also adds to costs. Overall the labour force is still basically a migratory force on what has been referred to as the 'tour of duty' method of earning a good salary. Earnings are roughly three times the national average, but productivity very much below it. The industrial worker in Siberia spent 163 days at work in 1975 (in the Far East 162) and construction employees spent only 140 days (the Far East figure was 150–60), whereas the average figure for European Russia was 230–40 days.[53]

General causes

Soviet trade with Japan is part of trade with the West and except for features peculiar to it, such as coastal trading, is formed and carried-out according to the same guidelines. Its original expansion paralleled the growth in ties with the West and the general amelioration in foreign relations. In that sense we would expect it to be just as susceptible to the fluctuations in the nature of that relationship as to fluctuations in particular Japanese–Soviet circumstances. Thus to attempt to depict the slackening of Soviet–Japanese trade as due to only two or three causes, as some analysts have done, would seem to be of doubtful validity. It is through the interplay of numerous factors, domestic and international, that the trade became limited.

The deterioration in relations with the United States by the mid-1970s may well have created a general climate within the Soviet leadership of 'suspicion' over the desirability of foreign trade. This is one of the arguments that Hanson has put forward.[54] However this would seem to be speculative. It is questionable whether dissatisfaction with the United States has the consequence of stimulating dissatisfaction with other capitalist trading partners. The United

Table 5 *Soviet imports of machinery and transport equipment from the West 1970–9*

Year	Value in current prices ($million)	Est. value in Soviet 1969 roubles (million)	Imports as % of domestic equipment investment of next year
1970	905	913	3.4
1971	840	792	2.8
1972	1126	979	3.1
1973	1574	1166	3.4
1974	2094	1378	3.6
1975	4184	2476	6.1
1976	4259	2462	5.7
1977	4571	2393	5.1
1978	4994	2254	4.6
1979	4851	2037	4.1

Source: Data selected from information presented in P. Hanson, 'Foreign Economic Relations', in A. Brown and M. Kaser (eds.), *Soviet Policy for the 1980's* (Oxford, St Antony's 1982), pp. 65–97. Data p. 80.

States was advocating a more politicised trading policy – grain sales excepted – than either the European allies or Japan, which, apart from grain sales, trade far more with the Soviet Union than does the United States.

Hanson cites as another contributory factor in the deterioration of trading conditions a perception by Moscow that by the end of the 1970s the Eastern European economies would be in need of financial support. He suggests that in order to be prepared for that eventuality, the Soviets by 1977–8 had taken the decision to stabilise and reduce hard currency debt, the easiest way to achieve this being through a reduction of technology imports. This move may also have been prompted by the Soviet fear of becoming more indebted to the West, losing its high credit rating and becoming more vulnerable to Western pressure.

The most convincing argument put forward by Hanson is in another article and is what he terms the 'backlash against technology imports'. This, he suggests, was due to growing economic concerns over a decline in the hard currency balance of payments in 1975–6 and a rise in outstanding hard currency debt. Consequently Soviet importation of machinery fell from *c*.$6 thousand million (1976) to $3.8 thousand million (1977) to $2.5 thousand million (1979–80). This continued 'despite the fact that the current account of the Soviet hard currency balance of payments quickly recovered after 1976 and despite the fact that the outstanding Soviet debt to the West had been reduced'.[55] Table 5 illustrates fluctuations in imports and their tendency to decline as a percentage of domestic equipment investment. Brezhnev summed up the attack on imports at the 26th Congress in March 1981 when he said that 'We must look into the reasons why we sometimes overlook our leading position in technology and spend large amounts of money to buy abroad such equipment and processes as we are fully able to produce ourselves, and moreover often of higher quality.'[56] Gorbachev's similar stance has contributed to recent falls in imports.

The Soviet economic slowdown as a contributory factor to trade limitation

The continual investment in the high cost Siberian developments had to be balanced against the continual successful performance of the Soviet economy. In the second half of the 1970s (the tenth five year plan 1976–80) economic growth had declined to 3% whereas it had been 6% during the first half of the decade (by 1982 it had declined to 2.5%). GNP growth declined to c.2.7% during the same period.[57] By 1986 it was down to 2%. In these circumstances the massive subsidies channelled into Siberia at the expense of other sectors had to be called into question. The continual favourable performance of the Siberian region lay entirely with oil and gas exploitation projects and that was reflected in the allocation of subsidies which strongly favoured these projects even compared to investment in timber and mineral extraction operations. Certainly by comparison the allocation to infrastructure and service facilities was particularly poor. The opportunity costs involved saw projects cancelled outright, existing delays increased and new ones created. Even priority developments in oil and gas and mining were not free from retrenchment to some degree, causing the Soviets to admit to the Japanese that in some cases they would not be able to fulfil their contractual obligations, for example, in the delivery of coal from the Neriungra field in South Yakutia.[58]

Dependence as a force for trade maintenance

Associated with the issues of cutting-back on the scale of trading have been the arguments – from both sides – of dependence and opportunities in each others' markets which would serve as a natural brake to a decline in trade. More radical commentators have suggested that each side was trying to manoeuvre the other into a position of dependence in at least certain sectors of trading (for example, in Japanese dependence on Soviet oil and gas).

We have two generally accepted definitions of dependence: a state of being determined or affected in some major way by external forces or 'a relationship of subordination in which one thing is supported by something else or must rely upon something for a fulfillment [sic] of a need'.[59] How does the state of relationships between the Soviet Union and Japan fit into these categories?

Let us consider the Soviet position first. At base the problem for Japan (and for the West) was that it paid too little attention to Soviet conceptions of trade, which had always been more modest than those shared by the Japanese. Let us posit the question: what exactly does imported technology do for the Soviet Union? Either the Soviets utilise it in combination with their own technology or they concentrate it in a specific area in which they lag seriously behind. Two good examples of each of these approaches are the automotive industry (a combination of technologies) and the chemical industry (almost solely based on Western skills). The incidence of the latter sort of application was rare and, as the Soviets quickly discovered, was a counterproductive strategy for development. Summing up, one trade commentator has written

> The greater the Soviet's existing level of skill in a particular industry, the more they are able to profit from technology transfer, and the harder it is to prevent them from doing so. The corollary is that the Soviets' ability to profit from technology transfer can be expected to increase over time *provided* that the Soviets have not handicapped their own innovators (as in the chemical industry) through an excessive reliance on foreign suppliers.[60]

A national technological ability is such a wide concept that it cannot be quantified. But this is excactly what the Japanese tried to do. If there was an area where the Soviets could be said to lag behind overall, it could well have been in the realm of technology diffusion rather than in research and development or in innovative ability. But even here the Soviets had tried – though we might question their success rate – to improve their deficiencies.

In particular, the areas of trade involving Japan were those which featured a higher than average participation by foreign investors, i.e. the oil and gas industries, timber, paper and pulp concerns. Even here the Japanese investment should be seen in its proper context. During talks in Moscow in 1981 on the Japanese position towards sanctions over Afghanistan, I. Grishin, the Soviet Deputy Minister of Foreign

Trade, pointed out to the Japanese that while there was Soviet interest in co-operation 'Japanese credits in the past five years had accounted for only 1% of Soviet spending for the development of the region'.[61] However, the further proviso should be made that Japanese assistance to these projects comes under the heading of contributions to 'existing plant'.[62] Investment in 'new plant' construction was more effective in promoting and channelling technology but investment in 'existing plant' projects applied Japanese technology to existing Soviet techniques. In these areas most analysts are agreed that the Soviet Union profited most; however these areas were *not* the main areas of foreign technology influx nor were they areas of excessive dependence on foreign inputs. Being able to profit from the application of Japanese technology does not imply dependence upon it. R. Campbell, in a case study of the Soviet pipeline industry, voices the opinion that Soviet dependence on imported pipe was overestimated, as

> Today the Soviet steel industry can itself produce, and is producing 1020, 1220, and 1420mm. pipe. One might therefore contend that the Soviet Union imports pipe not out of technological incompetence but to avoid production capacity bottlenecks or high costs at the margin from expanding domestic output.[63]

For these reasons the Soviet–Japanese relationship was not necessary, ineluctable, inevitable, inextricable or unavoidable.

A particular feature of Soviet–Japanese trade has been the central importance of compensation agreements and the large scale of credit funding made available through them. This peculiarity subjects the final trade figures between the two to particular fluctuation and hence misinterpretation. Either the signing of a new massive contract or the expiry of an earlier one can make significant differences to overall trade balances. As an *Izvestiia* correspondent pointed out when commenting on the decrease in trade by 1983:

> What has caused this slide? There are several reasons. One of them is the completion of the procurement of Japanese goods for the Urengoi–Uzhgorod gas pipeline. As well as this there is no longer any large scale undertaking involving co-operation between the two countries.[64]

How did the Japanese view their business with the Soviets? Japanese dependence on international trade with the Soviets was less than half of that of the major European nations. Yet at the same time Japan and the United States were the most important trading nations because of their absolute size of GNP and trade values. While in past years the growth in world trade had acted as a motor for Japanese growth, its decline by the turn of the 1980s was also having an adverse effect on the Japanese economy. Orders for Soviet timber were reduced due to the slump in the Japanese timber industry. Japanese members of the Japan–Soviet economic committee meeting in Moscow in September 1979 were willing to admit to that decline and expressed reservations about Japanese ability to fulfil their end of contracts. The decline in Japanese growth has by itself often been cited as the reasons for a fall in trade levels but it is apposite to ask whether trade would have fallen anyway due to other factors.

The Japanese have voiced discontent over a loss of substantial orders due to the sanctions imposed after the invasion of Afghanistan and have blamed the drastic decline in trade on these events. However the fact is that in Soviet trade with advanced industrialised countries, Japan had already slipped to fourth (Soviets say fifth) place in 1979 *before* sanctions had been imposed. The Japanese have always *ranked* highly; however if that rank is transformed into a total trade *value* comparison Japan's performance does not seem as impressive when compared to her main rivals in the Soviet trade market. Table 2 shows the trends and values in trade between Japan and the Soviet Union in a comparison with West Germany and Finland. Since 1972 the Japanese have always lagged behind West Germany and since 1978 even behind Finland. Tables 6 and 7 provide some data on Japanese energy-related trade with the Soviets; from these it can be seen that Japan fares very poorly as an oil purchaser from the Soviet Union even in comparison to Greece. By 1979 Japan was only taking 0.48% of Soviet oil exports. Japanese imports of Soviet coal (9.9% of Japanese needs) are the only significant area in an otherwise unimportant relationship, whereby by 1979 only 0.8% of Japanese energy requirements came from the Soviet Union.

Throughout the history of Soviet–Japanese negotiations there have always been problems over credit and interest rates. The Soviets tended to gloss over the problems faced by the Japanese in having to put up vast sums of money, especially when the pay-back period might be fifteen years in the future. In some cases, Sakhalin oil exploration being a case in point, the capital put forward by the Japanese was the only capital at risk. The peculiarities of compensation deals also caused their own sort of friction, as one economist has suggested:

> The Russians believe that joint partnership compensation deals should warrant low interest loans and credits, since foreign investors receive substantial benefits by way of low-cost energy sources and other raw materials. The Japanese answer this criticism by stating

Table 6 *Soviet oil exports to selected countries 1971–9 (thousand barrels per day)*

	1971	1972	1973	1974	1975	1976	1977	1978	1979
Total	2,110	2,140	2,380	2,340	2,600	2,970	3,130	3,300	3,280
France	75	66	95	23	57	72	95	104	128
Federal Republic of Germany	113	118	116	132	148	175	154	178	182
Greece	20	18	16	20	38	40	60	47	16
Japan	27	21	41	24	16	19	16	14	16

Source: Directorate of Intelligence, CIA, *International Statistical Review* (GI–IESR 82–007, 27 July 1982), p. 24

Table 7 *Japanese energy dependence to 1979 (million tons of oil equivalent)*

	Oil/oil products	Gas	Hard coal	Nuc-lear	Impor-ted elect-ricity	LNG	Total energy
Requirements	242.3	2.0	50.7	4.4	4.9	23.2	327.5
Imports from world	256.7	–	39.9	–	–	12.0	308.3
Imports from USSR	0.7	–	2.0	–	–	–	2.7
Imports from USSR as per cent of total imports	0.3%	–	5.0%	–	–	–	0.9%
Imports from USSR as per cent of requirements	0.3%	–	9.9%	–	–	–	0.8%

Note: Dashes indicate information not available.
Conversion factors: 1 kilolitre = 6.269 barrel = 0.1248 thousand metric tons oil equivalent; 1,000 mtce = 0.6859 mtoe
Source: US Congress, Office of Technology Assessment, *Technology and Soviet Energy Availability* (Washington DC 1982), p. 327

that their interest rates on Soviet loans are well below prevailing commercial levels for international trade.[65]

As a general trend Mathieson concludes in his otherwise very positive review of Soviet–Japanese trade that

Table 8 *Japanese coastal trade with the Soviet Union*
(millions of dollars)

	1977	1978	1979	1980	1981
Imports	34.74	39.74	50.62	54.32	54.17
Exports	31.61	34.94	43.46	54.79	68.75

Source: *Nisso Boeki Handobukku 1984* (Japanese–Soviet Trade Handbook 1984), (Tokyo, Nisso Boeki Kyokai, 1984), p. 243

> The co-partner's interests run counter to each other. On the one hand, the USSR's interest lies in obtaining the maximum amount of finance for each given project on very long period deferred payments at low rates of interest ... the Japanese rely on keeping credit extended as low as possible, with interest rates pitched at world levels ... they want to recoup as fast as possible their very onerous financial commitments.[66]

Let us now consider the issue of Soviet–Japanese coastal trade. As mentioned at the beginning of this section, coastal trade was the most rapidly expanding sector of overall trade between the two nations. But in spite of its impressive growth, it is relatively unimportant. It comprised approximately 2.5% of the total value of Soviet–Japanese trade in 1981 and by 1983 this had fallen to 1.6%, or in terms of value from roughly 90 million roubles to 50 million. (See table 8 for absolute values of coastal trade.) Thus the involvement of 'small and medium sized' Japanese companies, as sought by Soviet commentators, was very limited indeed. From the Soviet side, the main medium of transacting business was through the foreign trade organisation *Dalintorg* (established 1965). It operated under a barter agreement which limits the number of goods it may trade in. The lack of desirable products, poor Soviet quality control and relatively high prices effectively put the brake on trade beyond certain close limits. Given Soviet pricing policy – whereby Soviet selling agencies receive only the domestic price for goods destined overseas – any incentive to produce better quality goods for export is removed. That also had its effect on the market.

The myth of the complementary nature of the two trading economies is nowhere better illustrated than with the question of coastal trade. Japan had hoped to sell the Soviets primary products but they were not interested. The largest value commodity exported by Japan in 1981 came under the heading of 'clothes' ($14.03 million), the largest import commodity was 'food' ($23.61 million).[67] In practice the

83

economic activity on Hokkaido is least complementary with the structure of the Soviet Maritime province. Soviet imports in fact originate mostly from the Tokyo–Osaka region. Japanese economists the author talked with at Hokkaido University speculated that, while there was a rough balance overall in coastal trade, Hokkaido imported seven times as much as it exported.

The involvement of the Japanese in containerised shipment across Siberia was similarly constrained by Japanese involvement in other, more important markets that could not be served via the Asian landbridge. On closer examination the actual figures for container-ised traffic are not as impressive as might be thought. Tavrovsky[68] claims that the four Japanese ships which carry the freight can carry a total of 1,690 large containers, i.e. 400 each. (The four Soviet ships have the same capacity.) In 1981–2 a total of 138,000 containers were carried: this represents a maximum of 345 shiploads. From the figures it can be seen that approximately two-thirds of container traffic carry Japanese exports, which would represent 230 shiploads. Thus, *at best* one small (by Western standards) 400 container capacity ship would dock in a Soviet Far East port every one-and-a-half days. This figure must in turn, call into question Scherer's contention that this traffic represents 25% of Japanese containerised traffic to Europe.[69]

The benefits of relations have to be defined not in absolute terms but in terms of likely alternative solutions. For both parties involved there always was an alternative. For the Soviets it involved either finding another supplier or closing the doors entirely to foreign creditors. For the Japanese, as the accompanying table 9 shows, the total sums invested by individual companies were often a marginal percentage of their total capital; the losses themselves would not have been catastro-phic, other customers might have been found elsewhere, or most of the sum involved in Soviet dealings could have been compensated for by increased sales of other commodities or by diversification into supply of other goods. (Table 10 provides a wider comparison of Japanese trade with both the Soviet Union and the People's Republic of China.)

As one economist has argued:

> The 'benefits' of interdependence should be defined in terms of the values of the parties and the likely effects on those values of breaking the relationship. If there is little or no effect, or if the parties would actually be better off the relationship should not be described as interdependent. It is in that sense, *and in that sense only*, that interdependence involves mutual benefits.[70]

84

Table 9 *Major Japanese companies trading with the Soviet Union (millions of dollars)*

Companies	1980			1981			1982			1983		
	Total	Exports	Imports	Total	Exports	Imports	Total	Exports	Imports	Total	Exports	Imports
1 Sumitomo Shoji Kaisha Ltd	650	–	–	875.5	789.1	86.4	748.1	550.0	198.1	496.0	268.6	277.4
2 Nissho Iwai Co Ltd	461	–	–	700.5	569.8	130.7	510.7	407.3	103.4	476.3	371.5	105.3
3 Mitsui & Co Ltd	487	–	–	666.6	588.9	77.7	693.1	513.1	180.1	427.4	330.3	97.1
4 C. Itoh & Co Ltd	707	–	–	810.4	685.5	124.9	661.8	523.8	138.0	357.3	281.8	75.5
5 Nichimen Co Ltd	332	–	–	705.4	522.3	183.1	685.8	273.9	411.9	322.4	234.4	88.0
6 Marubeni Corporation	464	–	–	623.0	539.9	83.1	656.0	574.4	91.6	290.0	231.7	58.3
7 Mitsubishi Corporation	526	–	–	675.7	522.3	153.4	570.9	318.0	252.9	225.1	101.7	63.4
8 Toyto Menka Kaisha Ltd	153	–	–	133.9	75.1	58.8	168.2	73.9	94.3	138.9	90.1	48.8
9 Kanematsu-Gosho Ltd	241	–	–	174.8	96.8	78.0	169.9	68.0	101.9	134.8	77.8	57.0
10 Chori Co Ltd	167	–	–	169.4	49.3	120.1	169.4	49.3	120.1	96.8	42.4	54.4
11 Tokyo Boeki Ltd	74	–	–	–	–	–	–	–	–	73.5	51.6	21.9
12 Kyoho Tsusho Co Ltd	171	–	–	287.7	270.0	17.7	–	–	–	66.3	33.6	32.7

Note: These companies account for approximately 95% of all trade
Dashes indicate information not available
Source: Nisso Boeki Handobukku 1984 (Japanese–Soviet Trade Handbook 1984), (Tokyo, Nisso Boeki Kyokai, 1984)

Table 10 *Japanese trade with the People's Republic of China and the Soviet Union*
(thousands of dollars)

	PRC	USSR
1976		
Exports	1,662,568	2,251,874
Imports	1,370,915	1,167,441
Total	3,033,483	3,419,315
1977		
Exports	1,938,643	1,933,877
Imports	1,547,344	1,421,875
Total	3,485,987	3,355,752
1978		
Exports	3,048,748	2,502,195
Imports	2,030,292	1,441,723
Total	5,079,040	3,943,918
1979		
Exports	3,698,670	2,461,464
Imports	2,954,781	1,910,681
Total	6,653,451	4,372,145
1980		
Exports	5,078,335	2,778,233
Imports	4,323,374	1,859,866
Total	9,401,709	4,638,099
1981		
Exports	5,095,452	3,259,415
Imports	5,291,809	2,020,706
Total	10,387,261	5,280,121

Source: Japan External Trade Organisation (JETRO), *White Paper on International Trade*, Tokyo

In two of the main long-term projects that the Japanese are involved in, Yakutia gas and the Sakhalin shelf, the United States is also a party in Yakutia directly, and in Sakhalin indirectly as most of the technology utilised by Japan there is American. In both cases the recalcitrant attitude of the United States towards aspects of trading has complicated the Japanese involvement making negotiations more difficult and lengthening delays.

The last point begins to touch upon the politics of trade. There are other factors yet to be considered which influenced these developments: from the effects of abstract ideas, such as how two very different cultures view each other, or how the clash of different negotiating styles affected decisions. From the Japanese side, the functioning and limitations of bureaucratic organisations also had an impact on the course of relations. All of these factors we shall examine in Chapter 4 under the heading of Soviet policy and Japan.

3 THE SOVIET MILITARY AND JAPAN

SOVIET STRATEGY IN NORTH EAST ASIA AND THE PACIFIC

What has been termed the 'national security consciousness' of the Soviet military–political leadership has a decisive influence upon the leadership's perception of relations with the rest of the world. Military power is unquestionably of central importance for the Soviet Union in maintaining itself as a superpower; in this sense it is clearly an 'incomplete superpower'.[1] In the particular context of relations with Japan, many analysts contend that Soviet policy is overdependent upon the military aspects, to a degree where it has become counterproductive and merely acts to exacerbate the divide between the two nations.[2] Intimidation has not worked as a policy for the Soviets in north east Asia.

Inherent in such a critique of Soviet behaviour is a rejection, by and large, of the suggestion that in other dealings with the Japanese the Soviets have sought to adjoin military power to a political purpose and goals. The utilisation of military power, it is argued, had become (or indeed always was) an end in itself that had led, by the end of the 1970s, to a sharp perception on the part of the Japanese of a looming 'Soviet threat' to their future security. Thus one Japanese analyst has concluded that 'the answer to the question why Soviet Japanese policy has been self-defeating seems to lie in the fact that there is no other effective instrument of influence at the Soviets' disposal but the strategy of threat by military superiority'.[3]

We shall examine later whether this widespread claim can be substantiated. First, let us turn to some general propositions on Soviet defence policy as a whole and then in particular some likely theatre plans of operation in the Far East.

In the 1979 edition of *Asian Security*, its yearly survey of the military situation in Asia, the Research Institute for Peace and Security based in Tokyo wrote that 'The primary aim of Soviet strategy is the same as

88

that of any other nation: (a) to defend the country, (b) to ensure its survival, and (c) to protect her interests.'[4] This statement is unexceptionable but where contention arises is on the question of what level of defence is necessary for the Soviets to achieve these objectives. The debate throughout the 1970s concerning the idea of 'how much is enough?' continues; those problems involved in comparing Western–Soviet force levels and capabilities are numerous and fraught with methodological difficulties by now well known. For the moment it is not our purpose to be drawn into these considerations as they affect north east Asia but rather to try to picture how the Soviets view their security needs in the region.

Any consideration of Soviet strategic planning for the Far East has to confront four questions:

1 Which enemies will the Soviet Union have to face in the event of a war, either global or regional?
(The enemies the Soviets may well have to face in a global war may be different from those it might have to face in a regional conflict.)
2 What sort of war is it likely to be – nuclear or conventional?
3 What are the goals and missions of Soviet forces involved?
4 What level and deployment of armed force is necessary to achieve these goals?

The Soviet Union, unlike the United States, is faced with the particular problem of being confronted by 'enemies' on all sides. It has accordingly, as it sees it, to match and be able to counter the capabilities of each of these enemies in turn and provide itself with the wherewithal to defeat, or at least defend against, each in any potential confrontation. In the specific case of Soviet planning for the Far East, the Soviets must assure themselves that they have the capability to fight on the second of two major fronts (the other, more important, being in Europe). In the East they will have to face possible nuclear attack from the United States and perhaps also from China; conduct a distant and possibly prolonged war on land against China and Japan and perhaps against amphibiously-borne American forces. At sea the Soviets will have to consider conducting warfare in the vastness of the Pacific against a wide array of naval powers perhaps also including Australia and New Zealand. These formidable tasks require formidable force levels and equally daunting forward planning.

In fighting a nuclear war, the objectives for the Soviets in the East would be of dual nature, both offensive and defensive. They would seek from bases in the Soviet East to destroy the main heartlands of the enemy while preserving as much as possible Soviet resources that would contribute to their recovery and help them to emerge victorious over the long haul. Given the presumed list of Soviet priorities for nuclear missions, Europe and the war against the NATO alliance must figure as number one and operations in the East as a secondary imperative. However throughout the 1970s the distinction in priorities has become less straightforward as the Soviets, at both a nuclear and conventional level, have taken steps to upgrade the organisation and technical efficiency of their forces in the Far East and to integrate them more fully into overall doctrinal planning. The GK (High Command) of Soviet forces in the Far East was re-created in 1969, and it has been speculated that in 1979–80 General V. L. Govorov was appointed to head a new body in the Far East responsible for co-ordinating the operation of the Far Eastern and Transbaikal military districts as well as Soviet forces in Mongolia.[5] The significance of this reorganisation was emphasised by the highly unusual, and well publicised visit of Brezhnev and Defence Minister Ustinov to Siberia and the Far East in April 1978.

Since then it has become clear that this reorganisation of the Far Eastern Command was a part of a wider Soviet doctrinal and organisational revision that had taken place through the 1970s and is still in the process of implementation. Major strategic theatre commands were created for Central Europe and the Far East. The aim of creating these commands has been summarised by one group of noted commentators as to

> form a vital intermediate echelon which links central strategic control (exercised by the General Staff) with major operational field forces at theatre level, thus meeting the urgent requirement for both flexibility and effective command and control – facilitating the deployment of one 'force package' (or several such pacakges) in a particular crisis or operational area. This is the essence of *peregruppirovka*, strategic and operational *redeployment*, a theme explored in inordinate length in Soviet military writing.[6]

Associated with the refinement of the *peregruppirovka* concept has been the parallel development of the idea of the 'theatre strategic operation' which envisages large scale military operations co-ordinating Soviet forces from various fronts or armies into a major combined arms, multi-level offensive.

In this respect the Far Eastern theatre command (GTVD) encompasses not only the Central Asian, Siberian, Transbaikal and Far Eastern military districts and Mongolia, but also the naval forces assigned to the maritime (MTVD) or oceanic (OTVD) theatres of military operations. The Sea of Japan and the Kamchatka Sea have been designated as MTVDs, the Pacific as an OTVD. The Indian Ocean OTVD is also part of the structure. Each of these naval theatres may be further sub-divided into various zones according to the function and objectives of the military forces operating in them.[7] It is important to emphasise that actions envisaged in naval theatres are seen as not independent of actions in continental TVs or TVDs but rather as complementary to them.

Apart from a list of targets in the United States and China which would be attacked from bases in the Soviet Far East, targets in Japan would presumably be selected on the same criteria as those in Europe. There are advocates of the theory that the occupation and defeat of Japan would be a secondary objective to be accomplished after a main exchange designed to leave as much of Japanese resources intact (industrial, economic, agricultural) as possible so as to assist in rehabilitating the Soviet homeland after the cessation of conflict. Soviet targeting of Japan would therefore be what is euphemistically referred to as 'selective'. This argument, while depicting a possible scenario, should not be taken as definitive.

Various interpretations of the content of Soviet military doctrine are proposed by Western analysts. The differences lie mainly in the emphasis given to certain aspects of Soviet doctrine; perhaps the main area of difference concerns Soviet concepts of escalation. Some analysts tend to emphasise more the subtle nuances of Soviet thought which suggest that the Soviets conceive of escalation and thresholds in similar terms as Western strategists. However the other major school of thought on this question argues on the same lines as Lambeth when he sums-up the whole Soviet approach thus: 'For the Soviets, the key threshold is not nuclear employment but war itself.'[8] William Lee, an American expert on Soviet nuclear strategy, suggests that although generally the Soviets do not accept thresholds in the Western sense this might be subject to qualification as 'just as individual TVDs present different target arrays, Soviet politico-military objectives are not uniform for every TVD'. Thus in particular circumstances there might be 'practical considerations' which would limit a Soviet nuclear strike.[9]

Although Lee's views are shared by a wide body of opinion, they are far from generally accepted. On balance, the most persuasive interpretations still lie with that group whose views are represented by Lambeth.

> Perhaps the main point to be emphasised regarding Soviet attitudes towards thresholds is that Soviet defence planners simply do not preoccupy themselves with – or, in many cases, even recognise – the

sort of refined distinctions among levels and varieties of armed conflict that so heavily pervade Western strategic discussions. More to the point, they regard such notions as escalation ladders and comparable artifacts of Western discourse with a combination of bemusement and contempt ... For them, the purpose of military power is not to manipulate perceptions, manage crises, or otherwise play games at the edge of war but simply to underwrite key Soviet national security interests for which lesser means – such as diplomacy and coercive persuasion – have proven unavailing. In practice this means that the Soviets are not likely to be much inclined to respect thresholds governing the intensity of military commitment, even though they may be perfectly prepared to recognise distinctions among various objectives for which military forces might be employed.[10]

In another article Lambeth details the dissimilar rationales behind Soviet and American economic targeting in war. The major thrust of his argument is that if the Soviets 'spare' economic targets it is not necessarily because they can be of use in the post-war reconstruction, but rather because of the 'fundamentally countermilitary orientation of Soviet doctrine and operational planning'. In other words, 'those economic and industrial targets will be included in Soviet operational plans not so much because of whatever postwar significance they might have for the adversary as because of their tangible relevance to more immediate Soviet combat objectives'.[11]

The 'Lambeth school' reflects accurately the orientation of public statements by leading Soviet officials. Minister of Defence Ustinov in an interview with *Pravda* stated on the subject of limited nuclear war that

> Would anyone in his right mind speak seriously of any limited nuclear war? It should be quite clear that the aggressor's action will instantly and inevitably trigger a devastating counterstrike by the other side. No one but completely irresponsible people could mention that a nuclear war may be made to follow rules adopted beforehand, with nuclear missiles exploding in a 'gentlemanly manner' over strictly designated targets and sparing the population.[12]

In an interview with *Krasnaia Zvezda* in May 1984, Marshal Ogarkov echoed the same sentiment. 'The calculation of ... waging a so-called 'limited' nuclear war now has no foundation whatsoever. It is utopian ... arguments about "limited nuclear strikes without retaliation" against the enemy's main centres and control points are even more groundless. Such arguments are pure fantasy.'[13]

What or where would these likely nuclear targets be in Japan? Any suggestions we make can be only tentative at best but in terms of a list of priorities of targets in and around Japan we can present an approximate picture as comprising nuclear submarines, strategic air bases, naval bases, nuclear weapons sites, C3I centres. At a tactical nuclear level – nuclear equipped battle groups (US carrier task forces) and weapons systems/platforms capable of utilising nuclear weapons. Conventional targets which might be attacked with nuclear weapons would include weapons/fuel centres, smaller naval bases and airfields and logistic centres. Depending upon the extent to which the Soviets might want to spare Japan the worse effects, we can add economic and administrative targets, such as government centres, crucial industrial facilities and transportation nexuses. A basic list of these targets is presented in table 11.

It is axiomatic that the Soviets are gravely concerned about the prospects of a two-front war in Europe and Asia. The war in the West would be the decisive encounter and given that, there is a danger that operations in the East would be a drain on Soviet ability to win the decisive war. In this context even at a nuclear level, Soviet operations in the Far East have to be seen as oriented towards a strategic defensive war to limit the ability of the United States and China to inflict damage on the Eastern territories of the Soviet Union. In such a scenario the real enemy to be matched would be the United States as the Chinese forces are no real match for the Soviet strategic arsenal. (See table 11.)

Soviet conventional warfare plans

The waging of conventional war in the East alone or as part of a wider conventional global war would be a significant undertaking for Soviet planners. In the context of a wider war it could also well detract from the Soviet abilities to win that war – as maximum effort must be devoted to the European theatre. Even allowing for the prepositioning of stocks and the completion of the BAM line, the logistical tasks involved in sustaining any part of a prolonged campaign in the East while NATO forces were being engaged elsewhere would, realistically, be beyond the capacity of the Soviet Union.

A recognition of this by Soviet planners has resulted in the belief that any undertaking would undoubtedly be accompanied by the use of nuclear weapons, not least because the Soviets have never expounded publicly any plans in which the use of nuclear weapons has not been foreseen as an integral part of a combined arms offensive. There is evidence of division of opinion between Soviet planners and Soviet

Table 11 *Possible nuclear targets in Japan*

The following is an outline of a potential Soviet nuclear target list for any attack on Japan. The JSDF and United States forces share many facilities making them probably more of a likely target. Air training bases have been excluded from the list – there are five main bases used for purposes of such training. Also, GSDF mobile headquarters which might be targets, except for regional command HQs, have been excluded on the grounds that presumably in the lead-up to war they will move from their known locations. Nevertheless should their positions become known they would be high priority targets given their importance in the C3I network.

The regional command headquarters are: Northern army – Sapporo; North eastern army – Sendai; Eastern army – Ichigaya; Central army – Itami; Western army – Kengun. An important target for any Soviet attack will be American C3I facilities and electronic monitoring systems which are supporting and co-ordinating strategic systems. Some of these are located within American base areas but many are not. Consequently the target list should be expanded to include such targets also. Okinawa has not been included on the list but is without doubt a high priority target. Including bases on Okinawa unclassified sources list 118 American facilities in Japan.

JSDF bases

MSDF	
Yokosuka	Command HQ
Sasebo	fleet HQ
Maizuru	fleet HQ
Kanoya	fleet air force base
Hachinohe	fleet air force base
Atsugi	fleet air force base
Naha	fleet air force base
Tatsumi	fleet air force base
Iwakuni	fleet air force base
Kure	Submarine fleet HQ
Shimofusa	Major naval air training base
Ominato	fleet HQ

ASDF bases	
Chitose	Wing + air defence missile group
Misawa	Wing + air control and early warning + air defence missile group
Komatsu	
Hyakuri	
Iruma	Central air control and early warning, air defence missile group
Gifu	Air defence missile group
Nyutabaru	
Tsuiki	
Kasuga	Western air control and early warning, air defence missile group
Naha	Squadron and air control and early warning facility
Miho	Tactical airlift command
Fuchu	Air traffic control centre

The Japanese BADGE air control and early warning system consists of twenty-eight radar installations – all potential targets. A small number of ASW listening posts such as Cape Nosappu on Hokkaido might well also feature as important targets.

Major American bases

Yokota	HQ Japan, HQ 5th Air force, base fighter wing.
Zama	US Army Japan HQ. HQ Fleet air force
Yokosuka	US fleet HQ, submarine fleet HQ
Sasebo	US fleet HQ. Main base US SSN's
Kamiseya	HQ and command base of air patrol and reconnaissance force
Atsugi	Naval air base, fleet air force command base
Misawa	Wing + Japanese air patrol group, naval air base, location Electronic security group
Iwakuni	USMC HQ, air wing
Yosami	C3 centre for US SSBN

Sources: Defence Agency, Tokyo, *Defence of Japan* 1983. A comprehensive listing of C3I facilities – of which there are a significant number – can be found in W. Arkin and R. Fieldhouse, *Nuclear Battlefields* (Cambridge, Mass., Ballinger Publishing, 1985) and in D. Ball and J. Richelson, *The Ties That Bind* (London, Allen and Unwin, 1986). Further details can be found in P. Hayes, E. Zarsky and W. Bello, *American Lake*, (London, Penguin, 1987). See Appendices A–E. Estimates of Soviet strength can also be found in this book which presents an overview of American war plans and operations in the Pacific. American deployments in the Pacific and threat to the Soviet Union from the East are very much understudied areas. The Soviets constantly stress the need for adequate defensive measures against what they detail as a very substantial threat. There are odd elements of inconsistency in Soviet claims as, for example, Soviet defence spokesmen state that the SS-20s currently sought to be retained east of the Urals are needed to counter the US nuclear forces in South Korea, Japan, Philippines etc. Whereas, in fact, they principally seem to be intended to offset *Chinese* nuclear potential. In that sense Chinese nuclear capability is also considered very seriously.

officers who will have to operationally implement doctrine concerning the feasibility of 'selective' targeting or the 'limited' use of nuclear weapons in certain circumstances[14] but it would be unwise for Asian countries to conclude from this that the Soviet Union will omit to use nuclear weapons as an integral part of its conventional warfighting strategies in the Far East. More so as the dividing line between a regional/theatre system and a strategic system has become more blurred due to the deployment by the Soviets of advanced conventional weapons systems with the ability to carry nuclear warheads over longer ranges.

Depending upon the scenario the waging of conventional war against Japan could be greatly circumscribed. The Soviets stress the importance of carrying the battle on to the territory of the opponent. How does this concept relate to the Japanese case? Any attack on Japan depends upon Soviet ability to move forces and supplies amphibiously. Even in the best circumstances imaginable in any land war – when China is not involved and the Soviets only deploy 'holding' forces along the Chinese border – even an invasion of Japan limited to the purpose of holding the straits open for Soviet fleet operations would be a high risk undertaking, and perhaps altogether unfeasible. Consequently, apart from naval operations (to be discussed next) Soviet conventional operations against the Japanese homeland are likely to be confined to major air attacks against crucial installations. This would be carried out both as a means of limiting Japanese/American ability to inflict damage on Soviet forces (particularly naval) and as a 'softening-up' for eventual occupation of Japan.

As we illustrate in the following section the Japanese MSDF and ASDF possess a significant anti-submarine warfare (ASW) and air capability respectively. These capabilities are being steadily improved by the Japanese. Both of these constitute a threat to Soviet naval forces and are a particular threat to the successful defence of the submarine bastion in the Sea of Okhotsk (see below) and thus also to Soviet anti-carrier operations. It is therefore likely that Soviet attacks will be concentrated on destroying or immobilising these Japanese assets. Airfields and communication facilities are undoubtedly high priority targets.

The United States' air forces (fifty F-16s) that were based at Misawa from late 1985 onwards represent a formidable ground attack force. These high performance aircraft have the ability to carry a considerable weapons payload to Soviet bases. At a conventional level, this group of aircraft constitute the single most potent attack force based in Japan.

The Soviets have presumably taken this fact into account and planned accordingly.

Soviet naval operations in the Pacific

The Soviet Pacific fleet has been designed primarily for operation against the United States' naval forces. Its principal mission, the fulfilment of which has influenced naval developments throughout the 1970s, is to secure the Sea of Okhotsk where Soviet SSBN operate as an important component of the Soviet strategic strike force. It is in this area that the two considerations of offensive/defensive strategies overlap and the resultant complexity has caused Soviet planners difficulty.

The changes in mission requirements for the Soviet fleet have over the years generated an operational structure based on the requirements to carry-out long range missile strikes and counter Western ASW technology. In striving to fulfil both requirements Soviet maritime defence zones have expanded.

Any attempt to construct a list of Soviet naval targeting priorities for global war can only be speculative. In summing-up the various objectives, Soviet military commentators rarely rank them in explicit order of priority though one can sometimes be inferred; for example, it is reasonable to assume that those missions directly related to Soviet strategic strike plans have the highest priority. The problem comes in ranking other missions.

Sokolovskii stated that

> Nuclear rocket attacks against objectives in enemy territory, mainly against their nuclear devices, will create conditions favourable for the operations of other services of the armed forces. At the same time the strategic rocket troops, long range aviation and rocket carrying submarines will strike strategic objectives in the theatres of military operations as well, destroying simultaneously both enemy troop units, including reserves, and the bases of operational and tactical nuclear devices communications, the military control system etc . . . finally, military operations in naval theatres directed against groups of enemy naval forces to destroy his naval communications and to protect our naval communications and coast from nuclear attack from the sea must be considered an independent type of strategic operation . . . thus the theory of military strategy determines the following types of strategic operations by the armed forces during a future nuclear war: nuclear rocket strikes to destroy and annihilate objects which comprise the military–economic potential of the enemy, to disrupt the system of governmental and military control, and to eliminate strategic nuclear devices and the main troops units:

military operations in land theatres in order to destroy the enemy forces; protection of the rear areas of the socialist countries and troop groupings from enemy nuclear strikes; and military operations in naval theatres in order to destroy enemy naval groups.[15]

Admiral S. G. Gorshkov in his major work on naval power expanded upon the role of the navy in certain scenarios of war:

> Today, a fleet operating against the shore is able not only to solve the tasks connected with territorial changes but to directly influence the course and even outcome of the war. The most important of them has become the use of the forces of the fleet against the naval strategic nuclear systems of the enemy with the aim of disrupting or weakening to the maximum their strikes on ground objectives. Thus the fight of a fleet against the fleet of an enemy in the new conditions since nuclear weapons have appeared has become a secondary task as compared with the operations of a fleet against shore.[16]

Vice-Admiral K. Stalbo in *Morskoi Sbornik* concerned with 'Some Questions on the Theory of development and Uses of the Navy' talks of it being 'incorrect to underestimate the theory of the strategic utilisation of fleets, whose military might is based on submarine nuclear missile systems'.[17]

From these comments, particularly those by Gorshkov, we can infer that the Soviet navy's contribution to the strategic aspects of a nuclear war must be their paramount preoccupation – both through use of Soviet SSBNs in strategic strikes and through protection of this SSBN force as part of a retaliatory second strike force. The Soviet navy's concept of 'SSBN bastions' is designed to fulfil both these aims. It is arguable that Gorshkov's 'enemy strategic nuclear systems' include American carrier battle groups. Gorshkov pointed out earlier in his work (p. 185) that development and creation of forces capable of fighting aircraft carrier battle groups has been a prime preoccupation of the Soviet navy since 1945. A further indication that attacks on nuclear-capable battle groups would be of high priority is the probability that these groups would be assigned a major role in the assault on Soviet submarine bastions in either a nuclear or conventional war. Their strength, which makes them dangerous to the Soviet Navy and to shore targets, and the concentration of so much US naval strength in relatively few ships render them both necessary and tempting targets for Soviet naval operations, and likely therefore to be accorded high priority.

As we stated above another major threat to the SSBN bastion and to Soviet anti-carrier operations will stem from ASW and air-to-surface attack units. Ideally the Soviet fleet will have co-ordinated action against these targets in Japan with the Soviet air force.

What more can we assume concerning Soviet naval operations? Both Gorshkov and Sokolovskii had very little to say on aspects of naval operations such as support of ground operations or interdiction of an enemy's sea lines of communication, other than to stress their importance. Gorshkov argued however that traditional operations of fleet against fleet retained relevance only in terms of their contribution to success in operations of fleet against shore.[18]

From comments made by Sokolovskii and Gorshkov we can outline specific Soviet naval missions as : strategic nuclear strike; strikes on carrier battle groups, perhaps as part of action undertaken in strategic nuclear-strike; securing of contiguous waters; support of ground operations; interdiction of enemy sea communications.

We are still left, however, with the question of which priority to assign to each? To a large degree the first three missions are inter-dependent. So while the strategic strike must be considered first priority we should recognise that its success could be contingent on the other missions. Defence of the SSBN bastions must be seen as the vital mission for the Soviet Pacific fleet and all other missions secondary.

Naval co-operation with Soviet ground forces in a global war would be important. Such co-operative ventures are a possibility for Soviet forces in the Far East, specifically with regard to Japan and the seizure, or at the least denial to the enemy, of 'choke-points' to facilitate fleet operations. The Soviets would have the alternatives of nuclear attack and/or in the Japanese case limited invasion of Hokkaido. Should China be involved in any war the Soviets might also wish to undertake small scale amphibious operations against objectives on the north east Chinese coast in support of ground forces. It is also possible that the Soviets might undertake limited amphibious operations on the Korean coast. The final Soviet concern, that of interdicting Allied sea lanes, can be seen as of comparatively low priority.

SOVIET MILITARY POLICY IN OPERATION

In the foregoing sections we have sketched an outline of Soviet planning and targeting contingencies for possible war scenarios in the Far East. In the following we intend to examine in particular the circumstances which might in practice constrain the implementation of Soviet strategies and operational plans in the Pacific theatre. Also we intend to examine the political aspects accruing from the Soviet interpretation of Japanese revanchism, the Japanese military build-up and then finally consider the important question of how – if at all – Soviet military power in East Asia has been used coercively against Japan to achieve political ends.

In considering why the Soviets are active in Asia it is important to stress that they not only claim historical status as an Asian power but have throughout the 1970s been asserting their claim as a Pacific power also. The Soviets see their claim to this title as wholly legitimate since until the latter half of the nineteenth century Russia had far more substantial interests in the Pacific than had the United States, and had a longer period of involvement in Pacific affairs than America.

The major Soviet security objective in the Far East has been to prevent the formation of any sort of alliance between China and the United States and its allies, principally Japan. Bearing this in mind we can see that Soviet expressions of concern over Japanese militarisation relate not merely to the militarisation itself but to the fear that any real growth in Japanese military status will bring such an alliance closer to formation. Equally, it could be argued that Japanese armament could appear as much a threat to China as to the Soviet Union (indeed some of the latter Soviet pronouncements after the Japan–China treaty of 1978 were quick to suggest this), but for the most part Soviet public utterances have been eager to depict Japanese militarisation as directed against the Soviet Union alone. The Chinese, for their part, do not seem to see any serious threat to themselves from Japanese rearmament.

Writing some eight years ago Dzirkals in her Rand study suggested that

> In keeping with the characteristic sparseness of Soviet public pro-
> nouncements on the military aspects of Soviet security, there exists
> little in the way of media output that specifically treats the military
> dimension of Soviet policy towards Asian security. However, there
> do exist hints of possible active Soviet military measures as con-
> tingency options in support of Soviet security interests in Asia.
> Suggestions of such include (1) threats of retaliatory action against
> Japan in the event that United States' forces stationed there on
> Japanese territory should engage in unspecified armed action in Asia;
> (2) declarations stressing the critical importance of Soviet military
> assistance and successful military efforts on the part of Soviet allies
> and national liberation forces in Asia; (3) occasional advocacy of
> increased Soviet military force levels to meet the threat to Soviet
> security posed by possible adverse military developments in Asia.[19]

While the second of these features has diminished in salience since the mid–1970s, we can add a new category to the list in the form of increasing commentary on Japanese revanchism. Also we can cite a noticeably increased emphasis on statements stressing the necessity of Soviet counter-measures. Particularly, as a consequence of recent American deployment plans for Tomahawk cruise missiles in the Western Pacific and F-16 nuclear capable aircraft at Misawa airbase in Japan, Soviet threats of retaliatory action against targets in Japan have similarly increased.

The best example of this was the Soviet response to Premier Nakasone's remarks in Washington in January 1983 concerning Japan's position as an 'unsinkable' or 'big' aircraft carrier. TASS replied on 19 January that 'it is plain that there can be no "unsinkable" aircraft carriers – and that by deploying aboard it arsenals of armaments, including US ones, the authors of such plans make Japan a likely target for retaliation. For such a densely populated island country as Japan this could spell a national disaster more serious than the one which befell it 37 years ago.'[20]

Soviet concern over regional military developments is sharp, as may be expected in a region where the strategic interests of three major powers overlap.

In approaching the problem of ensuring stability in the area the Soviets have adopted various plans. Believing it politically impossible and militarily dangerous to acquiesce in stability based on a preponderance of US–Japanese forces, the Soviets have sought to involve (at least publicly) a wide number of Asian countries in their abortive collective security scheme. Japan has been approached at various levels concerning participation in, or bilateral association with this, but has rejected all Soviet proposals. Undeterred by Japanese reticence on the subject the Soviets continue to advocate that collective security is the only real path to security for the region, arguing that the Western approach, based around a 'balance of forces' idea can only lead to trouble and inevitable miscalculation. Indeed the Soviets note the relevance of the concept to Japanese expansionism, for they point out that Japanese commentators talk less and less about the 'defence of Japan' and more in terms of 'the Japanese contribution to the balance of forces in Asia'. The point which Soviet commentators are wary of raising is that this change in the Japanese view of their role in the region has been influenced by their perception of a growth in Soviet military power in the Pacific.

More to the point for Soviet analysts, the concern with the balance of forces concept is that it assigns the pivotal position to Japan. This in Soviet eyes is the evidence of, and rationale for, the expansion of Japanese military and political influence. Judging by frequency of press statements Soviet commentary on Japanese rearmament reached a turning point in 1978.

That year saw a noticeable increase in frequency of comment on Japanese association with the West. The Soviet press carried, amongst others, reports on the visits by Shin Kanemaru, Chief of the Japanese Defence Agency, to Washington (*Pravda* 25 February); Kanemaru's talks with NATO chiefs (*TASS* 12 June, *Pravda* 23 June); Japanese participation in US manœuvres (*Pravda* 11 July); Kanemaru's talks with Defence Secretary Brown in Washington (*Pravda* and *TASS* 5 August).

By this time it had become obvious that Japan's weight in the political and military sphere was growing significantly and was reflected in particular by 'the unprecedented frequency of US-Japanese summit meetings'[21] especially as these involved Japanese military chiefs.

The exact nature of the US–Japanese relationship in the military sphere is a matter of speculation for the Soviets who find themselves in a classic dilemma. Ideally they would wish to see Japan distanced from the United States, but they are also aware that an independent Japan might become more assertive in pursuit of its security, to the Soviet detriment.

Thus the Soviets are aware of the problems involved in the broad sweep of Japanese policy formulation but are hesitant to decide on the consequent policy to follow. This has led to a more noticeable than usual difference of emphasis of Soviet statements on the trends in Japanese–American military relations. How do the Soviets then view Japanese military links?

We can make the obvious distinction between public and private Soviet comment, but it is possible to make a further distinction based on which branch of the media is the source of comment. The most hard-line statements on Japanese revanchism, and in particular on the growth of a Japanese–United States–China alliance, can be found in *Krasnaia Zvezda* and in Radio Moscow broadcasts tailored for a particular Asian audience. Domestic publications and those intended for an English-speaking or Japanese audience, are less forthright in attributing blame or intent. Japan is sometimes depicted as an active partner of American imperialism in the Far East and sometimes presented as its passive victim.

As outlined above, 1978 seems to have been a turning point in comment not especially because of the China–Japan treaty of that year, but because of a new awareness that Japanese military growth really was beginning to take on substance. Japanese build-up through the 1970s and in particular the first half of the 1980s gave rise to substantial criticism and Soviet attacks began to be directed not merely at instances of Japanese co-operation with the United States in manœuvres but at a sharing of defence technology with the United States and, as the Soviets saw it, at Japan becoming a *de facto* Asian member of the Atlantic Alliance. The rise in volume of Soviet press criticism indicated growing concern but still no clear policy was enunciated to counter the problem.

Soviet commentary generally expresses the belief that Japanese policymakers retain an awareness of self-interest but circumstances have changed somewhat since Dzirkals wrote in 1977:

> (Soviet commentary of Japanese self-interest) . . . has been couched in reference to Soviet military power and has included explicit threats to employ that power directly against Japan, specifically in retaliation for action by US forces stationed there. Such statements are relatively rare however, and Soviet commentary generally does not go beyond depicting the potential threat that Japan's military preparations present to the Soviet Union and other Asian states . . . Soviet commentary is still regularly presented (particularly in the daily military press) depicting Japanese military policies as stemming primarily from United States' pressures.[22]

Explicit threats have become more frequent as a result both of the growth in Soviet capability to inflict damage on Japan and of the increasing probability of this occurring because of American nuclear deployments in and around Japan (cruise missiles and the Misawa deployment). An illustration of this was a broadcast to Japan by the Tokyo correspondent of Radio Moscow, V. Tsvetov, who commented that

> Prime Minister Nakasone's remarks at the Williamsburg summit signify a new stage of Japan's association with the NATO bloc. To be more precise, they mark a new step towards Japan's participation in the NATO aggressive bloc, an act which may entail many possible consequences, such as the deployment of medium-range missiles in Japan and Japan being turned into a theatre of nuclear war.[23]

By this time Soviet publications and news reports frequently accused Japan of being an active participant in the setting-up of a US–Japan–South Korean axis. This theme is still strongly underlined.

Gromyko could claim on 2 April 1983 that the deployment of Soviet SS-20 missiles in Asia was to help to counter the presence of American nuclear systems in and around Japan. At the same time *Izvestiia* drew an analogy between Japan's position in any future war in Asia and that of West Germany's in a war in Europe and threatened Japan, suggesting that it would make a particularly good target due to the density of

103

habitation, with a greater disaster than occurred in 1945. Gorbachev has repeated Gromyko's justification for continuing SS-20 deployments east of the Urals in more recent Intermediate-range Nuclear Forces (INF) proposals.

In similar vein the Soviets were more determined to suggest the independence of at least 'certain circles' when it came to Japanese military developments.[24] That closer co-operation with the United States by the 1980s was taking place was not in doubt but more stress was attributed to the Japanese developing their own momentum in this field. The potential inherent in Japanese advances into 'dual technology' fields is a case in point. In January 1983 Japan agreed to lift its ban on the export of military technology to the United States. In January 1987 it committed itself to research in the Strategic Defence Initiative (SDI) programme. Japanese electronics firms have a large share in the world market in micro-electronic circuitry and advanced telecommunication equipment. For a few years they have been 'racing' the United States in the development of the next generation of computers, the so-called 'super computer'. Keal argues that 'were Japan to gain a significant lead over the United States in the development of the fifth generation computers it would at the same time lessen its dependence on the United States and might achieve similar results in other core technologies'.[25] He continues to argue that Japan already produces a wide range of systems which 'enhance Japan's own military potential and are in demand by armed forces of other countries' (p. 30). This is of vital significance for it is Japan's possession of these dual technologies which gives it the ability to develop its own state-of-the-art arms industry.

Growth of Japanese forces – Soviet comment

The manpower of the Japanese Self Defence Forces has actually declined over the last fifteen years. The basis of Soviet attacks on the course of Japanese militarism lies not with the numbers involved but rather with the substantial improvements in quality of the equipment of the Japanese forces. Now that Japan has officially abandoned the self-imposed 1% of GNP bar on the defence and budget level, the Soviets expect that the modernisation of Japanese military equipment will continue apace.

Comparison of present-day figures with those of 1970 shows a dramatic upgrading of the artillery component of the Ground Self Defence Forces and also of the anti-tank guided weapon (ATGW) element. A significant improvement has also been made in the force's air defence capabilities.[26]

These are improvements in the defensive sphere, which could only contribute to making any Soviet invasion of Japan more difficult. But improvements which have taken place in the quality of the Air and Maritime Self Defence Forces cannot be dismissed as having no applicability outside Japanese territory, and these are worrying to the Soviets.

Since 1970 the Japanese naval forces have been re-quipped with more modern ships and equivalent weapons systems, such as the US-designed Harpoon surface-to-surface missile system and the anti-submarine rocket (ASROC) system, both of which are standard NATO armaments. Constant emphasis on the development of anti-submarine capability throughout the 1970s has produced a highly formidable force, while the upgrading of the air force to some 270 combat aircraft, many of latest US designs, also marks an impressive advance on its 1970 position. The Self Defence Force also has a significant construction and procurement programme in hand. Its requests for the 1985 budget, for example, excluding purchases of tanks and artillery, sought to lay-down three destroyers and one submarine as well as purchase eleven P-3C Orions (ASW and surveill-ance aircraft) and thirteen HSS-2Bs (ASW helicopters).[27]

These developments are the source of Soviet concern. Numerically the Japanese Self Defence Forces are of significant size and formidably equipped. However, major doubts have been expressed in Japan about the efficacy of Japanese forces and their likely performance in war.

A general complaint is that the Japanese defence effort has lacked shape and direction – the Japanese are unsure about the kinds of missions they want to accomplish and the nature of the threats they want to counter. Nakasone's 'commitment' to the naval defence of a '1000 mile zone' is a good example of the gap between capability and objectives. Such an undertaking was far beyond the resources of the huge Imperial navy of the 1940s and is thus beyond those of the Maritime Self Defence Force. Admiral Long, former Commander in Chief US Pacific Fleet, has commented that while the Japanese defence forces are substantial 'there are serious deficiencies in the sustain-ability of their forces, in their ability to conduct combat over an extended period of time'.[28]

Criticisms have been made of the decentralisation of the command and control systems of the forces, lack of thorough training, infre-quency of exercises, low stocks and low issues of equipment.

A report undertaken by the Centre for Strategic Studies in Tokyo, an organisation with strong affiliations to the military and staffed in the

105

main by conservative analysts, entitled *The Defence of Japan – An Alternative View from Tokyo* stated the opinion that both the Self Defence Forces and the Japanese government have been overly optimistic with regard to the threat posed by the Soviet Union and that in consequence the Self Defence Forces leave 'much to be desired in both quantity and quality'. The Centre characterised the major deficiencies as:

· an inadequate intelligence apparatus
· an insufficient air defence capability, lacking depth and endurance as well as bases, particularly in the North
· an insufficient ability to maintain control of the sea, and to secure and blockade the straits around Japan
· land forces unable to check, counter-attack or undertake tactical/strategic manœuvres
· a dangerously low level of readiness. Insufficient reserves, no mobilisation system established. Virtual lack of fortification of strategic locations
· stockpiles of munitions, fuel, food, extra equipment, spare parts and reserve material all low. Thus bringing into question the factor of sustainability.[29]

Much of this criticism is of a general nature; its validity depends upon the particular scenario, the nature of the initial attack, duration of action and level of Soviet forces committed. More telling specific points can be made on the abilities of the Self Defence Forces to conduct operations.

Although by the end of 1981 the Ground Self Defence Force was some 14% undermanned this has no real significance of itself. Against a high level sustained attack, even a larger force could not defend Japan without extensive American assistance. The main contingency which Japan has to plan for (and one which we shall later dismiss as being beyond the present capability of Soviet forces in the East) is an invasion of Hokkaido. In defending against this specific scenario the Japanese forces may have major obstacles to surmount. The United States Arms Control and Disarmament Agency summed-up the Ground Self Defence Force's overall problem as being that 'It is presently limited in its mobility and ability to concentrate forces rapidly. Transport assets are inadequate for moving large numbers of troops and much of the equipment, such as artillery, is not readily transportable. Anti-tank and air defence capabilities in support of ground forces are not impressive judged by contemporary standards. Further compounding all of these difficulties are inadequate logistics'.[30]

Criticisms of the Self Defence Forces' capabilities have sometimes been overstated, circumstances seldom being quite as bad as the critics would have us believe. The problem of transport support is a case in point. While a case can be made that the Ground Self Defence Force lacks organic transport, Japan's extensive civilian communications networks and transport resources could probably provide sufficient transport for Self Defence Force requirements in an emergency.

As indicated above, the primary mission for which the Japanese have planned is to counter the Soviet Pacific fleet. In operational terms this has meant developing a significant ASW capability. Of the thirty-two destroyers available in 1984, four could carry three helicopters each; four were equipped with two helicopters each and seven with one each. Where the fleet is deficient is in its quotas of surface to surface missiles: only thirteen of the fleet's destroyers and three of the frigates are equipped with a surface to surface or ship to ship missile. The main armament of the remaining ships is guns, though most are also armed with an air-defence missile system (*Sea Sparrow*), now somewhat dated.[31]

Although the ships are amongst the most modern, nearly 30% of the fleet is confined to minesweeping operations, and the surveillance capabilities of the fleet are similarly constrained. The submarine fleet is by and large obsolescent, and limited to coastal operations, although in the enclosed seas where the Japanese will be mostly operating this may not prove a serious deficiency. It is also a diesel-powered fleet; this is to some extent advantageous in these enclosed waters, as the submarines are more difficult to detect than nuclear submarines. Much of the fleet's reconnaissance capability lies with the ageing P-2J aircraft but modern Orion P-3C are being acquired. The Maritime Defence Force lacks organic tactical air power as it has no carriers, and is also deficient in ship-based air defence systems. Given the high priority the Soviets will likely assign to air attack protection of Maritime Self Defence Force surface ships would in large part fall upon an air force already heavily engaged in carrying out its other tasks.

The Air Self Defence Forces suffer from lack of an electronic counter measures (ECM) ability but their largest drawback stems from their orientation to air defence, i.e. they are an interception force not designed to undertake ground attack missions. Their ground attack capabilities are marginal and revolve around the indigenously designed F-1 aircraft. This deficiency may be compensated in future by the fact that the American F-16s deployed in Misawa from 1985 onwards are equipped for a ground attack role, not interception. Questions have been raised concerning the early warning system's ability to pick-up low level penetrations – but this may well be somewhat alleviated with the introduction of the F-15J which has a look-down shoot-down capability. There has also been an apparent failure to train Air Self Defence Force pilots in the conditions likely to be encountered in attacking targets at sea, partly because of a lack of the appropriate surface attack technology and partly through bad planning by the command of the Self Defence Force. These limitations must call into question the ability of the Air Self Defence Force to support the Maritime Self Defence Force. The Air Self Defence Force Nike ground-to-air missile system, deployed in 1962, is widely held to be inadequate against modern aircraft. Their BADGE, aircraft control and early warning system, operational since 1967, is similarly constrained by obsolescence, though it has been somewhat updated.

The conclusions suggested above are mixed. Japanese forces, while relatively large, and equipped in some respects with very up to date weapons systems and platforms, are not capable of offensive operations outside Japan, and are still suffering in the 1980s from deficiencies which the very recent acquisition of modern technology (P-3C for example) may begin to put right; but the benefits of the modernisation will not begin to materialise for perhaps another five years or more. The lifting of budget restrictions *may* increase the pace of modernisation but this would seem to be dependent upon other factors, such as public acceptance and commercial willingness, both as yet unsure quantities.

Soviet capabilities in the region: military competence or military omnipotence?

An estimation of Japanese defence capabilities cannot be made in a vacuum but has to be related to the potential threats perceived by policymakers. The circumstances of the outbreak of war, its duration, its geographical location and the stength of forces committed by the Soviet Union all have relevance to the Japanese ability to fight successfully.

We stated at the beginning of this chapter that military power is the pivotal component of Soviet status as a superpower. We also stated that the Soviet Union was an 'incomplete superpower'; the rise of military capability which has carried it to, and assured it of, that status has been dramatic in certain areas. Many Western analysts would agree with a summation of this rise to power given by Levin in his Rand report:

> this change in status is particularly noticeable in East Asia, where a
> remarkably rapid build-up of Soviet military capability over the

course of the 1970s was accompanied by a concomitant diminishing of those of the US . . . this build-up took place in two broad stages. The first, from the late 1960s to the early 1970s, emphasised the rapid build-up of Soviet ground forces deployed primarily against China. After a hiatus of some five or six years, the Soviets resumed their build-up. This second stage involved the deployment of a new generation of intermediate range nuclear weapons, the major expansion and qualitative improvement of the Pacific Fleet, and the development and extension of Soviet bases in the territories North of Japan.[32]

This growth, Levin concludes, serves wider interests which are the interdicting of air–sea communication in the region: giving the Soviet Union the ability to operate in Europe and the Middle East without sacrificing their position in the Far East; an ability to tie down US forces and impede their move elsewhere; attainment of global power standing (the Far East has become the focal point of these efforts).

Levin's conclusions can serve as a good benchmark for our following section which will examine Soviet capabilities within the region. For while representing accurately the general trend in the development of Soviet capabilities, Levin's remarks do not tackle the fact that the actual abilities of Soviet forces still have to be measured against the tasks set them by military circumstance. It is apposite to ask what is militarily within the ability of the Soviet Union to accomplish in north east Asia and the Pacific.

Nuclear warfighting

We have argued above that at a strategic nuclear level the Soviet Union needs the capacity to counter, or to attack first, the nuclear capabilities of an array of enemies and a widely dispersed range of targets in the United States, Europe, China, Japan and elsewhere. We have also outlined – in terms of mission priorities – a list of targets that Soviet planners would probably desire to attack.

For those targets in Japan the Soviets have sufficient warheads to devastate any series of potential targets. However, on a regional basis, whereby the Soviets have to take into consideration the survivability of their own systems and their ability to attack, with a reasonable probability of success, targets in China, Southern Asia and the Pacific, 'success' becomes more problematical, not to say questionable.

Throughout the 1960s and then into the 1970s the limitations of SS-4 and SS-5 missiles curtailed Soviet chances of success in such a scenario. The replacement of these systems by mobile SS-20s, armed with three warheads and a range sufficient to reach Guam from Soviet territory, undeniably constitutes a major alleviation of the uncertainty about achieving targeting objectives in difficult circumstances. At present there are reportedly 136 SS-20s deployed against Asian targets.

Throughout the 1970s the Soviets have also enhanced their capability to fulfil regional nuclear missions by deploying more varied nuclear-capable systems: SU-24 and TU-22M aircraft are good examples of these. These modernisations replacing suspect systems with better ones, are however, occurring at a time when the United States and to an extent China are themselves diversifying their nuclear delivery systems thus causing Soviet planners recurrent problems of having to attack more diversified and perhaps better protected targets.

The position and involvement of the two Koreas in Soviet strategy is uncertain. Immediate North Korean involvement on the Soviet side could have disadvantages for the Soviets, particularly in terms of nuclear escalation as American forces on the peninsula are geared to defending the South with nuclear weapons. Further, North Korean involvement may have ramifications for the Chinese position. Should China decide to remain initially netural in any Soviet–American/Japanese confrontation, North Korean intervention may precipitate Chinese intervention under circumstances not favourable to the Soviets (i.e. when they were not prepared for it). Even in circumstances of co-ordinated Soviet–North Korean action, Soviet support for the North Koreans is likely to be limited only to air support and possibly assistance in amphibious operations on a small scale. Ultimately the eventual occupation of South Korea is a likely Soviet goal as it would enable the Soviets to secure the southern end of the Sea of Japan from American penetration. But this goal should be seen, realistically, as very much a long term proposition.

Questions raised with respect to Western Europe about the feasibility of 'selective' targeting are equally, if not more, valid in the circumstances of any attack on Japan, where industrial and population centres are not only geographically more concentrated but also more densely populated. The Yokosuka port complex is only 40 kilometres from the centre of Tokyo: an estimated 30 million people inhabit the greater Tokyo area, at present this constitutes the largest concentration of people in the world. The world's third largest concentration of population lies along the Osaka–Kobe–Kyoto axis. Thus the question remains how can a 'selective' nuclear targeting strategy be implemented in such an environment?

Conventional war and Japan

The scenario of conventional warfare involving Japan and the United States, and possibly China, against the Soviet Union can be seen either as a straight conventional war in its own right or as the conventional phases of a nuclear conflict.[33] In the Far East the major mission of Soviet conventional land forces would be the defeat and occupation of certain sections of China; certainly the north and perhaps western sections also. Even such limited holding operations would be logistically highly demanding. It seems unlikely that any further operations would be undertaken further into China, because of demands those operations would place on Soviet forces. Rather, the likely Soviet approach would be to deliver a rapid 'knock-out blow' in a geographically limited operations context sufficient to leave Chinese potential for waging war at an absolute minimum. In a situation where China is neutral the Soviets might choose to deploy 'holding forces' and utilise remaining forces elsewhere.

In interpreting Soviet strategy in the East we must be aware of the 'big picture' as seen by Soviet planners. In a global war – according to Soviet theory quite possibly a prolonged war – the Soviets would have to fight on two major fronts (Europe and the Far East) and on a third front in the south (the Gulf/Indian Ocean region) probably having to undertake operations against American forces that could threaten Soviet success elsewhere. A successful war on two fronts, and a possible third, may well be beyond the capabilities of Soviet conventional forces.

In waging war in the East the Soviets have to consider the effect of American and (possible Chinese) strikes upon the transportation network in what is termed a 'broken-backed' scenario when Siberia is 'detached' from the European districts of the Soviet Union by destroying its communication links. To serve to counter this the Soviets have given constant attention to improvements in the communications infrastructure as well as in stockpiling and prepositioning material for forces in the East so that they can conduct at least a defensive battle as independently as possible, not least because Soviet planners are aware that the demands of any war in the East could detract from Soviet abilities to win the crucial battle against NATO.

The past Soviet historical experience of the problems of conducting a war against Japan (1904–5, 1938–9, and 1945) involved major logistic efforts. Not surprisingly the Soviet military have been constant supporters of the BAM development. Placed at an average distance of 250 kilometres from the Chinese border it is a far more defensible line than the trans-Siberian. According to Pentagon estimates up to one-fifth of all the military material for the Far Eastern military district (a total of 11 million tons) is prepositioned along BAM. The Pentagon suggests that this material is sufficient to sustain operations for up to two months for Soviet forces.[34]

However we should be careful not to exaggerate the impact of this new development. Whiting summarises its real significance when he suggests that it has 'more value in a pre-military combat situation than in an actual war'.[35] Looking at things overall in the Far East he contends that 'Soviet development offers only a limited increase in Soviet strategic capability . . . its greatest contribution is in its strengthening of the region's logistic and support capacity before hostilities begin. Once a war starts, however, the defensive liabilities appear to outweigh the offensive advantages.'[36] Despite the benefits to be gained from the construction of BAM, Soviet communication and supply to the Far East is still tenuous. Though large Soviet air forces are interposed between China and BAM it is not inconceivable that low-level intruding aircraft could still attack the railroad. Conventional missile attacks, especially on 'choke points' (e.g. there are three major bridges of 400 metres length and numerous smaller ones as well as two major tunnels on the line), could pose serious threat of disruption.

Let us now consider in detail the Soviet threat to Japanese security. In this context the principal focus would be on Soviet naval power and the Pacific fleet. The major threat to the Soviet Far East stems from the nuclear capabilities of the American 7th fleet but a secondary, conventional threat, which the Soviets cannot dismiss lies in the substantial amphibious capability of the fleet. Moreover the increasing emphasis of Western navies on offensive operations against the Soviet submarine bastions, in this case the Sea of Okhotsk, have worried Soviet strategists sufficiently for them to develop since the 1970s and into the 1980s a capacity for the Soviet navy to push out its defensive barriers as far from Soviet coasts as possible.

The requirements of operating in distant waters led to changes in naval strategy and ship design towards systems capable of maintaining command of selected sea areas over an extended period of time. To this end new types of frigates, destroyers and ship-borne aircraft units were deployed in modernisation programmes through the 1970s, while shore-based air capacity was also increased with the introduction of more advanced, longer range aircraft, the most obvious of these being the TU-22M.

112

Table 12 *Strength of Soviet Pacific Fleet, 1983–6*

	Assumed percentage of total fleet, 1983	Total number, 1983	Estimated total number as of January 1987
Strategic forces			
All SSBN	35	22	27
*Active long range maritime forces**			
SSGN	41	20	23
SSG (J)	22	3	5
SSN	33	19	22
SS	33	25	22
Surface strike			
CVHG	33	1	2
CGN/CG		4	5
CG/CL Sverdlov	33	2	2
Surface ASW			
CG (Kara, Kresta II)	–	6	7
Surface escorts			
DDG	–	10	10
FFG	–	11	11
Amphibious			
LPD	–	1	2
LST	–	10	10
Long-range aircraft			
Bombers (TU-22M)	–	20	135 (total figure)
MPA<ASW (Bear F)	–	25	–
*Active theatre maritime forces***			
SSBN (H II)	35	2	–
SSB (G II)	53	7	7
Attack submarines			
SS	28	20	20
Theatre surface			
DD (Kotlin, Skory)	31	8	5
FF/FFL	30	43	41
Mine warfare			
MSF/MSC	24	62	61
Amphibious			
LSM	19	10	10
Theatre aircraft			
Bombers	33	103	(see above)
Fighter bombers	18	14	–
MPA/ASW	39	55	65
Reserve attack sumbarines			
SS/SSC	25	27	–
Reserve surface			
CG/CL, DD, FF	–	10	–

Note: * Active long range maritime forces in general refers to those units capable of distant water operations – generally ships in excess of 1,000 tons and amphibious transports and long range aircraft.
** Active theatre maritime forces generally refers to units likely to operate under a protective umbrella of land based aviation. The table does not include coastal defence/patrol units, KGB forces patrol ships.
Dashes indicate information not available.
Source: J. J. Tritten, *Soviet Navy Data Base: 1982–83*, (Santa Monica, California, Rand Corporation, Rand Paper P–6859 April 1983), pp. 14–16; *Jane's Defence Weekly*, 27 June 1987, pp. 1383–4; N. Polmar, *Guide to the Soviet Navy*, 4th edn (London, Arms and Armour Press, 1985), p. 5

Table 13 *Soviet bases and deployments in the Far East*

Prior to consideration of the information presented below it is necessary to place it in a wider context. The Soviet Far Eastern Military District is part of the 'Far Eastern Strategic Theatre' (GTVD) which comprises the Central Asian, Siberian, Transbaikal, and Far Eastern military districts as well as Mongolia and the Pacific and Indian ocean 'Oceanic TVDs'. In the Siberian and Transbaikal military districts and Mongolia the Soviets deploy a total of 4 tank divisions, 18 motorised rifle divisions, 2 artillery divisions and just over 520 combat aircraft. These divisions, as with divisions in the Far Eastern military district, are maintained at different levels of readiness. These forces are normally counted in the Soviet–Chinese balance; however it is important to register their existence as a ready-to-hand reserve to provide elements for any campaign against Japan depending upon the scenario. This is a particularly appropriate consideration in the case of aircraft, where the Soviets have a geographically proximate large reserve on which to draw but where the Japanese and Americans basically do not. For them air-reinforcement of Japan is a far more complex and time consuming problem.

Army strengths

In the Soviet Far Eastern military district there are deployed 2 tank divisions, 18 motorised rifle divisions, 1 airborne division, 2 motorised rifle brigades and 2 independent air-mobile brigades. The majority of these land forces are of course earmarked for operations against China. In evaluating the numbers likely to be involved in the scenario of war against Japan there are many variables to consider, e.g. the state of readiness of Soviet forces: bearing that in mind and with the proviso that the Soviets can of course reinforce those forces which they choose to utilise against the Japanese and American forces in North East Asia the following table outlines, from unclassified information those forces deployed mainly in the Far Eastern military district.

Kamen-Rybolov	29th Motorised Rifle Division
Komsomolsk-na-Amure	73rd Motorised Rifle Division
Ussuriisk	HQ 5th Army, Motorised Rifle Division
Poronaysk	79th Motorised Rifle Division, 1st Artillery Division
Slovania	Motorised Rifle Division
Yuzhno-Sakhalinsk	HQ 15th Army, 342nd Motorised Rifle Division, 1 Artillery Division
Barabosh-Kraskino	17th Motorised Rifle Division
Petropavlovsk	22nd Motorised Rifle Division
Magadan	Independent Motorised Rifle Brigade
Kuril Islands	3rd Motorised Rifle Division

Lesozhavodsk	Motorised Rifle Division
Khabarovsk	194th Motorised Rifle Division HQ Military District
Svobodnii	Motorised Rifle Division
Belogorsk	6th Guards Airborne Division
Birobidzhan	Air Assault Brigade, Spetsnaz Brigade

Pacific Fleet
The fleet is based around two squadrons, the 5th and the 7th

Vladivostok	60–70% of all vessels (mainly surface). HQ of 5th squadron. 2 naval infantry regiments also deployed
Petropavlovsk (Talinskaia Bay)	HQ of 7th squadron. 75% of submarines – most of the SSBN, SSN. 18–20 major surface combatants
Nakhodka	Base for submarines, frigates, minor combatants
Sovetskaia Gavan	Second largest base for surface fleet: 7–10 major surface combatants
Vladimir	Frigates
Olga	Frigates
Korskov (Sakhalin)	Destroyers and frigates
Magadan	Submarines (5–6)

Comment: Most of the Siberian Far Eastern ports tend to be frozen for up to six months of the year. Peter the Great Bay (Vladivostok) is greatly hampered by ice in winter. Magadan is usually ice bound from November until April.

Naval Aviation (HQ Sovetskaia Gavan)
Total of 350–60 aircraft

Anadyr	Forward Staging base Tu-22M
Sovetskaia Gavan	Mixed squadrons of patrol, reconnaissance and bombers. Estimated at: Tu-22M (30–5), Tu-22 Recce. (10–15), Tu-142 ASW (20), Tu-16 EW (15–20)

Table 13 (cont.)

Kamchatka (South)	Tu-16 (60–70)
Kamchatka	M-12 ASW (10), Il-38 ASW (15–20)
Korsakov	ASW patrol and helicopters
Alexandrovsk (Sakhalin)	ASW patrol, TU-22M, Su-17
Alexsyevskaia	Bomber base TU-22M
Khaka	(No information available)
Khabarovsk	(No information available)
Carrier-borne aviation (on the Minsk and Novorissisk)	Yak-36 (24), Ka-25 ASW (60)

Soviet Air Forces: Far Eastern Military District (HQ Khabarovsk)
US intelligence reports suggest that up to 90% of the aircraft deployed in the region are now (1984) third generation as compared to only 50% in 1978
Total air strength 1000–1100 (includes 200 helicopters)

Vladivostok	3 large bases
Nikolayevska	2 bases (Voyska PVO/Frontal aviation)
Dolinsk/Sokol	Base complex. Voyska PVO (SU-15)
Provideniia	Staging base, long-range bombers
Ussuriisk/Spassk-Dalnii	2 bases Tu-16 Bombers (130–140)
Khaka lake	3 bases
Sandagou	2 bases
Khabarovsk	VA – VGK base (formerly long-range aviation)
Velikaia	(No information available)
Sovetskaia Gavan/Komsomolsk	Voyska PVO base
Nikolayevsk-na-Amure	?
Okhotsk	?
Blagoveshchensk	?
Petropavlovsk	Major concentration; Voyska PVO

Sakhalin South   6 bases. Korsakov, Yuzhno-Sakhalinsk Dolinsk (Voyska PVO) SU-15s
Sakhalin North   Leonydovo (Voyska PVO)
Kuril Islands   2 bases, Burevestnik (Iturup) 20 Mig-23, 10 Mig-21, SU-15)
From these bases Frontal aviation deploys an estimated:
Mig-23 : 120–180   Su-7/17/20 : 75–100
Mig-25 : 100–120   Su-15 : 120–180
Mig-27 : 50–75   Su-24 : 70–80
Yak-28P : 40   Tactical Recce : 70–80 aircraft

Long Range Missiles
SSM's deployed which have the range to hit Japan if launched from areas of the Maritime Province are SS-22 and SS-23 (number unknown)

Transport Aviation
It is estimated that the VTA deploys 100–130 aircraft in the Far East base principally around the Sovetskaia Gavan and Komsomolsk-na-Amure complex of bases

Comment: It should be pointed out that neither Anadyr, Magadan nor Petropavlovsk are linked by either railway or sealed road. They are totally dependent, as in Sakhalin, upon supply by sea or air transportation.

Sources: Various, major works are: J. Moore (ed.), *Jane's Fighting Ships 1984–85* (London, MacDonald and Jane's). N. Polmar, *Guide To The Soviet Navy*, 3rd ed. (Annapolis, Maryland, Naval Institute Press, 1983). *The Military Balance 1984–85, 86–87*, (London, International Institute for Strategic Studies, 1984, 1986). *Asian Security 1980* (Tokyo, Research Institute for Peace and Security, 1980), W. Arkin and R. Fieldhouse, *Nuclear Battlefields*, (Cambridge, Mass., Ballinger Publishing, 1985). *Jane's Defence Weekly* 1:4 (14 April 1984) 560–2; 19 January 1985, p. 89. 'Soviet Air Power', in *Asian Aviation* (April 1983), 44–59. 'Soviet Air Defence Systems Showing Increasing Sophistication', in *Defence Electronics* (May 1984), 75–86. *Jane's Defence Weekly*, 3:10 (9 March 1985), 406–7

Estimates of Soviet fleet strength in the Pacific vary considerably. Table 12, mostly compiled by Tritten, is based on a comparison of unclassified figures from various sources. Table 13 presents Soviet force levels and deployments in the Far East.

We have said that the first Soviet priority is to maintain the survivability of the submarine component of its strategic nuclear arm. However it is generally accepted by Western naval analysts that at any one time only approximately 15% of the Soviet SSBN fleet is ever on station. (This compares with 55% of the American force.) The average number of Soviet SSBN boats on station for 1980 was thirteen out of approximately sixty.[37] Thus in a Soviet worse-case scenario, when war is instigated by the United States and the Soviets are caught relatively unprepared, a major portion of the Soviet SSBN fleet may lie vulnerable. An estimated 35% of Soviet SSBN are based with the Pacific fleet. While the *Delta* class of boats may have the range to attack the continental United States from Soviet coastal waters, their survivability would be greatly enhanced by deployment outside the Sea of Okhotsk.

In the event, or likelihood of a major war it is probable that the Soviets will pursue a strategy of deploying as many submarines to sea in as short a period as possible, not merely to coastal sea areas but also out into the wider Pacific. This may well take place as a 'surge mobilisation'. Certainly it is plausible that *Yankee* class boats would be deployed to forward positions in the Eastern Pacific ('politically desirable as an escalatory statement and as a demonstration of resolve'); certain analysts also believe it possible that a number of *Yankees* might be held back in relatively closer waters to act as a *theatre* nuclear strike reserve. There are arguments which are supportive or dismissive of both hypotheses. Tritten sums-up the position on deployment patterns by suggesting that, 'From the evidence of the hardware alone, it is impossible to conclude with certainty whether Yankees retained in home waters would be used in theater strikes or as part of the theater or strategic reserve.'[38]

Delta and *Typhoon* class boats, as suggested above, would also probably be deployed to sea as quickly as possible in order to maximise their survival chances. There are again both political and military reasons for this in that they can act as *naval* contributors to any *overall* strategic reserve in the context of Soviet strategic theory which includes the potential for an initial conventional phase or a total conventional war.

> Hence the long range of SLBMs and deployment in home waters maximises submarine survival. Coupled with their lack of accuracy

which limits use against hardened targets, this tends to support a reserve vice immediate use role. The one main advantage of the Delta/Typhoon is that it further guarantees a Soviet 'assured destruction' strike against the US no matter what else happens to other Soviet strategic forces.

This reserve role does not necessarily mean *only* for inter- or post-war bargaining or coercion but *also* as a hedge against the possible but unlikely destruction of Soviet bombers, submarines in port, and ICBMs. No matter what happens sufficient capability remains at sea to make a nuclear response.[39]

Western superiority in ASW makes the long term survivability of these submarines, and certainly the older and 'noisier' classes (*Yankee*) doubtful. The Soviet problem has been compounded by the Western response to the development of bastion areas, which has been the evolution of a counter strategy designed to carry the attack right into the secure areas relying on superior Western technology and ECM ability. This has been pursued to the extent that 'the growing importance of naval strategic assets and concern about the budding US determination to wage offensive operations in Soviet home waters have prompted Soviet military planners to opt for an even more rigorous and systematic pro-SSBN strategy'.[40]

Thus Soviet strategy has evolved throughout the 1970s and 1980s. But even though more of the fleet has become SSBN oriented, the task of defending the bastions has become more problematic and more of a preoccupation for Soviet planners. In other words we can still pose the question that planners asked in the 1970s: how secure and survivable can the Soviet SSBN component be?

Included in the strategy for SSBN survival in the Pacific is the need to seize and control – possibly for a long period – parts of Japanese territory, or at least deny their use to Japanese and American forces. We shall consider the mechanics of this in a following section, and speculate on actual Soviet assault plans for such an operation. But let us first examine other missions the naval forces will be required to undertake.

The second priority for Soviet naval forces would be the destruction of opposing forces. The main objective in this category is the detection and destruction of Western SSBN and American carrier battle groups. While the detection of battle groups would not pose a significant problem, their intrinsic defence capabilities – high ECM ability, air and air defence/ASW forces – mean that their actual destruction would require the commitment of sizeable Soviet naval resources and readiness to incur significant losses.

The Soviets might seek to counter American carrier battle groups by using nuclear weapons against them. Two American analysts see the forces in these groups as being at risk in a nuclear scenario, 'In preparing for nuclear war at sea, Soviet planners have sought to exploit the fundamental weakness of the US navy – an extreme concentration of combat power . . . given the relatively low number of major US combatants, each battlegroup is an important percentage of the Navy's aggregate capability'.[41]

The targeting of Western naval forces by the Soviet Strategic Rocket Forces (SRF) is an historical declaratory policy dating from the late 1960s – although it has been mentioned very little since, especially after the early 1970s. More hypothetical is the question of Soviet naval forces utilising nuclear weapons against Western naval elements. One commentator's view of this is that

> the author must conclude that once nuclear weapons are used ashore, they will be used at sea as well. The decision to initiate tactical nuclear war at sea appears to be neither a Soviet navy decision nor one that will hinge upon naval matters. Rather it will depend upon the political context, such as participants in and the desired length of the war.[42]

The Soviets are aware that if they wish to 'win' at sea they must win quickly. That belief alone indicates that the use of nuclear weapons at sea must be considered a distinct possibility.

In contrast to American battle groups, the detection of American SSBN would pose a very difficult problem. American SSBN are far quieter in operation than their Soviet counterparts and are more geographically dispersed. In the Pacific theatre they are capable of operation in remote waters, thus making it very difficult for the Soviets even to reach them to conduct ASW operations. Even then it is generally recognised that Soviet ASW technology lags far behind that of the West.[43]

Hence both these tasks (attacks on carrier battle groups and ASW operations) are 'resource intensive' and would constitute a major drain on the numbers of available Soviet naval units. The trade-off in terms of likely Soviet losses might well prove to be crippling. Given the relative fleet strengths in the Pacific it is not unreasonable to suggest that in this high attrition environment the Soviets are not well placed to emerge the victors.

As we suggested in our list of Soviet naval mission priorities, the disruption of Japanese–American communications across the Pacific via the interdiction of sea lines of communication (SLOC) would probably rank low compared to other tasks for Soviet forces in the

Pacific. Reinforcement of Japan with American troops or supplies is not likely to compare in scale or urgency with reinforcement and supply of Europe across the Atlantic, and consequently the Soviets are unlikely to devote sizeable forces to counter it.

The Soviet Pacific fleet is neither strong enough nor well equipped enough, with organic air power for example, to conduct a sea-denial campaign in the wider Pacific. This would involve the denial of sea areas to all enemy shipping, including warships, but implies that one's own forces would not necessarily be able to operate successfully in the contested areas. In the Sea of Okhotsk the Soviets would not seek merely to deny the area to enemy operations but to actively control it for their own purposes. We should note therefore the differences between sea control, sea denial and sea (SLOC) interdiction.

Given the vastness of the Pacific any interdiction operation would require a large input of resources to have any real chance of success. Obviously sea traffic has to become concentrated in the approaches to Japan thus making it particularly susceptible to attack, but equally we can expect Japan and the United States to put a maximum effort into defending traffic at that point precisely for that reason. Presumably in the run-up to confrontation the Soviets would try to put as many of their submarines to sea as possible but their ability to remain at sea for long periods – as would be required by an interdiction campaign – is doubtful. Soviet air-cover is unavailable outside a limited distance, and any Soviet submarines on long-range station will be particularly susceptible to ASW countermeasures. Given the other Soviet priorities what Soviet forces in the Pacific could be spared for an interdiction campaign? Bearing in mind that the Pacific fleet also supplies out-of-area forces for deployment in the Indian Ocean and South China Sea (the China Sea squadron consists, on average, of two submarines, three to four cruisers/destroyers and one assault LCM; the Indian Ocean deployment is usually about five submarines and six major surface units) and that the defence of the submarine bastions holds an overriding priority, that any attacks on American surface battle groups will be of high attrition, we can realistically only expect a small number of submarines to be available for allocation to the task. Moreover, it is probable that these submarines will be predominantly older class boats – thus more easily detectable. Assigning a figure to this can only be speculative, but some Western assessments, such as the Atlantic Council's, have put the number of available submarines as low as fifteen boats. The accompanying table (14) from a study by the Atlantic Council depicts what they envisaged as the division of roles for Soviet forces in the Pacific and Indian oceans in 1979–80.

121

Table 14 *Theatre Allocation by Mission: Pacific and Indian Ocean Current/obsolescent*

Naval forces	Designation	Soviet Navy — Class of assets	Fleet allocation — Pacific fleet	Strategic strike	Theater strike	SSBN Protection	Outer area attack	Counter-carrier	Counter-SSBN	Support of ground forces	Command contiguous waters	Port & SLOC interdiction	Allocated to Indian Ocean
Submarines	SSBN	DELTA, YANKEE	20/0	20/0									
	SSB/N	HOTEL, GOLF	0/8		0/8								
	SSG/N	CHARLIE, JULIETT, LONGBIN	8/2					8/2					
	SSGN	ECHO II	14/0					13/0					1/0
	SSN	VICTOR	6/0				3/0		3/0				
	SSN	NOVEMBER, ECHO	0/9				0/6					0/2	0/1
	SS	TANGO, FOXTROT, ZULU	14/4				6/0					6/4	2/0
	SS	B., R., W., Q CLASS	1/10								1/10		
Aircraft		BACKFIRE											
		BADGER, BLINDER	0/95					0/60				0/35	
Major surface combatants	CLG/M	KARA, KRESTA II	2/0				2/0						
	DDG	KRIVAK, KASHIN, KANIN, KOTLIN	14/0				12/0						
	CLGM	KRESTA I, KYNDA, KILDIN	4/0					3/0					2/0
	CLG	SVERDLOV	0/4							0/3	0/10		1/0
	DD/DE	KOTLIN, SKORY, RIGA	0/15							0/5	7/0		0/1
	FF	New. GRISHA, MIRKA, PETYA	19/0				10/0				6/0		2/0
	PM	NANUCHKA	6/0										
Other		Small Patrol Craft	70/35								70/35		
		Amphibious Support Ships	73/0							73/0			

Source: P. Nitze and L. Sullivan, Atlantic Council Working Group, *Securing the Seas* (Boulder, Colorado, Westview Press, 1979), p. 115

Table 15 *Japanese oil consumption*

Year	Average consumption (thousand barrels per day)	Oil stocks at end of month (thousand barrels)	Supply period stock (days)
1972	4,311	–	–
1973	5,000	322,000	64
1974	4,872	–	–
1975	4,568	335,000	73
1976	4,786	350,000	78
1977	5,015	390,000	78
1978	5,115	394,000	77
1979	5,171	420,000	81
1980	4,674	480,000	102
1981	4,444	480,000	108
1982	–	460,000	–

Note: The International Energy Agency *Oil Market Report* (June 1986) claimed that as of March 1986 Japan held an oil stock sufficient for 127 days. The average West European stock supply stood at 96 days.
Dashes indicate information not available
Source: Directorate of Intelligence, CIA, *International Energy Statistical Review* GI IESR 82–007, 27 July 1982, pp. 14, 18

There are likely to be further problems in that Soviet submarines, especially in any prolonged war, could well have their performance impaired by disruptive attacks on the Soviet C3I system. Even in the age of technology ships and convoys still have to be 'found' and tracked, submarines have to be guided to an intercept point and attacks with other submarines co-ordinated. The secure communications and information flow that are a necessary prerequisite cannot be guaranteed, and the availability of the latter tends to decline with greater distance when the Soviets would lose, for example, the support provided by high-powered coastal search radars. At a tactical level many Soviet attacks on shipping will be carried out at long range by cruise missile carrying submarines (SSGNs). Many of these missiles require mid-course guidance to target; this can be done by aircraft, more often by helicopters. Here the Soviets are hampered by a lack of mobile naval airpower and once again the distance factor has a role to play in mitigating against physically being able to deploy such co-ordinating aircraft to a combat zone lying to the south or east of Japan.[44]

Some analysts point to Japan's particular vulnerability to blockade. Available statistics on Japanese oil reserves and consumption show that to be significant any blockade would have to be sustained over a long period. The statistics show that Japan has oil stocks adequate for at least 127 days. This is a figure higher than the West European average. (See table 15.) The rationing that would be instituted in wartime could extend this period considerably. Commenting on the blockade scenario one analyst suggests that 'the passive solution is to reduce wartime import requirements. By one calculation this could be done for a six month emergency . . . by austere standards ship arrivals could be reduced by 80%.'[45] To counter any Soviet campaign would undoubtedly require sizeable naval forces which might better be used elsewhere, but it seems within Japanese and American capability to at least limit the threat if not nullify it entirely. Attacks on shipping (particularly on shipping in waters close to Japan, as opposed to for example, attacks conducted on shipping at the extremities of the South China Sea) by Soviet aircraft could only be conducted at heavy loss to Soviet aircrews, and the danger from this source is therefore likely to diminish the longer the conflict lasts.

The effects of attacks by submarines on shipping in Japanese waters are problematic. As we indicated above, Soviet attacks in the area, given the concentration of shipping, may prove very damaging but the losses incurred by submarines could be prohibitive and force the Soviets to operate further out from the concentrations of ASW technology.

A possible Soviet tactic would be the disruption of SLOCs, in the indirect sense, by attacking shipping terminals with nuclear weapons. This is in fact Soviet declaratory policy and a recent major survey of declaratory policy on the uses of the Soviet navy has concluded on this point that

> There is only modest evidence of a declaratory Soviet SLOC disruption mission associated with traditional at-sea operations rather than by missile strikes against terminals. Occasionally, the Soviets state they intend to use aviation, surface ships (missile boats, especially) and submarines against SLOCs but some of this commentary has specified coastal areas and closed seas. It appears that the declaratory strategy, to disrupt distant SLOCs is by fleet versus shore missile strikes.[46]

We have already speculated on possible nuclear attack on Japan and its consequences but what are the conventional options open to Soviet forces? First, it must be said that it is difficult to conceive of any situation outside a general war in which the Soviets would invade Japan – the most likely point being Hokkaido. The obvious disadvantage of such an attack in a general war situation stems from the limited Soviet amphibious capability which places constraints on the

Table 16 *Soviet amphibious lift capability in the Far East*

Class type	Combat personnel	Vehicles	Cargo	Number
Ivan Rogov/LPD	Naval inf. btn.	20 tanks	13,000t.(l)	1
Ropucha/LST	250	35 tanks	2,000t.(c)	(8)
Alligator/LST	125–250	25–30 tanks	1,700t.(c)	(7)
Polnochny/LSM	Vehicle crews	6 tanks	350t.(c)	10
Kiev/CV Airlift of *c*. 20 helicopters. (Ka-25:12 man capacity)				2

Sources: Figures in parenthesis are quoted from G. Jacobs, 'A Soviet War for Northern Japan' in *Asian Defence Journal*, 1:83, pp. 6–17. Moore, *Jane's Fighting Ships 1984* gives a total number for these LST as being 10. See also, B. Hahn, 'The Soviet Union's RDF', in *Pacific Defence Reporter* (April 1984) 17–21. P. Young, 'Soviet Amphibious Capabilities', in *Defence Update*, 54, (1984), 35–40. The vehicle figures represent maximum loads: composition of loads can therefore vary. Cargo tonnages are given as either loaded (l) or as capacity (c).

initial lift and the subsequent reinforcing and supply of the landing force. Demands might also be pressed on available Soviet resources by plans to mount small amphibious operations against the Chinese, and possibly Korean, coasts.

The most probable scenario envisaged is invasion and attempted seizure of areas of Hokkaido. A main landing is anticipated on the Wakkanai–Sarafutsu–Teshio peninsula followed by a subsequent advance over the rest of Hokkaido to secure the bridgehead supported by air assault troops and heavy air attack. A second landing might possibly be undertaken along the Nemuro–Kushin axis adjacent to the Soviet occupied islands north of Japan.[47]

The largest of the Self Defence Force armies has been deployed on Hokkaido to counter this contingency; four of the thirteen divisions of the Self Defence Force, supported by formations such as missile and helicopter groups and a tank brigade. One of the divisions, the seventh, is the only fully mechanised division in the Ground Self Defence Force.

Table 16 lists the available Soviet amphibious lift capability in the Far East. The spearhead of any assault would presumably be the naval infantry of which there are at present some 8,000 deployed based at Vladivostok. Army formations would also be utilised supported by airborne assault troops. Where necessary the available shipping capacity would be supplemented by standard merchant ships or by passenger cruise liners (there are approximately twenty of these in the East) and Ro/Ro ferries. However these could probably not be fully utilised until a major port had been captured. Except for a heliborne

Table 17 *Selected Distances between Soviet bases and Hokkaido*

Korsakov–Sarafutsu (Wakkanai peninsula)	165kms
Yuzhno–Sakhalinsk–Sarafutsu	198kms
Khabarovsk – Wakkanai peninsula	700kms
Vladivostok–Wakkanai peninsula	770kms
Sovetskaia Gavan–Wakkanai peninsula	420kms
Petropavlovsk–Wakkanai peninsula	1430kms
Vladivostok–Sapporo	710kms
Kunashir (Kuril islands)–Sapporo	380kms

assault – likely only to be of regimental size – the Soviet air contribution would be confined to air attack and escort patrol for the invasion fleet. Although at its closest point Hokkaido is only 180 kilometres from Soviet air bases at Yuzhno-Sakhalinsk (and of course even closer to the northern islands) the main Soviet air cover and air supply forces will have to launch their sorties from the Maritime province over 700–800 kilometres away. For combat aircraft this would only leave them a loiter time over target of roughly twenty minutes or less if engaged on their way to the ground combat zones by enemy aircraft. To give an impression of the problems involved, table 17 gives some selected distances between Soviet bases and Hokkaido.

Such an operation could not be mounted with any degree of surprise and it can be assumed that Japanese and American forces would try their utmost to deplete the amphibious forces while still afloat. The main force's journey from Soviet ports to Hokkaido would take in excess of thirty-five hours, allowing ample opportunity for attacks on it. Even if Hokkaido were successfully invaded the Soviet forces would then face their greatest obstacle, that of supply and logistical support. In a high density combat zone over which the Soviets could not be sure of air superiority, logistical capacity could prove inadequate to supply the initial landing force. No adequate supply of a major follow-up force could be ensured unless a major port and airfield were captured in reasonably usable condition; these would then have to be successfully defended and kept operable in the middle of a combat zone.

Soviet study of amphibious operations is a massive subject in itself and it cannot be hoped to do justice to it here. Suffice to say in conclusion that all of the above provisos *contradict* main guidelines derived from Soviet experiences during World War II of amphibious operations. The Soviets claim to have undertaken more than 110 amphibious operations during the war and have learned that: the greatest success is achieved when amphibious operations are combined with a land offensive (which meets-up with the amphibious force within a few days); *the* most important prerequisite for success is surprise; *large* amounts of air support are needed for protection, suppression, and air superiority; generous provision must be made for logistical support. One final point needs emphasising – Soviet amphibious operations during the war were very small scale affairs and were basically 'coastal-hopping' activities. Even current Soviet rehearsals of amphibious operations, for example, in the *Zapad-81* and *Shchit-82* exercises, were on the same scale. The Hokkaido operation would be a *massive* undertaking the like of which the Soviets have never experienced before.

The point has been raised[48] that it is plausible – given the Soviet preoccupation with the American threat, and since American combat forces constitute the overwhelming majority, both qualitatively and quantitatively, in the region – that in a conventional phase of any war Soviet forces will give priority to neutralising and destroying US assets over those of the Self Defence Forces. Implicit in such suggestions though would be the proviso that dealing with US forces would absorb such a large proportion of Soviet conventional resources that direct major attacks on solely Japanese installations and military targets may be few and far between. Numerous small scale, limited operations would thus be envisaged. Should this prove to be the case it must have an impact on any plans for invasion of Hokkaido as the resources to mount a complex multi-arm invasion might be committed elsewhere; thus any invasion would be an affair limited to a small holding operation to secure passage from the Sea of Okhotsk to the Pacific.

Soviet forces as a political instrument

It is often stated with regard to Soviet–Japanese relations that the Soviets have pursued a counter-productive policy in choosing to forego normal diplomatic interactions and follow instead a deliberate policy of coercion to encourage Japan to adopt a more acquiescent position. This line of approach has, it is argued, produced an adverse reaction in Japan which has encouraged increased Japanese defence efforts and fuelled a bitter resentment against the 'Soviet threat'.

The Soviet Union's rise to military parity with the United States has been its greatest achievement; that the capability of Soviet forces has greatly increased cannot be doubted. However what cannot be deduced from this observation is whether this growth in power is the product of a deliberate policy or is the result of other variables. Theses on the nature of military procurement patterns, opportunism, action–reaction relationships etc. are well known and need not be gone into here.[49] Furthermore, even if we accept that acquisition of more capable forces has been the product of conscious decision we cannot extrapolate further as to their probable or potential use. Although intent may change over time, possession does not of itself imply intent. However it does provide the Soviets with an enhanced capacity and readiness to exploit opportunities and indicates a concern about regional security.

In attempting to posit a relationship between military power and political influence we are concerned with an abstract concept. We can measure and quantify the components of military power but how do we measure 'influence'? We cannot posit a simple equation that more power equates with more influence, for this is demonstrably not always the case. Also it would be a further mistake to depict influence as being related to a perception of an ability to project power.

Can we outline some sort of categorisation of types or objectives of influence? Bull outlined some basic parameters which are useful starting points: persuasion can be sought through the symbol of national power and commitment rather than of a particular situation; it can be directed towards compulsion or deterrence of certain actions; it can be 'latent' in the sense that it occurs through routine actions; or it can be 'active' in the sense that it involves a deliberate attempt to invoke a specific reaction.[50]

A complicating factor arises in examining the concept with regard to Japan because implicit in the statements made by Western analysts positing a Soviet counterproductive policy is the connotation of a deliberate and continuing policy of coercion. Other commentators have explicitly stated this.[51] Our problem is that it would seem to be difficult to sustain an argument of 'deliberate intent' not least because we are not privy to policy decisions within the Kremlin.

Kaplan in his seminal work on the use of Soviet armed forces as a political instrument delimits the following categories and definitions.

> A political use of the armed forces occurs when physical actions are taken by one or more components of the uniformed military services as part of a deliberate attempt by the national authorities to influence, or to be prepared to influence, specific behaviour of individuals in another nation without engaging in a continuing contest of violence.[52]

For this situation to have occurred four elements must be present according to Kaplan: a physical change in the disposition (location, activity, readiness) of an armed unit, including exercises or demonstrations or the movements of any units away from or toward a specific location; behind this activity there had to have been a consciousness of purpose aimed at achieving some specific outcomes abroad; Soviet decision-makers must have tried to attain their objectives at least initially by gaining influence in a target state rather than physically imposing their will; and Soviet leaders must have tried to avoid a sustained contest of violence.[53]

Kaplan suggests that regular or routine occurrences do not constitute coercive incidents. He further excludes the 'continued presence of forward deployed forces, non-discriminating political deployments, and operational deployments' as well as flights over territory to test readiness and defences and the 'large number of seizures by Soviet patrol ships of foreign – usually Japanese – fishing vessels operating in or said to be overfishing waters claimed or protected by the Soviet Union'.[54]

If we accept Kaplan's definitions and criteria it is difficult to see any real cases in which the Soviet Union could be accused of coercing Japan. Even the notable cases of the deployments of SS-20s in the Eastern military districts of the Soviet Union would be discounted as Kaplan excludes deployments or modernisations associated with strategic nuclear questions and the improvement of warfighting capabilities.

But is this really where we should be directing our appraisal? Even if, by some criteria, we find it difficult to substantiate an argument of coercion we should be aware of a Japanese perspective which might be very different. Each nation has an interpretation of the present that is always to an extent the product of earlier events – for many nations this proves to be the tyranny of historical experience. The constant feature of twentieth-century Russian/Soviet–Japanese relations has been hostility: even now no peace treaty has yet been signed, and the two countries are thus still technically at war. There can be little dispute that the Japanese perception sees a significant and growing threat from the Soviet Union which has for the most part materialised in the early 1980s; or at least this is the image with which we are confronted. But some qualifications should be made to views of Japanese interpretations of the Soviet Union.

Japanese public opinion polls indicate that the Soviet Union is the foreign country least liked, or most feared. But probing what that fear means in real terms qualifies the image of antipathy. On the question of threats to national security, 'Do you feel threatened . . .' responses in 1979, 1980, 1981 ranged between 'greatly threatened' – 6.0%, 7.5%, 5.1% respectively; 'certain extent' – 24.5%, 32.4%, 24.0%; 'a little

Table 18 *Violations of Japanese airspace*

1977	1
1978	2
1979	1 (November 15)
1980	1
1981	1
1982	1 (April 3)
1983	2 (October 15(?), November 16)
1984	3 (November 12, 20(?), 23)

Note: Between 1955 and 1977 there had been five confirmed violations of Japanese airspace by Soviet aircraft. By the end of 1983 this confirmed total had risen to thirteen. These figures are still very much speculative due to the reticence of the SDF to release specific details. Often information in non-official sources conflicts with what little is released by the SDF.
Sources: Defence Agency, Tokyo, *Defence of Japan 1982*, p. 79; *Defence of Japan 1984*, p. 155. *Asian Security 1980*, p. 42. *USSR and Third World*, 1 September to 15 December 1977, p. 99, 1 February to 30 June 1978, p. 28, 1 January to 28 February 1979, p. 4. *Canberra Times*, 17 November 1983

threatened' – 41.6%, 36.0%, 34.3%; 'not at all' – 10.2%, 5.6%, 8.7%; 'do not know' – 17.8%, 18.6%, 27.9%.[55]

In the same surveys, 77.3%, 83.6% and 77.4% of those surveyed replied that the Soviet Union posed the greatest threat to Japan, but only 7.6% thought that there would be any conflict between Japan and the Soviet Union. Only 27.3% viewed conflict between the Soviet Union and China as likely.[56] Thus even though a threat is perceived, the majority does not appear to consider it great.

We can take the argument a stage further by asking what form the Japanese see the Soviet threat as taking. Psychological, political, military, etc.? In a study of a specific sector of the Japanese population, the 'defence influentials' as he terms them, Young C. Kim's results suggest that it is seen in psychological and political terms; 'by psychological is meant the intimidation resultant from the Soviet military build-up. Political refers to the political use by the Soviets of this military capability. In either case the threat perceived is one of gradual Finlandisation of Japan.'[57] However Kim qualifies his comments by stating that these views are held by a very closed group, even within the spheres of the 'defence influentials'. These perceptions of the Soviet threat are related to other factors; 'in general, those who perceive a Soviet threat to Japan tend to ... have an especially favourable attitude towards the United States' military presence'.[58]

What is the threat based upon in real terms? The Japanese Defence Agency compiles statistics of violations of Japanese airspace and

Table 19 *Scrambles by Japanese aircraft*

		Royal Norwegian Airforce Scrambles
1970	370	–
1971	345	–
1972	306	–
1973	257	–
1974	323	–
1975	305	–
1976	528	–
1977	496	–
1978	798	–
1979	636	–
1980	783	–
1981	939	–
1982	929	–
1983	–	290 (estimated)
1984	–	471

Note: To put these figures into a more useful context it had been hoped to compare figures with the number of scrambles launched by the Norwegian airforce or with the RAF in Britain. However only the information cited above on Norwegian airforce scrambles has been forthcoming. This is cited from 'Moscow apology for drone cheers up Scandinavians' in *The Times*, 17 January 1985. Coincidentally the Norwegian report confirms a speculation made in our examination of Japan – that an increase in scrambles may well be due to use of more sophisticated detection equipment rather than an increase in the number of Soviet flights. Specifically it states that 'A (Norwegian) defence ministry spokesman said the increase was probably caused by improved Norwegian detection equipment and not by an increase in Soviet flights.' D. van der Aart, in *Aerial Espionage*, Airlife, Shrewsbury UK, 1985, claims that in 1983 the Royal Norwegian Air force carried out about 300 'interceptions' and in 1984 about 125 'interceptions' (see p. 132)
Dashes indicate information not available
Source: Defence Agency, Tokyo, *Defence of Japan 1984*, p. 155.

scrambles by ASDF aircraft are presented in tables 18 and 19. Movements of vessels around Japanese waters are also listed in table 20. (The geographical features of the Japanese straits are also indicated (table 21), showing the problems confronting the Soviets with regard to these straits. The Soya strait is so shallow that Soviet submarines often transit it on the surface.)

The Defence Agency is very reticent in presenting its own data regarding Soviet military actions around Japan, so that it has been necessary to compile these incomplete tables from various sources. The information presented by the Agency tells us very little; moreover it presents a rather distorted picture of Soviet movements. The Agency

Table 20 *Soviet naval vessel movements through Japanese straits*

	1979	1980	1981	1982
Tsushima Strait	140	150	165	165
Tsugaru Strait	50	55	60	60
Soya Strait	130	155	205	230
Totals	320	360	430	455

Source: Defence Agency, Tokyo, *Defence of Japan* (relevant years)

Table 21 *Geographical features of Japanese Straits*

	Narrowest width	Average depth	Deepest point
Soya (La Perouse)	43 kms	50m (164ft)	74m (243 ft)
Tsugaru	20 kms	210m	449m

Source: *Kodansha Encyclopedia of Japan*, Vol. I–IX (Tokyo, 1983). Ministerstvo Oboroni SSSR, Voenno-Morskoi Flot, *Atlas Okeanov: Tikhii Okean* (Moscow, Glavnoe Upravlenie Navigatsii i Okeanographii, 1974), p. 282.

figures represent five year averages, without indicating whether they derive from steady growth or from high activity in some years followed by decline.

This is particularly to be borne in mind regarding Soviet air and naval movements through/over the Tsushima strait in 1979–80. Following the invasion of Vietnam by China the Soviets undertook a substantial resupply mission that obviously necessitated more numerous flights and sailings. Given the growth of ties between Vietnam and the Soviet Union these increases would have to be expected anyway, especially with the growth of the Soviet base at Cam Ranh bay. This is a specific point acknowledged by *Kyodo* the Japanese newsagency, which has stated that: 'In the year to 31 March 1982, ASDF aircraft were alerted on 263 occasions, compared with 137 the previous year against Soviet aircraft over Kyushu ... the Force attributed this to more frequent (166) flights by Ilushin transports between Moscow and Hanoi, and also by more frequent flights by TU-95 aircraft to Da Nang.'[59] The Self Defence Forces have chosen to make this point public only in the 1983 edition of the *Defence of Japan* yearbook.[60]

Qualification must also be made concerning what can reasonably be inferred from the total number of scrambles by the Air Self Defence Force. An increase in the number of scrambles could as well result from an increase in the sophistication of the Air Self Defence Force's detection equipment, as from an increase in Soviet flights. There is also an obvious discrepancy between the figures quoted by *Kyodo* for transits over Kyushu as compared to the official Agency figure. This might be explained if the Agency incorporated most of these flights in the 'over the sea of Japan' category, but that can only be speculation.

The balance of air scrambles is not favourable to the Soviets. There is no specific information available on this subject but the author has not encountered references to Soviet air force scrambles to intercept Air Self Defence Force flights, though these doubtless occur, but not on a comparable scale. More so is this the case where the Air Self Defence Forces have supposedly penetrated Soviet airspace. Both the United States and Japan place strict limits on how close aircraft and naval vessels can approach the Soviet Union, though the United States operates electronic surveillance and eavesdropping flights along the limits of Soviet airspace and probably within Soviet airspace when specially authorised.[61] But nevertheless the Soviets are clearly far more active and provocative in their use of air operations than the Japanese and United States combined.

The calculations involving naval figures are fraught with similar pitfalls as in the interpretation of the air activity data. The figures provided by the Defence Agency categorise 'Vessels' but make no distinction between 'warships' and 'other' vessels. Major Soviet settlements in the Far East such as Anadyr, Magadan, Petropavloysk or Sakhalin have no rail access so supply has to be undertaken by air or sea especially to the Northern islands close to Japan. Consequently a proportion of the totals cited are in fact a movement of transport ships – icebreakers, water supply, or oil tankers and the like. The Tokyo correspondent of *Pacific Defence Reporter* has written

> Another little-known element that casts doubt on the battle-worthiness of the Soviet Far-Eastern Fleet is its relative lack of mobility. According to data collected by the Japanese Maritime Self Defence Force, a total of 450 Russian naval vessels last year passed through the Soya, Tsugaru and Tsushima straits. This count is the number of units entering or exiting from the Sea of Japan to the Pacific Ocean and contains some duplication. This tally was made not only of warships but also of supply vessels, landing ships and barges. However, during 1983 only 19 ships larger than corvettes passed through the Soya and Tsushima straits.[62]

Soviet naval activities are, on the whole, geographically limited, certainly in comparison to the number of ship days at sea accumulated by opposing Western navies. The prevailing tendency has been for the

Soviet surface fleet to hug coastal waters, rarely engage in long-range cruising and spend much time in port. The Japanese raised a great deal of concern over the arrival in the Far East of the Soviet carrier *Minsk*, but in the slightly more than three years it has been with the Soviet Pacific fleet it has spent most of its time either in port or in short coastal water sailings. It has participated in only one long-range cruise in August–November 1980 and in one distant exercise in the Tonkin Gulf in April 1984. Between 1 and 17 April 1985 the carrier *Novorossiysk* participated in what has been termed the Soviet navy's 'first carrier battle group' cruise. The group of seven ships sailed in a circular route out round Japan; at its furthest point the group was about 1,500nm from Japan (1,200 km north-west of Midway). The *Novorossiysk* has cruised only in the Sea of Japan since. Its most publicised sortie was at the end of June 1987, when it was accompanied by the *Frunze*, *Tashkent* and *Varyag*. Collectively they were described as 'the most powerful force of Soviet surface vessels ever to be observed by the JMSDF'.[63]

The Soviets also conduct conventional live firing practices in waters around Japan as well as rocket launching tests. Normally the Soviets give advance warning and designate the danger areas. On occasions the Japanese government has lodged protests over these practices, because they claim they are taking place in Japanese waters, usually the disputed waters around the northern islands. The requests for cancellation of a practice in disputed waters are usually turned down, but the Soviets agree to other requests.[64]

There is also a difficulty in trying to interpret Soviet air or naval manœuvres or deployments as attempts to influence specific events. On 11 January 1978 the Japanese press reported that the sailing northward of two Soviet vessels, 400 kilometres off the Japanese coast in the east China Sea, when talks between the Japanese and Soviet foreign ministers were breaking-up 'may be considered as a flagrant show of force'.[65] Later, on 7 June 1978, the Japanese claimed that the Soviets had begun manœuvres in the Kurils to dissuade them from concluding the China treaty, particularly as the manœuvres had been announced on 31 May, only one day after the Japanese had announced the recommencement of negotiations with the Chinese. However between 13–15 June the Japanese themselves changed their minds, and Foreign Minister Sonoda retracted the original condemnation, and stated his government's belief that the manœuvres were 'only part of usual firing practice' and had no political design. 'It would be excessive to consider the manœuvres as causing a strain in Japanese–Soviet relations. But it was extremely regrettable that the military exercises were staged on Japanese–claimed territory.'[66]

If anything the evidence points to Soviet deployments as a result of a trend of modernisation. The Soviets have justified their moves by claiming that certain things have been reactions to American or Japanese initiatives. The most noticeable instance of this is the Soviet deployment of Mig-23s on the Kuril islands. Soviet commentators have openly claimed that this was a response to the American announcement of their intention to deploy advanced F-16s at Misawa. Similarly, Andropov was reported[67] to have stated that the Soviet decision to deploy SS-20s in eastern Siberia was specifically a response to the planned stationing of the F-16s at Misawa. These arguments are unconvincing. Given the Soviet trend of modernising their forces in the Far East, it is probable that these deployments would have taken place in any case: deployment of nuclear-capable F-16s in Japan would certainly be a worrying factor for the Soviets but would not be the basic reason behind the decision to deploy SS-20s.

That an increasing number of 'incidents' have taken place demonstrates growing Soviet activeness. The important proviso on the above view of instances of Soviet behaviour is that while we might find fault with Japanese interpretation of specific cases, there can be little doubt that the Japanese perceive a threat from the overall trend.

Can we conclude anything from the above? That the capabilities of Soviet forces in the Far East have increased dramatically is an observable fact. The argument has to centre around relating this new military power to a political purpose; incidents involving Soviet forces have taken place but the question is whether they are, *per se*, proof of Soviet intent to intimidate Japan.

Perhaps the most useful concept would be the idea of 'latent' influence. In the case of Soviet behaviour towards Japan it is difficult to correlate specific military actions with specific political aims, i.e. there is no pattern of Soviet manœuvres or flights etc. taking place at the same time as negotiations or Japanese policy announcements. In this sense the categories suggested by Kaplan, where he rules out certain factors, are applicable to the Japanese case. But his guidelines are not entirely satisfactory; there is a 'threat' there – if only because the Japanese, or some of them, perceive that one exists – and the idea of a 'latent' threat might be the best way to interpret this situation.

The definitions provided by Bull become pertinent. If 'suasion' is there at all then it is being sought by the Soviet Union through the symbol of national power and commitment and not by specific action. To take the case a stage further – at what is this suasion directed? Is it to constrain Japanese behaviour or to achieve specific Soviet goals; is the suasion aimed at deterring unfavourable actions or at prompting new developments or courses of action from Japan? The answer here would have to be that Soviet suasion has been directed towards gaining the former rather than the latter, to deterring Japan from pursuing a course it has declared it wishes to follow. In this context it can be argued that Soviet efforts at suasion have been reactive rather than initiatory. That Soviet moves have been reactive prompts the thought that there has been, on their part, a lack of firm direction in the policies which they seek to pursue *vis-à-vis* Japan. This point we shall explore further in our examination of the general aims of Soviet policy towards Japan.

4 SOVIET POLICY AND JAPAN

UNDERSTANDING THE JAPANESE: A BARRIER TO EFFECTIVE POLICY?[1]

In all situations of interaction the actions of the participants on each other create their own effect. Thus, while our concern is with a study of the Soviet Union, to be comprehensive we must be aware not only of the peculiarities of the Japanese policy processes but more importantly of whether or not the Soviets are aware of these peculiarities and if so, of how they took account of them.

It is therefore proposed to outline the major significant features of the Japanese style of government and then to elaborate upon those in the context of a Soviet interpretation.

In a general sweep of Japanese affairs the consensus of Western analysts (though not of their Soviet counterparts) has been that Japan has never achieved internal consensus on what foreign policy goals should be, nor on how Japan should participate – if at all – in the 'international system'. The Japanese tradition of isolationism (both cultural and geographical) has served to reinforce Japanese unease about playing a greater role in international affairs in this case. Japanese ideas of 'distinctiveness' have made Japan wary of too deep an involvement. The emphasis of observation on Japan's position changed by the late 1970s to suggest that while Japan could afford the luxury of such a stance while her economy boomed it could not be maintained as Japan became afflicted with the ills which affected other economies, and as the political climate in north east Asia began to assume a more complicated form. It was postulated that pressure from these changing circumstances and from the United States would force Japan to assume a less distant stance.

This however would seem to have been the theory rather than the actual course of events. Statements by Japanese politicians in the late 1970s that Japan was striving to avoid non-participation, did not manifest themselves in concrete action. The vacillation apparent in the

Japanese position has led one commentator to characterise policy within that country in the following manner: 'the Japanese strong desire to avoid international isolation and to conform to world trends have made Japanese foreign policy *ad hoc*, reactive and equivocating. Thus at best Japanese foreign policy is characterised by a shrewd pragmatism and at worst, by an incomparable immobilism'.[2]

Despite some cultural affinities Japan holds no identification with Asia as a whole, though her relationship with China is well developed and of long standing. On the other hand, for all that Japan is fêted as a member of the camp of Western nations, she is only so in terms of her industrial development and in the superficial framing of her democratic system of government. Japan is still the 'odd man out' among advanced industrial nations in terms of the employment structure in industry, the organisation of the union movement and the organisation of the workforce. Japan is an Asian giant in a Western-oriented world economy.

Japan's foreign policy in light of the country's stable position assumed a form of omni-directional diplomacy until the 1970s, when a renewed debate on resource supplies encompassed the direct concerns of Japanese security. The new term of 'comprehensive security' came to be applied as a description of policy. But the nearest that anyone in Japan has ever come to defining this vague term was former Prime Minister Ohira who said merely that 'Japanese security has to be comprehensive . . . we can only maintain security effectively when not only military power but also political power, dynamic economic strength, creative culture and thorough-going diplomacy are well combined.'[3]

The vacillation claimed by Western analysts still to be a feature of Japanese government can well be illustrated by its response to the Soviet invasion of Afghanistan. Ohira's government, although quick to condemn the invasion, was rather slower than the other Allies to initiate sanctionary steps against the Soviet Union. It was not until February 1980 that, under pressure from within the LDP (which according to some reports was resisted by certain Japanese business groups), the government began to undertake serious sanctions, and not until 13 March that the House of Representatives passed a resolution requesting the withdrawal of Soviet troops from Afghanistan. Within this time frame Premier Ohira moved from the neutral position stated on 22 January that 'Japanese foreign policy was based on co-operation with the United States . . . the Soviet Union is a defensive, cautious, diplomatically skilful and experienced country – not a reckless country' and that on the Olympics boycott, 'for the time being the government intends to observe the reactions of Western and other countries',[4] to one of anti-Sovietism, which aligned Japan with Western nations on 1 February when he stated in the Diet that 'It is a stark objective fact that recently the Soviet Union has been greatly reinforcing its military forces, judging from the Soviet military deployment in the northern islands (and in other areas). Thus I cannot help but regard the Soviet troops (there) as a potential threat to Japan.'[5] This was the first time in the postwar Diet that a Prime Minister had openly labelled the Soviet Union as a 'threat' to Japan.

Kimura sums-up the entire process when he suggests

> The slow and inconsistent foreign policy strategems of the Ohira administration must be seen in the context of the indirect process of decision-making which characterises Japanese leaders and often involves their waiting patiently until the 'last minute' when there is no alternative but finally to decide. Unlike their Western counterparts Japanese leaders do not dictate, initiate or discuss various plans and alternatives with the general public and others concerned. Instead they create an environment out of which they can later insist certain policies have evolved naturally.[6]

By May the government had resumed credit of the Export–Import bank of Japan to the Soviet Union which had been cancelled in February, and requested that exceptions to sanctions be made in the cases of Sakhalin oil development and sale of steel pipe to the Soviets.

A major phenomenon of the Japanese political process is the factional system of politics. Let us outline some descriptions of this system. Stockwin, Director of the Nissan Institute of Japanese Studies at Oxford, makes the following comments on it:

> *oyabun – kobun* is commonly encountered in contemporary descriptions of Japanese politics ... it signifies that a fictive-parent status is being attributed to a certain prominent or powerful political individual, while his coterie of personal followers (*kobun*) are demonstrating family-like loyalty their *oyabun* [p. 30] ... Another closely related usage is the ubiquitous term *batsu*. Given a variety of prefixes, the term signifies 'clique' or 'faction', with overtones of some quasi-familial relationship. [p. 30] ... It may be more accurate to, therefore, regard political parties as coalitions of self-standing and independent-minded *habatsu* [p. 31] ... The Japanese do not confine *habatsu* to political parties. They are regarded as fairly ubiquitous phenomena within government ministries, industrial firms ... What the phenomena have in common is that personal connections *kankei*, often of a quasi-familial kind, are utilised for purposes of advancement [p. 31].[7]

One of the results of such a system is that anyone seeking to rise to pre-eminence and high office in Japan needs to be a manipulator of that system as well as a product of it. Consequently it has been the case that experience and knowledge of foreign policy has not been considered an important stepping-stone to a successful political career. The Foreign Ministry is not held in especially high regard as a career path, certainly not in comparison with the Finance Ministry or the Ministry of International Trade and Industry. The case of Suzuki illustrates this point. Suzuki was elected to the Diet by a fishing constituency and prior to his appointment as Prime Minister his only experience of foreign policy was in representing Japan, as Minister for Agriculture and Fisheries, at the annual fishery negotiations with the Soviet Union.

Factionalism has other relevant consequences. Writing as far back as 1969, Hellmann, while commenting on the factional units in Japanese politics as constituting the basic mechanism by which business gets done, pointed out two consequences:

> the practice of unwavering party discipline in the Diet votes, together with the responsibilities of the Prime Minister, both in selecting the cabinet and assuring day-to-day party leadership, has made the politics and policies of the ruling party the main domestic influences on Japanese foreign policy ... issues, particularly international issues, come to be considered not only as to their merits as policy but to their worth in advancing the party position of faction leaders ... fractions and individual rivalries and petty personal ambitions are thus projected into the heart of the policy formulation process, thereby complicating the situation and virtually proscribing decisive action.[8]

Hellmann may be overstating the case, in that all policy processes are subject to individual rivalries or preferences, but it would be fair to draw from the argument the point that the Japanese arrangement makes such influence more likely. One associated point not mentioned by Hellmann is worth stressing; that is that unlike other nations where factions or lobbies etc. can interact to influence policy from a predominant economic, social or ideological base, the Japanese situation is unique in that these factions are not so organised but are based purely on loyalty to an individual in a client–patron relationship.

Concerning another consequence of the factional system, J. A. A. Stockwin has written that

> Factional competition within the LDP is the principal reason why Japan since the early 1970s has experienced a quite rapid turnover of Prime Ministers, with the average Prime Ministerial terms lasting

about two years. It also tends to result in cabinet reshuffles, since factional claims on government posts need to be satisfied. This in turn makes it difficult for ministers to dominate portfolios, and facilitates the exercise of effective power by a highly meritocratic and self-confident public service. There have been times (most recently 1979–80) when factional rivalries threatened to tear the party apart.[9]

Stockwin argues that on balance 'consensus mechanisms' have developed those situations into a 'rolling compromise'. Nevertheless it may be suggested that these circumstances of interfactional conflict cannot have been conducive to the pursuit of effective policy and negotiations with the Soviets nor can the resultant image projected abroad, of instability or indecisiveness of purpose, have contributed to the idea of a resolute Japan. In the popular Soviet journal, *New Times*, for example, the Tanaka bribe scandal and its ramifications was constantly exploited for propaganda in the second half of the 1970s.

The responsibility for conducting foreign affairs lies with the Prime Minister and the Cabinet. It is assumed that the Cabinet has the support of the ruling party in the Diet. Differences between the ruling party and the government rarely occur in Diet debate as all important policies are decided upon beforehand by informal agreement between the party and the bureaucracy. One Japanese political commentator has pointed out that 'the Japanese Diet has never originated any legislation that had to do with foreign or defence policy'.[10] The same statement can be made with regard to treaties. The Diet can only approve or reject an already written treaty, it cannot alter or draft a treaty. To date the Diet has approved every treaty submitted to it.

Constitutionally the Japanese Diet is the sole law-making authority and the highest organ of state power. It is divided into two Houses: the lower, the House of Representatives and the upper, the House of Councillors. The power of the House of Councillors lies in its ability to delay bills and to act as a forum which the Opposition utilises to hinder legislation it finds disagreeable.

In the field of international economic policy-making the influence of the Keidanren, and through them the Keiretsu, are a factor to be considered.[11] The predominant attitude taken by the Japanese government towards deals with the Soviets has been to categorise projects as the responsibility of the private sector and accordingly not to participate in them. As a result the representatives of Japanese business abroad in fact conduct diplomacy on behalf of their country, and the results of their contacts are reported to the government. Thus it has been the business representatives who have been in the forefront of contact with the Soviet Union. This, superficially, appears to be no different from the situation of Western trading partners of the Soviets. However there is a difference of degree as the Japanese government takes considerably less of a role in business with the Soviets than its Western European counterparts.

While it is possible to delineate a clear hierarchical path of authority in negotiations conducted by the Soviets it is not clear whether a similar exercise can be conducted in the Japanese case. Trade policy is a case in point. A former Japanese trade official comments that:

> All of MITI's [Ministry of International Trade and Industry] trade responsibilities are more or less duplicated by the Ministry of Foreign Affairs. The distinction between the two ministries' responsibilities however is clear. MITI is in charge of trade policy which in turn not only affects but is also affected by domestic industrial policies and conditions. The Ministry of Foreign Affairs, on the other hand, is responsible for international negotiations and agreements . . . nevertheless, MITI takes the position that the collection of information through direct contacts with trade partners is essential for effective policy formulation, therefore the ministry should be allowed to engage in international negotiations. To retain control over international relations the Ministry of Foreign Affairs naturally seeks to bar MITI from such direct contacts. Thus the two ministries are frequently involved in jurisdictional conflicts.[12]

Soviet interpretations of the Japanese policy process

In the preceding paragraphs we have set out briefly some of the major mechanisms and components of the Japanese political process. We must now seek to see how the Soviets would be likely to interpret those components. Are the Soviets aware that the Japanese system functions in this manner? Do they recognise the difference between the theory and practice of Japanese policy making? An awareness of those problems depends to an extent upon a knowledge of Japan and an example of the obstacles which the Soviets have to overcome can be found in the testimony of former intelligence officer Stanislav Levchenko who served in Japan and wrote for *New Times* as their Tokyo correspondent. When asked why he could successfully function as a journalist he replied:

> The general rule is that most KGB officers under journalistic cover do not write in the field. Stories are filed on their behalf. My case in Japan was somewhat unusual. I actually sent one or two articles back to *New Times* each month. Two reasons may explain this. First, I had an extensive understanding of Asia because of my postgraduate studies. Second, *New Times* had no one at its headquarters who was knowledgeable about Japan.[13]

That an international journal, published in nine languages, should have no-one on its staff competent to comment on Japanese affairs would be a deficiency of some impact. It does not provide an impressive picture of Soviet expertise on Japan in the mid 1970s.

Foreign Minister Cheysson of France reputedly said of Prime Minister Suzuki that 'it is no use smiling in a language nobody understands'. It is not sufficient for the Soviets in their contact with the Japanese to be able to identify the differences in communication; they should also be able to *understand* those differences.

If we were to try to establish a general theme of the history of Russian/Soviet–Japanese relations it would on balance have to be one of distrust and fear. Long before Commodore Perry obtained his treaty which 'opened-up' an isolated Japan, Russian traders and naval expeditions had been in contact with the Japanese. The treaty of Shimoda, (the Russian equivalent of Perry's treaty) was vague enough over territorial boundaries to leave the problem open as the source of future conflicts. Those clashes which were the later result of expansionist policies on mainland north east Asia are well known. But the years after 1905 proved to be a period of stability with the signing of the Russo–Japanese ententes of 1907, 1910, 1912 and 1916; the intervention of Japan in Siberia brought that abruptly to an end. The continual engagement of the two powers in northern China was only successfully brought to a close by the Soviet defeat of the Kwantung army in August 1945. It is a process characterised by a cycle of revenge and counter-revenge. Territorial disputes tend by their nature to leave deep memories, in this case particularly for the Japanese. Another feature noticeable in past relations and arguably still very applicable today, is that of mutual contempt and under-evaluation. Commentators otherwise favourable to the Japanese still are prone to assert that the Japanese tend to be overbearing; 'There is a certain smugness in Japan about the failure of all foreigners to cope effectively with modern industrial challenges. This effects the Japanese assessment of the Soviet Union, among others', is how two Western analysts see things.[14]

The Soviets for their part, have a respect – even if grudging – for Japanese industrial capabilities, mixed with a degree of antagonistic envy, fuelled by the constant impression that Soviet leaders have wrestled with, of Soviet backwardness and of the need for the Soviets to 'catch-up'. Vadim Zagladin, deputy head of the International Department of the Central Committee of the Communist Party of the Soviet Union commented after a recent visit to Japan

> I had visualised Japan as one of the most up-to-date countries of the non-socialist world. This was fully confirmed, though some notions

143

had to be corrected. Perhaps – let my friends in the Western countries not take offence at this – Japan has left the Western countries far behind in many respects. And it not only ranks among the foremost today. It looks ahead. The technical blueprints of Japanese researchers and engineers are projected to the 21st century. Indeed, one cannot but marvel at and admire Japan's accomplishments in gradually going over to less and less material and energy intensive production processes. (In our age of global problems this is of particular importance.)[15]

Similar sentiments have been expressed publicly by at least one prominent economist at the forefront of the current reforms in the Soviet Union. In an interview with *Der Spiegel* on 5 July 1987, L. Abalkin, a member of the Academy of Economic Sciences of the Central Committee, commented that of all the economies in the capitalist world the system he respected most was Japan's. He then went on to praise Japanese 'dynamism . . . high productivity and the quality and variety of their products . . . management methods not just in individual firms but in the whole state strategy . . . they are very successful'.

Yet the suspicion must remain that because of Japan's relative military insignificance the country does not carry sufficient political weight in Soviet eyes. To the Soviet Union in its capacity as a military superpower it could conceivably be perplexing as to why an economic giant should not wish to have military power commensurate with that economic strength. An example of this 'lack of respect', as the Japanese see it, could be the draft treaty on 'Goodneighbourliness and Co-operation between the Soviet Union and Japan' unilaterally published by the Soviets in *Izvestiia*, 23 February 1978. Its publication was viewed as discourteous by the Japanese, but some articles were interpreted as actually insulting to Japan. The treaty required Japan to revoke the security treaty with the United States and contained a clause concerned with 'security in case of emergency' – such a clause is only included in Soviet treaties with Eastern Europe or developing states. Nor was there a clause which provided for the termination of the proposed treaty.

It is not at all clear that the Soviets have estimated well the force of Japanese nationalism. Some writers, Hellmann and Christopher for example, are prone to attribute to the Japanese a strong sense of cultural homogeneity; the idea of a 'national family'. On the whole the evidence suggests that the concept has been over-emphasised (aside from the problems of how we quantify its influence) – the Japanese are much like everyone else in this regard. What has served as the motor of resurgent post-war nationalism has been the force of the Japanese economy, but at the same time that confidence has tended to breed arrogance and aloofness, and these attitudes have irritated the Soviets. The Soviets have tried to avoid purposely taking action that fuels the undercurrents of nationalism but because they have not been able to gauge accurately its strength and premises their actions have more often than not stirred that nationalist sentiment. An indication of this can be gauged from the results of Japanese opinion polls which throughout the 1970s showed a rise in the degree of anti-Soviet sentiment, or of the rating of the Soviet Union as the nation 'least liked'.

The Soviets voice the opinion, however, that it is unlikely that the fanatical ultra-nationalism of the 1930s will recur; though loath to state it openly the orientation of their moderate critiques of Japanese militarisation imply that the political conditions necessary for that to occur just do not exist. Yu. Tavrovsky details the frequency of 'pro-militarisation' meetings and demonstrations and describes the 'great deal of clamour around the revival of militaristic chauvinistic tradition'.[16] He continues to list those against the trend: the 'ordinary people', all the opposition parties, and businessmen 'who are convinced that the policy of militarising the economy is baneful'. 'Even within the Liberal Democratic party, of which the Premier is the leader, there is growing criticism' according to Tavrovsky.

Soviet experience of Western processes of political decision-making, especially their extensive experience of the American system, has presumably given them knowledge of the fluctuations and delays as well as 'policy somersaults' that are inherent in such systems. Therefore they could reasonably only have expected similar trials from the functioning of the Japanese system. It should not be surprising, then, that an analyst contends that the Japanese stand has 'lacked consistence'.[17] Arguably these 'inconsistencies' are only superficial[18]; rather than being inconsistent, Japanese policy, has demonstrated by and large a pattern of continuity and only relatively recent *public* utterances have been inconsistent with what has been voiced before.

Very few Soviet authors comment on the Japanese policy process but it is evident that at least one commentator has a clear appraisal of the mechanics of the Japanese policy process as the following excerpts show:

> The specifics of Japan's postwar development have conditioned the complex nature of her foreign policy mechanism, which involved the Diet, government, ministries, monopoly organisations, political parties and the mass media. Quite naturally, the influence of each of

those factors was far from equivalent and depended on the specific policy issue in question and on the domestic and international situations ... some Japanese historians even assert that the Prime Minister is the country's most powerful political leader whose status is similar to that of the British Prime Minister, who in critical periods exercises great power to no less a degree than any dictator. International issues enjoy the special attention of every new Japanese Prime Minister. This is largely because of a desire to associate his name with some significant foreign policy act ... in the post-war period the bureaucracy and the top officials of ministries ... have had great influence on the planning of Japan's foreign policy. Most of them were from the Ministry of Foreign Affairs, Ministry of International Trade and Industry, Ministry of Finance and the National Defence Agency ... despite the existence of constitutionally stipulated official institutions designed to shape the country's foreign policy, relevant control in the post-war years was largely exercised by the ruling party, whose leader automatically became Prime Minister and formed the cabinet. Due to its majority in the Diet, the ruling party can control the Diet committees concerned with foreign policy issues.[19]

Though a brief description of the Japanese political process, Verbitsky has summarised aspects of its effective functioning. The main constitutional theory behind the Japanese system was to produce a bureaucratic central government; however, though this has been achieved, it has been distorted by the peculiarities of a Japanese approach. Factionalism is perhaps the biggest single influence in causing the distortion of the original idea.

We have pointed out that constitutionally both Houses of the Diet have a say in policy. In practice this constitutional counter-balancing has been nullified in recent times as both Houses have been dominated by the LDP.[20] The system of House committees, to which Verbitsky refers in his closing comments, serves as an important forum for debate on foreign policy issues but this too has been dominated by the LDP. While the House of Councillors can delay legislation, it can delay the most important bills such as the budget, passing of treaties or the election of the Prime Minister, by only thirty days.

Though individual parliamentarians may propose that certain bills be debated in parliament this is merely a pre-arranged method of operation between Cabinet and parliament. The Cabinet, through dint of practice, has established a superior position over the House of Representatives and in fact proposes the bills to be debated in House and merely agrees that a particular parliamentarian should raise them on its behalf.

146

Critics (including Hellmann and Higashi) have made plain what they see as the rivalries between the Ministry of International Trade and Industry (MITI) and the Ministry of Foreign Affairs, and may have tended to exaggerate the extent to which MITI 'makes' Japanese foreign policy. If anything the more issues oriented themselves towards defence policy in the latter 1970s, the more the pendulum of influence swung back in favour of the Foreign Ministry. Stockwin in 1975 argued that

> The Ministry of International Trade and Industry (MITI) is now seen as one of Japan's best-known and powerful ministries largely as a result of the central role it has had in formulating industry and trade policies during the period of spectacular economic growth . . . The status of other ministries reflects changing national priorities. Thus the Ministry of Foreign Affairs was not highly regarded during the post-war period, but has slowly been rising to a position of greater prominence with the emergence of Japan into a somewhat more active role in international affairs.[21]

Stockwin's judgement is echoed by a Soviet analyst. Head of the Japan section at the Institute of Oriental Studies in Moscow, K. O. Sarkisov, expressed the opinion that by 1980 the Japanese were pursuing a more diplomatically oriented course and that 'therefore the Gaimusho (Japanese foreign ministry) had moved to the fore in policymaking'.[22]

It is impossible to state with confidence how the Soviets interpret that realignment of influence as in public they do not go beyond speculation that it is the top groups of bureaucrats, the administrators who are a part of the 'ruling circles', that dictate a particular policy line, rather than the bureaucracy as a whole which propounds a cause. Sarkisov, for example, stated that those in the 'Soviet desk' at the Gaimusho were 'quite good at their job'; however he also added that the Gaimusho 'constantly puts forward an anti-Soviet position'.

In the above we have tried to stress the fact that aside from the obvious concessions to Party doctrine which appear in their writings on Japan (mainly with regard to the status of 'progressive forces' or the influences of the 'ruling circles') these Soviet *academics* (and a few others, Lukin and Zagladin, for example) concerned with contemporary politics and foreign policy demonstrate an informed appraisal of the details. The difficulty that we face in trying to establish inputs behind Soviet policy, however, is that we must include not only inputs from academic researchers but also from government personnel. We must also evaluate the problems inherent in the process of transferring available knowledge to policymakers.

Soviet researchers on international politics have to act as transmitters of the Party line as well as encourage the 'creative development' of the theoretical foundations of current Soviet policies: there is always then a conflict between academic credibility and *partiinost'*. Institute staffers are regularly called upon to brief TASS, or *Izvestiia* or *Pravda* on appropriate issues and through their writings are also used to disseminate Soviet policy positions. Oriental studies is one of the few areas which holds opportunities of study outside the Moscow or Leningrad complex but even the 'China school' is not held in such high regard nor has such a high profile as ISSHAK (Institute of the United States and Canada) or IMEMO (Institute of World Economy and International Relations). It would be wrong to interpret the position of members of these institutes as analogous to those in some Western 'Think-tank'. To date, only a handful of their number have risen to political appointments as advisers, chiefly the *Amerikantsi* – the Soviet experts on the United States – and some staffers from IMEMO, while a few others, like R. Ulianovskii and K. Brutents, have obtained Party posts in the Central Committee apparatus. The main exception to the concentration of top appointments being from the *Amerikantsi* or IMEMO, is personified by the sinologist Mikhail Kapitsa, formerly a Deputy Foreign Minister, and now director of the Institute of Oriental Studies. Interestingly enough, Kapitsa also has some expertise on Japan. To what extent an adviser can influence policy via the policy-maker is still a matter of great controversy and speculation. While the Brezhnev years saw an expansion of the number of specialists overall it is questionable to deduce a resultant increase in effectiveness from that expansion.[23] But under Gorbachev at least the prominence of such advisers is hard to refute.

Soviet assessments of Japan are primarily economically oriented. *MEMO*, the Journal of the Institute of World Economy and International Relations, regularly features such articles. The largest grouping of contributions to the Japan Yearbooks published by the Academy of Sciences is similarly economics-based.

From the results of our literature survey (summarised in table 22) most attention, as we would expect from Marxist–Leninists, centres around economic appraisals of Japan and of its influence. Military questions probably rate a second place in terms of frequency, especially by the latter half of the 1970s. Lastly comes the purely political coverage. Tables 23 and 24 present more data drawn from literature surveys.

It seems fair to conclude that the expertise of the Soviet 'Japan watchers' is mixed. In interviews with the author it was commented

Table 22 Coverage devoted to Japan in selected Soviet journals

Year	International Affairs 12 issues per year	Narodi Azii i Afriki 6 issues per year	SShA 12 issues per year	Novaia i Noveishaia Istoriia 6 issues per year	New Times 52 issues per year	Foreign Trade of the USSR 12 issues per year	MEMO 12 issues per year	Kom-munist 18 issues per year	Kommunist Vooruzhennikh Sil 24 issues per year	Vneshnaia Politika Sovetskovo Soiuza: sbornik dokumentov
1970	2A 1c	4A	1A	None	–	1A	5A (3c)	None	1A	None
1971	1A 1c	(H19) 2A	1A (1BR)	None	–	1A (BR)	1A (1c)	None	2A 1BR	None
1972	4A 1c	5A(H19) (H)	2A	None	–	1A	3A (2c)	1A	2A	2
1973	None	1A(H19)	3A (1BR)	None	–	None	2A (1c)	None	None	1
1974	1A 2c	3A(H19)	None	1A	–	None	2A (2c)	None 1BR	None	None
1975	2A(H)	2A(L)	None	None	–	1A	2A	(1st on militarism)	None	1
1976	1BR 1A 1BR	1BR 1A(H19) 1BR	None	1A	12A(4)	None	(1c) 2A (1c)	1A 1BR	None	1
1977	None	3A(H10) 1BR	None	None	9A(4)	3A	5A (1st on militarism) (2c)	None	1A	None

Table 22 (*Cont.*)

Year									
1978	3A	1A	1A	None	14A(6) 1A (1st on militarism)	3A (2c)	None	None	1
1979	1A(S-J Treaty)	3A(H6) 1BR(L2)	1A	None	11A(4) None	(1c)	None	1A (1st on militarism)	None
1980	1BR	3A 1BR	None	None	9A(3) 1A	4A	None	1BR	None
1981	1A 1BR	–	None	None	9A(4) 1 (Document)	4A	None	None	1
1982	2A 1BR	–	None	None	10A(3) None	1A (1c)	1A	None	–
1983	1A	–	1A(H)	1A(H)	13A(6) None	2A	1A	–	–
1984	2A	–	1A(H)	None	20A(6) None	6A (1c)	None	–	–
1985	–	–	–	–	–	–	–	–	–

Key to table

A : Article (for *New Times* the figure in brackets indicates the number of articles of the total which were of one page or less in length)

c : Commentary. Usually a maximum of two to three pages long

BR : Book review

(H) : Indicates that one of the articles was of historical content (20th Century) The number following, e.g. (H19) indicates the century concerned, i.e. (H6) indicates an article about 6th century history

(L) : Indicates an article concerned with literature

None: No articles, commentaries on book reviews for that year

– : No information available

General comments on table 22 by journal

International Affairs

This is the main English language journal published in the Soviet Union on international politics. Although articles on collective security in Asia, South Asia and China are relatively common, coverage of Japan is minimal. Articles on, for example, the Federal Republic of Germany, France, Italy and Britain occur more frequently.

Narodi Azii i Afriki (Peoples of Asia and Africa)

Coverage devoted to Japan compared with other subjects is low. The main orientation of what little coverage there is focuses upon historico-cultural and linguistic concerns.

SShA (United States and Canada)

This is the journal of the Institute of the United States and Canada. Within these terms of reference comment on Japan occurs in the context of Japan as a trading partner/rival of the United States or on Japan as the main military ally of the United States in the Pacific. As the table indicates these comments are very few in number; we might expect, given the declared importance of Japan to the United States in the eyes of the Soviets, for them to be more numerous. Apart from comment on the United States itself the mainstay of content deals with American relations with Europe. However Japanese involvement with the United States fares badly as an issue of comment even in comparison with the coverage given to United States' association with non-European nations or with non-European areas of the world, e.g. South East Asia, Gulf.

Novaia i Noveishaia Istoriia (New History)

Nothing to be said in the case of this journal except to state that obviously Japan holds no interest as a subject for the compilers of the journal.

New Times

The Soviet popular weekly journal published in English and other languages. As a 'popular' journal the content of the articles varies accordingly. Features cover a wide range of subjects from conversations with Japanese fishermen, articles on crime in Japan, travel, to comment on Japanese politics and trends of militarisation. Increasingly by the late 1970s some comment on militarisation was a regular feature of the Japan coverage in each issue.

Foreign Trade of the USSR

An English language journal on Soviet foreign trade. We might expect that, given the attention drawn in public statements by the Soviets to trade with Japan, comment on dealings with Japan would be fairly frequent. This is not the case. Trade with the Federal Republic of Germany, France and even the United Kingdom occurs more frequently as a topic. Overall, even trade with quite minor partners such as Portugal or Greece features almost as often as a subject for comment as does trade with Japan.

Table 22 (*Cont.*)

MEMO

The journal of the Institute of World Economy and International Relations. The strongest area of Soviet expertise is probably economics – both domestic and international. The main concentration of this expertise is at IMEMO and is reflected in the coverage given to Japan in the house-journal, *MEMO*. However, as a comparison with other areas, Japan once again fares poorly. As the comparative information on table 24 shows, the journal is dominated by work on the United States and Europe. In fact the imbalance is actually greater than indicated on the table as the numerous theoretical articles on trends in (European) capitalism which appear in each issue of the journal have not been included in the figures. Commentary on Latin America or particular nations (Chile, Brazil) is fairly common and in quite a few cases coverage devoted to Japan during particular years is at a comparable level even with that of individual Latin American nations.

Kommunist

The theoretical journal of the Communist Party of the Soviet Union. Given the nature of the journal there is no special reason why Japan should feature as a regular subject of contribution. However, given that other nations do feature as such, it might be of interest that Japan does not. An interesting indication of the poor state of relations between the CPSU and the JCP can be found in the later 1976 editions which covered the 26th CPSU congress. Reports of speeches of the visiting guest communist parties were printed in *Kommunist*, including speeches by parties from Sri Lanka, Lebanon, Cyprus, Canada, Iraq and South Africa. The report given by the JCP is not mentioned at all.

Kommunist Vooruzhennikh Sil (*Communist of the Armed Forces*)

The Party journal of the Soviet armed forces. Apart from providing for the political education of the Soviet armed forces the journal carries articles, as we would expect, on the threat to peace posed by actions or designs of other nations. Developments within those nations which are labelled as 'militaristic' or 'trends towards militarism' are a standard subject of comment. The attention drawn in public by Soviet leaders to what they characterised as resurgent Japanese revanchism is not reflected by the comment in the journal. In fact in all the journals (e.g. *SShA*, *International Affairs*) including this one, which might have been expected to devote space to the militarism question, scant space is devoted to it. This journal, which we might expect to be the most aware of the concern proved to be the *last* (all the others published before it) journal to publish an article on Japanese militarism. It did this in 1979.

Table 23 *Coverage of Japan in RSFR Oblast' newspapers April–May 1983 (in column lines)*

Oblast'	Japan total	Militarism	Anti-war	China total
West of Urals				
Murmansk	975	515	205	260
Leningrad	525	90	250	550
Moscow	85	10	0	200
Novgorod	850	110	280	70
Kursk	985	345	125	135
Riazan	1100	110	345	90
Vologda	1190	505	180	120
Western Siberia				
Tiumen	615	225	230	170
Novosibirsk	840	200	235	175
East Siberia				
Krasnoiarsk	1020	250	250	40
Irkutsk	1270	130	605	180
Chita	1510	385	150	505
Far East				
Iakutiia	450	95	155	275
Magadan	1040	515	235	185
Kamchatka	1330	275	485	320
Amur	1820	295	115	1205
Khabarovsk	1915	1210	115	950
Sakhalin	2325	980	375	400

Note: The term 'Oblast'' used here includes the terms 'Krai' and 'ASSR'. The column 'militarism' covers those articles concerned with the threat from Japanese militarism. 'Anti-war' refers to those about peace issues. Both totals are sub-totals of the first column.

Source: Data selected from J. Hough, 'The Evolution of the Soviet Political System', in *Acta Slavica Iaponica*, 2, (1984), 127–58. Figures pp. 139–40.

Comment on table information: The results here indicate nothing for certain other than that there seems to be no fixed policy of comment on Japanese affairs. As a *general* proposition, it is fair to say that the closer the Oblast' is geographically to Japan the larger the amount of coverage is likely to be. However in the face of this proposition we have to explain the high coverage given by Riazan, Murmansk, Novgorod and Kursk and the almost nil coverage by Moscow. Murmansk might be explained by the presence of navy personnel, the others probably by the preferences of the individual editors. From the results it would also appear that there is no necessary relationship between proximity to Japan and coverage (either as a percentage of total coverage or as a total) of militarist issues. For example, as a percentage of the total coverage devoted to militarism, Khabarovsk – 63%; Sakhalin – 42%; but Murmansk – 52%; Kamchatka – 20%; Amur – 16%. In Iakutiia and Tiumen oblasts, where because of the continuing economic connection, we might expect the coverage of Japan to figure quite prominently – in fact comparatively speaking, the opposite is the case.

Table 24 *Total number of articles for period 1970–84*

Journal	Japan	PRC	W Europe	US	FRG	UK	France
MEMO	42	None	24	121	39	21	27
Kommunist	4	3	5	9	1	3	2
KVS	7	7	3	26	2	6	None

Comment: The heading for Western Europe does not include articles which deal with NATO or the EEC, thus the European bias is far more pronounced that might appear from the table.

that traditionally Japanese specialists in the Soviet Union/Russia had been quite numerous. This is not the case today (see table 25). Predominantly the traditional areas of study had been language, literature and history. One academic lamented that there was not sufficient emphasis on modern-day concerns thus, he thought, 'we fail to see the subtle perceptions'. The same lament is obviously behind statements made by another Soviet writer when he suggests that 'Soviet scholars attach much importance to analysing present-day relations between labour and capital in Japan. Nevertheless, the substantial changes in this field in recent years have not been adequately studied in Soviet literature.'[24]

The bureaucracies present an altogether different picture. By comparison with the Institutes we know very little about internal functionings and structure of, for example, the Ministry of Foreign Afairs or Trade. The bureaucracies themselves in the late 1970s became increasingly concerned to encourage their own 'in-house' research staffs, if only to promote their own perspectives on issues. For example, the Scientific Research Marketing Institute (NIKI) is part of the Ministry of Foreign Trade and its job is to explore profitable markets for Soviet goods. The Research Institute of Economic and Technical co-operation was established in 1979 to handle foreign aid assistance also under the auspices of the Ministry of Foreign Trade. Research in these organisations, as we would expect, is more tailored towards specific objectives than the work undertaken by the formal research institutes. The Ministry of Foreign Affairs and the Trade Ministry of course have their own sources of information from their posts abroad.

An area where the talents of the staffers and bureaucrats may overlap is in the operation of the International Department of the Party.[25] This is now recognised as the main co-ordinating body in relations with non-ruling Communist parties and is thought to have an important voice in formulating foreign policy. The department is

Table 25 *Staff numbers of Japanese sections of Soviet research institutes*

Institute of the Far East
Total Institute staff: 300–500
Japan section: 20 (mainly foreign policy oriented)
Institute of World Economy and International Relations
Total Institute staff: approx. 700
Japan section: 14 (with 10 more involved in Japan study scattered through the institute. There is a special section within the section which deals with the Japanese economy and Japanese labour politics.
Institute of Oriental Studies
Total Institute staff: 800 (of which 200 in Leningrad)
Japan section: 40–45 (approximately 15 of which concentrate on language and literature)
Institute of the United States and Canada
Total Institute staff: 300
Section on US policy in the Far East (including relations with Japan): 9

Source: Author's conversations with Soviet academics at each of the above Institutes

Table 26 *Soviet radio broadcasts*

To:	Radio Moscow	Radio Peace and Progress	Totals
Europe	406	–	520.5
Americas	63	–	206
Central/South America	81.5	10.5	92
Middle East/ North Africa	–	–	197.5
Sub-Saharan Africa	126	3.5	129.5
South/South East Asia	297	21.5	318.5
Far East	245	91	336

Dashes indicate information not available.
Source: Foreign and Commonwealth Office, *Soviet External Propaganda* Background Brief (London, October 1984). The 'Total' figure includes hours broadcast from regional stations not listed. Also it does not include the Moscow 'World Service' broadcasts nor the clandestine radio stations' output for the Middle East (this represents a few hours a week in Persian or Turkish).
Comment: Although a breakdown of the total figures was not available, it is reasonable to assume that in the case of the Far East category most of the output is in Chinese and English. The 91 hours of Radio Peace and Progress broadcasts are, for example, solely in English or regional Chinese dialects. Given that as a representative distribution, it is probably the case that total broadcasts to Japan will constitute less than 100 hours out of the 245 broadcast by Radio Moscow. Actual hours broadcast in Japanese (rather than English) will therefore be even smaller. Japan therefore receives less coverage than the major European nations.

155

organised into geographical sectors. Each of these sectors is in turn composed of 'desks' usually given a country or geographical area as its administrative responsibility. I. I. Kovalenko has, for example, been identified as Head of the Far East sector which comprises South East Asia and Japan. Interestingly, within the Far East sector Japan is given the designation of 'sector' rather than 'desk'. Kovalenko is himself a former academic and Japan specialist (he still occasionally contributes articles under the pseudonym of I. I. Ivkov) with extensive experience of Japan. Amongst his past positions was one responsible for the political education of Japanese prisoners of war in Siberia and according to Japanese who have met him, he often adopts an overbearing attitude towards Japanese.[26]

One report suggests that in the late 1970s the International Department maintained a staff of four Japan specialists under a sector chief called Senatorov. The Japan Sector has been known to consult with I. A. Latyshev (Chief of the Japan department of the Institute of Oriental Studies), D. V. Petrov (Head of the Japan section of the Institute of the Far East) and V. B. Ramzes of the Institute of World Economy and International Relations.[27]

The re-organisation of foreign policy administration under Gorbachev seems to have increased the nominal influence of the International Department of the Central Committee of the Party. Moreover Japan also holds an anomalous position within the rearranged structure of the Soviet Ministry of Foreign Afairs in that in the newly created Directorate responsible for Pacific Ocean and South East Asian affairs, Japan is the only regional nation accorded a department to itself. All other departments are amalgamations which cover two or three countries. (As of 30 June 1987, V. V. Alexseyev headed the Japan department in the Soviet Ministry of Foreign Affairs, with I. Abdurayakov as his deputy.)

The *images* which nations form of each other and of each others' actions have been accepted in the literature of foreign policy research as a crucially important factor in international politics. If the information which the Soviets receive about Japan is deficient then we must expect that any Soviet policies involving Japan will be lacking in some way.

The difficulty is that the Soviets (like other governments) are not necessarily aware of the extent of their deficiencies and of the irritation which they arouse in the Japanese. We have tried to argue that the Soviets have, for example, probably under-estimated the strength of Japanese nationalism. We must differ from Vadim Zagladin's (Deputy Head of the International Department of the CPSU) statement that

> One cannot agree with the contention advanced in some Japanese press organs that the USSR underrates Japan or does not regard it with sufficient respect.[28]

This is not to say that the Soviets underrate the Japanese, but that the Japanese think that they do. Some incidents of provocation against the Japanese have been deliberate (from the petty snubbing of diplomats to larger scale concerns), others not so, have undoubtedly been exacerbated by mutual misunderstanding.

Soviet–Japanese negotiations

In considering the course of Soviet policy towards Japan there are certain important factors, the impact of which can only be estimated because of their abstract nature. One of these areas covers the images or impressions of each other created by interaction during meetings or negotiations.

The point to be made at the outset, at the risk of stating the obvious, is that Japan and the Soviet Union are very different from each other. To the Soviets the Japanese are still very much an alien race with which they have had comparatively little contact and correspondingly little substantial experience. In these respects the Soviet Union shares with the rest of the world in the exclusionary nature of Japanese society and culture. The specific characteristics of a Japanese style have manifested themselves in negotiation with the Soviets.

Except for the early post-war negotiations with the Japanese, the Soviets have kept their demands and positions in negotiation free from any obvious influences of ideology in the sense that they have entered into negotiations in a businesslike manner and subsequently steered a pragmatic course. This general observation is applicable whether the negotiations have concerned trade questions, the northern islands issue or fisheries. What may we say then about Soviet approaches? An American survey undertaken for Congress characterises the Soviet approach to negotiations as 'not only sitting down and haggling over language at the bargaining table but rather manœuvering for position, and achieving certain adjustments by one means or another, including the threat of force or agitation, or bribery or inducements or any number of things'.[29] Other general attributes of a definitive Soviet 'style' have been suggested as comprising an attention to detail (hard-line Western critics argue that we can rely on the Soviets to adhere to the letter of an agreement but not necessarily the spirit); a tendency to let the other side take the initiative; there is also a traditional view which depicts Soviet negotiators as being aggressive and unwilling to compromise easily.[30] It is always a dubious business to attribute 'national' characteristics, let alone make deductions from them. No nation 'invariably' possesses the attributes assigned to it. We can substantiate particular points by example but should always be wary of the problems involved in moving from the general to the particular. Bearing that in mind let us move to some estimation of Japanese methods of operation.

In a study of Japanese negotiating techniques the concluding remarks were made that 'the Japanese approach to negotiations was dominated by a philosophy of risk minimisation and confrontation avoidance. They seemed to prefer doing nothing when it was safe to do nothing and acting only when the pressure of events forced them to act.'[31] Japanese conduct during the annual fishery negotiations illustrates well this trait; often Japanese negotiators would only act when the Soviets imposed a deadline or threatened unilateral action. The principle of confrontation avoidance – whether it be group-based or individual – seems to be part of the Japanese ethic. A corollary of this attribute is that the Japanese will operate by a consensual process of decision-making in order to avoid the prompting of confrontation. Operating by consensus is in some circumstances a benefit but in others a distinct handicap. In either case it is a mode of operation which is very time consuming.

The Soviets, for their part, are renowned for their willingness to 'sit-out' negotiations and grind down an adversary's position almost by a process of attrition. The fact that Soviet negotiating positions are always determined from the centre, forces Soviet negotiators to refer back for new instructions thus adding to the drawn-out process of delays and frustrations. This can be advantageous or disadvantageous depending upon the circumstances.

An initial observation then is that both parties, though for different reasons, utilise a tactic which results in the taking-up of great amounts of time. The difficulty in such a situation is self-evident. Moreover the Japanese idea of consensual decision-making has led to accusations, from other Japanese negotiating partners as well as the Soviets, of duplicity. The problem seems to be that until consensus is reached on which line to take in negotiations the Japanese negotiators concerned will say differing things simply because at that point they are not sure of what they are supposed to be saying.

The Japanese interpretation of the role of concessions in negotiations differs markedly from other nations. When they do make a concession they

158

do so on the assumption that whatever 'concession' they make will
be accepted by the foreigners as a gesture of good will and an effort to
reach a solution that saves face all round. And they never cease to be
astounded when the foreigners, who are interested not in saving face
but in achieving concrete goals, denounce the Japanese gestures as
meaningless or deceitful and interpret them as tacit admission of
guilt.[32]

Related to this is a peculiarity of the Japanese 'style' whereby they tend
not to appear at negotiations with a structured agenda of points or
demands. This has been a common feature in negotiations with the
West and we have no reason to assume it would be any different
where the Soviets are involved. This approach, coupled with a desire
to avoid open confrontation, leads to the Japanese constantly being
disadvantaged by placing themselves on the defensive in negotiations. This situation clashes directly with two of our assumed Soviet
methods of operation: the Soviet tactic of trying to let the other side
take the initiative (hopefully so that they end up negotiating with
themselves) and the Soviet approach to signs of weakness which is to
adopt a harder stance.

The Soviets have an especial penchant for attention to detail on
agreements and to the legal foundation of documents. Always aware
of the propaganda bonus of being seen to operate within legal norms,
the Soviets like, when possible, to be seen to be adhering to international legal stipulations and in this they are no different from most
other nations. It follows from this assumption, then, that a legal
document is more important than some sort of informal understanding: arguably, this principle can be demonstrated in the case of the
Soviet reaction to the Japan–China treaty of 1978 and in the Soviet
approach to their peace treaty with the Japanese.

In the first example, the Japanese–Chinese treaty of 1978 is almost
exactly the same text – in some places it is identical – as the Japanese–
Chinese protocol of 1972. *Both* documents contain the much vilified
'anti-hegemony' clause. Yet why then was the Soviet Union so critical
of the latter document of 1978, especially as the document also
contains a qualifying clause (which had been omitted from the 1972
protocol) to the 'anti-hegemony' clause? The important difference is
that the former was a 'protocol' whereas the latter was a 'treaty' and
hence legally binding upon the signatories. The context in which the
two documents were agreed was different but with the 1972 protocol
coming so soon after the Nixon visit to China and the Nixon doctrine
there must have been cause for worry then also, yet no noticeable
furore was made by the Soviets on that occasion. Presumably, if the

'anti-hegemony' clause was in itself a hostile act against the Soviet Union in 1978, then it was also so in 1972.[33]

Pressure behind the Soviet moves to conclude a peace treaty seem to be based on a desire to have things 'tidied-up' with the Japanese and put on a regular footing – a visible sign for all to see of Soviet acceptance and legitimation in north east Asia. Although both parties have developed relations to a satisfactory level without a treaty, the Soviet longing for one is still there for the reasons given. 'Of course, both states can get along without a peace treaty. However, considering that the USSR and Japan faced each other across the frontline during the last world war, the placing of their relations on a strong legal basis would be an important and useful thing.'[34]

In examining the course of Soviet–Japanese negotiations it appears curious that a nation such as the Japanese which is conscious of the importance of rank or formal status should put itself constantly in the position of being 'outranked' in negotiations by the Soviets. It is possible that because of the very significance which the Japanese give to formal status they have not sent high ranking officials to meetings with the Soviets as this would be seen to confer status on the Soviets. That apart, in general the Japanese have always been put at the disadvantage of having to travel to the Soviet Union to negotiate and have often been confronted by high ranking Soviet personnel. Heads of Japanese parliamentary delegations and business groups were regularly met by Politburo members such as Kosygin, Gromyko or Suslov, though very rarely by Brezhnev. This may have been done by the Soviets as a matter of courtesy but it can also be seen as an attempt by the Soviets to emphasise their authority. In practice the tactic has quite often backfired on the Soviets, for the Japanese would take at face value the statements made at meetings by such high leaders and then would subsequently be disappointed and frustrated when the promises they made or implied (or that the Japanese thought the Soviets had made) were not subsequently implemented.

The most obvious example of where the Japanese negotiated on an equal footing concerns the annual fishery negotiations. Even here, although formal rank can be equated, the Soviet team had a vast experience always lacking in the official Japanese minister, due to continual changing of portfolios within the Japanese Cabinet. Moreover, the actual portfolio is that of 'Agriculture and Fisheries' and any minister is therefore required to divide his time between both concerns. The Soviet team leader and Minister of Fisheries, for most of the period examined, A. A. Ishkov, had twenty-five years of experience behind him. The closest the Japanese came to matching that sort of experience was in the person of Zenko Suzuki, who was elected in a fishing constituency, but he was in office for only two and a half years. By all accounts Suzuki was constantly advised by his team of civil servants from the Ministry, and in particular by one top official with great experience of negotiations. Potentially there exists in that kind of arrangement a source of friction between formal status of the 'top man' and the status of the person with 'greatest experience'. This is a phenomenon found throughout pluralist systems and in some instances one-party systems; it appears particularly acute in the case of Soviet–Japanese fishery negotiations.

In conducting negotiations in the private sector with Japanese companies the Soviets again were at the tactical advantage in that the Japanese, by and large, had to come to them to do business. The advantage was reinforced due to Japanese companies not being able to establish suitable premises in Moscow to use as a base. The Soviets were therefore able to make on-the-spot decisions unlike the Japanese deputations who often might have to refer back to Japan for instructions; in these circumstances of competition against other companies it was the Japanese who needed to be able to make the on-the-spot decision. Also, faced by hints from the Soviets of alternative terms being offered by competitors (the Soviets were indeed negotiating with major competitors of Japanese companies, as was common knowledge), Japanese businessmen were inclined to accept less favourable terms on the spot rather than return home empty handed.

CONCEPTUALISING SOVIET POLICY TOWARDS JAPAN

Analysts are divided over the question of whether the Soviets have formulated any specific policy with regard to Japan. Some observers remain sceptical, arguing that Soviet policies towards Japan are merely an extension of Soviet global policy or of policy towards the United States and China in the north east Asian region. At least one leading Japanese sovietologist takes a different standpoint, contending that 'such interpretations may have been credible in the past; however with the growing Soviet realisation of the significant role which Japan occupies in North East Asia, the Kremlin leaders have recently been increasingly recognising the need to formulate a specific policy for Japan.'[35]

The 'do they or don't they have a policy' controversy still dominates the analysis of Soviet behaviour towards Japan. In this sense there is not an approach which we could label as 'the conventional wisdom' *vis-à-vis* Soviet policy and Japan, though it would probably be accurate to say that on balance the largest group of analysts tend to come-down on the side of ascribing policies to the Soviets – if only to argue at a later point that these policies have 'failed'.

We have seen how in the analyses of Soviet foreign policy towards Japan, commentators have utilised terms such as 'failure', 'bad', 'counter-productive', 'coercive'. The use of these concepts implicitly entails a comparison with either earlier Soviet policy or with Soviet policies involving other nations or the policies of other countries towards Japan. It also entails an implied notion of some objectively ascertainable set of Soviet goals attainment of which is also ruled-out by the meaning implied in the concept. What might these objectives be? What can we say concerning Soviet strategy in East Asia?

The Soviet Union: perceptions, objectives and strategies in East Asia

Writing in 1983 Paul Dibb concluded on the Soviet security outlook that

> At its most basic level, the view from the Kremlin is informed by a perception of the contemporary international situation that is tense and potentially threatening to Soviet state interests. Militarily stronger than ever before, the USSR does not necessarily feel more secure. Although the Soviet Union has attained broad nuclear parity, or in Soviet parlance 'equal security' with the United States it does not feel confident of its position.[36]

It is accepted that the 1970s saw, as the Soviets would interpret it, a swing in their favour at last in the correlation of forces that proved decisive in propelling the Soviet Union to a situation where it was perceived by other states to hold equal status with the United States. The SALT agreements and Helsinki were a legitimation of that status and the increased Soviet activity in the Third World a manifestation of it. The litany of successes and failures of Soviet policy in the 1970s and early 1980s illustrates the global reach of a rising power out to assert its place in the sun.

Central to the Soviet conduct of its international affairs is its relationship with the United States. The United States is, and will remain for the foreseeable future, *glavni protivnik* – the main enemy. That global evaluation of the position of the United States is as applicable to the role that the Soviets assign to it in the Pacific. That apart, Soviet preoccupation with the United States has not obscured perception of the sources of other potential threats in the Pacific region. Nor has it prevented sophisticated analysis of American policy changes in the region.

V. P. Lukin, head of the Pacific foreign policy section at the Institute of the United States and Canada, made it clear in an interview with the author that as American interests have moved from continental Asia to a new centre in north east Asia the United States has striven hard to encourage a new relationship with its allies in the region, akin to the one it has with its NATO allies, in the shape of a 'division of labour'. The earliest signs of this redefinition of interest could be seen as coinciding with a period when Soviet inactivity in East Asia and, most obviously, in Africa, was coming to an end. The Soviets are also aware that the process of realignment was the product not only of American unease and dissatisfaction but also of the allies' own changing perceptions of their responsibilities and the threats which confronted them. The superficial manifestation of that trend, with regard to north east Asia and Japan, so the Soviets argue, is that the term 'ally' as applied to Japan has come to carry with it more the connotation of 'partner'.

Soviet interpretation of the extent of Japanese 'partnership' has not been fully resolved by Soviet analysts. The more sophisticated analyses propose a balanced judgement of the Japanese–American relationship; Lukin, in his own contribution to an edited collection of works entitled *SShA i Problemi Tikhogo Okeana: Mezhdunarodno–Politicheskie Aspekti* (The United States and the Problems of the Pacific: International Political Aspects)[37] suggests that Japan has, from the beginning of the 1970s, slowly and cautiously become more forceful in presenting its own approaches to questions. It has developed its own dynamic on matters of defence and other international concerns.

Other analyses have sought to stress the continuing primacy of the United States as the driving force.[38] Lukin has commented that the relationship between the two powers is complicated, in that while Japanese forces have grown significantly in quality, and that while Japan is possibly America's closest ally, Japan has proved less willing than the NATO allies to convert its economic potential into an appropriate military effort. Many of the initiatives taken under Nakasone have been cosmetic in terms of fulfilling some of the more exaggerated promises outlined below.[39] This was the case under previous premiers also. Premier Ohira asserted in 1980 that 'The days are gone when we were able to rely on America's deterrence' yet the pace of Japan's reply has not been hurried. But they have made, and are making, incremental advances. The defence budget, for example,

163

escaped the strict public spending cuts applied in August 1984 and thus allowed projected spending to rise by 7% in 1985.[40] The recognition of the importance (some would argue, the ٴ. ɛakness) of the air and naval defence of Japan has been met by the JSDF's plans for 1986–90. The stress has been laid on the continued fast procurement of the F–15J and P–3C and the upgrading of squadron strength to twenty-five aircraft. At the same time the Maritime Self Defence Force hope to be equipped with AGM–84 *Harpoon* and *Phalanx* close-in weapon systems. Japanese capabilities in advanced high technology are enabling a general future upgrading of JSDF electronic counter measures capabilities, and in particular a programme to be launched into development of a new indigenous high technology aircraft, the 'FS–X'.[41] Lukin's point is that they (the Japanese) could be doing much more.

The Soviets are probably as uncertain as other observers about the most likely course that Japan will follow. However, it should be emphasised that probably mere Soviet perception of American indecision (especially in the Carter years) and of Japanese hesitancy would have been enough to encourage them to pursue initiatives already under way more forcefully and to launch new ones. The Brezhnev–Andropov proposals on confidence building measures in north east Asia are a good example of this.

Commentary on the main axes of Soviet strategy in the Pacific has centred upon the limitations to Soviet intervention in the region.[42] The Soviets themselves have little in common with the nations of the region and in the economic sphere have little to offer either on a scale desired or in terms of type of goods desired.

At various stages in the discussion of military, and now of wider policy questions, it has been suggested that the Soviets see themselves as facing a coalition or 'array' of powers that stretch across the Pacific. The military dimension of this view is that the Soviets see a line of military bases dominated by the US presence on 'islands beyond the horizon'. For example,

> New bases are being built and old ones modernised on the perimeters of the Asian continent – in the Persian Gulf, along the coast of the Arabian Sea, in Australia and in Japan. Bases are being established on the islands of Micronesia in the Pacific such as Tinian, Saipan, Palau, Kwajalein and others. Along with the base at Guam, these form a frontier from which the Pentagon would like to exercise strategic control over vital passageways from the Pacific to the Indian Ocean.
>
> In addition, the recent talks between the USA and the Philippines have ended with the former retaining its bases in that country. The

Pentagon has also 'frozen' the decision on the withdrawal of its land troops from South Korea.[43]

Soviet views of being confronted by such an amalgamation are predated by Russian perceptions of the same – if on a smaller scale. In both cases there was/is a sense of a barrier set by the US (the dominant power) and Japan; in the present-day context to these can be added South Korea, Taiwan, Hong Kong, the Philippines, (arguably) Indonesia and Australia and New Zealand. Some of these states the Soviets view as not necessarily being naturally anti-Soviet, but amounting to as much by default, in that they come under a large degree of American influence. Beyond this main barrier lies a collection of smaller island states which might be more susceptible to Soviet influence. From a Soviet grand strategic viewpoint the aim is to break through the barrier using whatever means are most appropriate. Most recently Gorbachev's speech in Vladivostok (28 July 1986) gave notice of an increased Soviet interest in the wider reaches of the Pacific. In August 1985 the Soviets finally concluded a fishing agreement with Kiribati and in December 1986 with Vanuatu. Negotiations are also under way with Papua New Guinea and Fiji.[44] Soviet Foreign Minister Shevardnadze toured South East Asia and Australia in March 1987, emphasising the heightened Soviet interest. Soviet 'penetration' in this case has been primary economic and thus should be containable. The importance of Japan and of the Soviet–Japanese relationship to the Soviets stems at a high level from the Soviet perception of Japan's position in this barrier.

Although it has only been in the later 1970s that the Soviets have acquired a limited military capacity to project their influence to the far flung corners of the Pacific, influence in the region predates the military capacity. Indubitably that interest has been of a lesser priority than elsewhere but that has not of itself made it negligible. As we shall propose, the Soviet relationship with Japan has been in fact of a far more positive nature than critics of it would contend.

The most fragile aspect of regional relations has been the economic. If it were not for the levels of trade with Japan (even though the Soviet Union's trade with Japan has slackened, Japan remains its most important trading partner in East and South East Asia) Soviet trade with the nations of East and South Asia could reasonably be categorised as pitifully small. On average, trade with Japan constitutes 50% of total Soviet trade with the region. Therefore trade with Japan for the Soviets should be evaluated not only in the context of their bilateral relations, but also be seen as of value in projecting their trade position in East Asia generally. Trade with Japan serves to legitimise Soviet interest in trading developments in the other parts of the region and the wider reaches of the Pacific. Although the Soviets have continually attacked the ideas of a proposed 'Pacific Community' as providing the framework for another military alliance, (as well as implicitly denying the Soviet Union membership) they have expressed genuine interest in participation in creating a trading organisation in the Pacific, even though expressing doubts as to its feasibility. However the Soviets have not brought forward any detailed proposals themselves on Pacific co-operation or its mechanics. The most recent proposals, in Spring 1986, for an all-Asian conference on economic and military security were still general.

From the Soviet viewpoint ensuring 'sufficient' national defence is a daunting prospect. The range of contingencies which the Soviets must plan for in a potential war against an array of powers is too large for them to be confident of success. In prolonged hostilities against the Western coalition, the additional support of operations in the Far East would probably be beyond the logistic capabilities of the Soviet forces.[45] The main preoccupation in their search for security has been with the nuclear balance and part of their answer has emphasised a growth in commitment to the SLBM component of their nuclear forces. That in turn has prompted a change in their approach to maritime strategy and defence. The concomitant change in mission has imposed changes in the force structure of the Navy, in the design, numbers and size of its ships and in the missions of the surface fleet. Gorshkov has explained that 'command of the sea' for the Soviets is based not on the old concept of dominating every sea but on that of dominating the areas in which theatre operations are envisaged. In other words it is a local command concept. However, even with a qualitatively improved Pacific fleet the Soviets are still not in a position to command or deny the north-west Pacific to the US navy. The north west Pacific constitutes the outer defence region of the Sea of Okhotsk and the inability of the Soviets to fight effectively in the north west Pacific would force them to fight from a position that lacks strategic depth. That cannot give Soviet planners much reassurance.

The Soviet build-up in the Far East has not been prompted by a relatively sudden desire to exploit perceived weakness, nor has it received special attention in comparison to other theatres where the Soviets deploy substantial forces.

> When we examine Soviet behaviour in other parts of the non-Western world (Africa or the Middle East, for example) or compare the military build-up in the Soviet Far East with that on the European front, we find no convincing evidence for the contention that Asia

during the 1970s has *suddenly* and dramatically gained special prominence at the expense of other areas where the Soviets have an
important stake. In other words, the growth of Soviet military
capabilities directed towards Asia on the ground, in the air, and on
the sea has proceeded during the past decade not markedly faster
than in other theatres . . . it appears that the Soviet military build-up
in Asia is in essence part of a world-wide, relentless process transforming the USSR into a truly global power.[46]

The notable feature of Soviet forces in the Far East is not that they have
increased in numbers – in fact the ground forces and air forces have
decreased numerically from their early 1970s levels – but that they
have improved qualitatively. In practice the Soviets have stabilised the
manpower levels of their forces-in-being in the Far East and have set
about to improve their capabilities and correct their shortcomings by
organisational restructuring and equipment modernisation.

We shall start our examination from the premise that the Soviets do
indeed have discernible policies and objectives. As we have already
pointed out, some commentators express certainty over Soviet aims in
the region but this view cannot be ascribed to the majority of
commentators. In the opening sections of a recent book, Zagoria states
unequivocally that 'the principal unsatisfied power in Asia is the
Soviet Union'[47] because with the exception of Indochina the Soviets
have so far not been very successful in realising their ambitions,
particularly towards the Great Powers, the United States and China.
He goes on to suggest that the two major Soviet efforts have been
centred on the containment of China and keeping it weak and the
weakening of the American alliance system in East Asia. In Zagoria's
view the Soviets have failed to achieve either of these. Zagoria has
highlighted two objectives; a complete list of objectives would probably comprise the following:
- the containment of China
- a reduction in the role played by the United States in East Asia
- The establishment and acceptance of the Soviet Union in some
  regional role (preferably in place of the United States)
- the legitimation of the territorial status quo
- the neutralisation of Japan, or as a minimum aim, the keeping
  of Japan as distanced as possible from the other main regional
  powers.

As we would expect, in a regional setting these aims largely interact
with each other. However the attainment of any one might well not
have a beneficial effect on another. For example, attainment of the
second objective on the list (reducing the American role) may superfi-

cially seem to aid in containment of China but equally it could also provoke a counter-reaction based on increased Chinese fear of the Soviet Union, or it might prompt the Chinese to try to replace American influence with their own and in the process heighten competition between themselves and the Soviet Union.[48] This same kind of effect has been observed in a wider Asian setting: 'the success of Soviet policy is debatable ... in fact the build-up of Soviet military power has led to a greater political co-operation among the East Asian states ... and it has increased their co-operation with the United States. It has also increased China's role in the region.'[49] It is not unknown for policymakers to pursue contradictory policies simultaneously, certainly over the short term, though over a long term it is likely that their behaviour will be consistent with the attempted attainment of specified goals.

Accepting the above as constituting a list of Soviet objectives only surmounts one obstacle. Questions left to be answered are whether we can attach a priority to each and how Japan fits into Soviet plans to attain each goal. For example, China is clearly the unspoken enemy, but the threat from the United States is more immediate and far greater. In relation to the latter, Japan occupies the pivotal position in the region due to its geographical location and its industrial/technical capability. Without a presence in Japan, the ability of the United States to intervene effectively in Asia would be severely circumscribed. But this does not necessarily accord any significance to Japan *per se*. The Soviet Union may see itself able to achieve its goal of nullifying American influence by other means than by action directed via, or against, Japan. Japan as the linchpin may be the obvious target – but it is not necessarily the best nor easiest target.

The Soviet Union, Japan and China

The containment of China is often described as the major Soviet goal in East Asia. Possible extension of the United States–Japanese alliance into one involving the People's Republic of China (PRC) has been a recurrent fear for the Soviets, and the idea is commonly expressed that in order to avoid this singular catastrophe the Soviets have always been willing to make concessions to the Japanese. One writer cites the events of 1972 as evidence of this. After the Nixon visit to China in 1971 he suggests that the Soviets were very quick to react to a Japanese invitation for ministerial talks involving Gromyko. According to this writer,

During his 1972 visit, Gromyko offered the Japanese a compromise on the issue of the northern islands; access to Siberian resources; an expanding Siberian market; verbal support against the PRC; and political co-operation where possible on East Asian issues, preferably with Japan as an independent power, but even with Japan as an American ally if Japan so desired. In return Gromyko asked for a pledge that Japan would not develop a relationship with China that was detrimental to Soviet interests.[50]

Aside from vague suggestions of a compromise on the northern islands what of the other 'concessions'? Siberian co-operation, as we have discussed in our examination of Soviet–Japanese trade, was initially to both parties' benefit; verbal support against the PRC was likely to be forthcoming anyway; political co-operation can be deemed highly unlikely in practice, in what realistic areas of co-operation might it occur? Expressing a willingness to enter into a dialogue with Japan – even if she still desired to be an ally of the United States – is giving nothing away.

In practice the Soviet 'concessions' did involve giving nothing away. The quotation cited above is symptomatic of the overemphasis some analysts place on Soviet fears of Japanese collaboration with China. In practice, the Soviets have undertaken no substantial initiatives nor changes of course, in response to Japanese moves towards closer ties with China, arguably not even in the military sphere, where the growth in quality of Soviet forces in the East since the early 1970s has been the product of long term modernisation plans and an acceptance of a stable situation on the Soviet–Chinese border, not an obvious response to any manifestations of a Japanese–Chinese alliance.

Japanese–Chinese relations, either in peace or war, have a long historical background. The period of substantial contact between the two nations is considerably longer than that of Russian/Soviet–Japanese association. As recent trade figures show, Japanese trade with China has been greater than with the Soviet Union; indeed, the Soviets only appeared as a trade rival to the Chinese during the 1970s. For the most part the Soviets are aware of the history and nature of the relationship between Japan and China and moreover of its limitations. Many of the barriers which contained the development of ties between Japan and the Soviet Union, particularly in trade, can be seen to be operable in similar circumstances of Japanese trade with China. There are factors which are pertinent only to the Chinese case, but these are to an extent double-edged and have on occasion militated against favourable developments between China and Japan.

For example, in the 1950s the Chinese, in line with their concept of 'people's diplomacy', adopted a more lenient approach to the repatri-ation of Japanese prisoners of war than the Soviets chose to. Also in the early 1950s, the Japanese parliament called for the widening of trade associations with China but the gains made here were lost due to an incident in 1958;[51] however the situation had corrected itself by the early 1960s. Politically, due to domestic upheavals brought on by the Cultural Revolution in the 1960s, the Chinese were more vociferous than the Soviet Union in their public criticism of Japanese foreign affairs. The Chinese openly attacked the Japanese role in ASEAN, the Asian Development Bank and the Asia Pacific council as attempts by Japan to achieve regional leadership and build an anti-Communist alliance detrimental to Chinese interests.

We have mentioned specific points of Japanese–Chinese relations not notable in Japanese relations with the Soviet Union. One example of this is the existence in Japanese politics of a sizeable pro-Chinese lobby, which was particularly active during the six years of negotiation which preceded the signing of the peace treaty with China in 1978. This lobby's influence can be seen to vary from issue to issue and is mainly oriented towards self-gain in trade. Its influence and alle-giances are also very much determined by the structure of Japanese politics which functions around a system of factions within parties rather than around the actual parties themselves. The pro-China group is a product of the long history of ties which Japanese govern-ments and traders have developed with China. Certainly no similar grouping exists so oriented towards the Soviet Union; although by 1980 evidence was beginning to emerge of some sort of movement in certain Japanese businesses involved in trading with the Soviets, it was clearly not comparable in size or influence with the pro-China lobby.

There exists a degree of parallelism in both Soviet and Chinese relations with Japan which constrains both parties. Of relevance to our investigation is the question of whether or not the Soviets were indeed aware of the limitations of any Japanese–Chinese partnership and acted accordingly.

The most pressing Soviet fear in the East is of a war with China simultaneously with a coalition war with NATO. The Soviet concern is not with suffering defeat at the hands of the Chinese (it is gen-erally accepted that the Soviets would achieve their (probably) limited objectives, namely the occupation of northern China, the destruction of the core of Chinese forces and the curtailment of Chinese ability to wage a prolonged war), but rather with the unknown factor in that war which could lead to a global nuclear escalation. Because of the unwelcome possibilities, war with China is not to be sought or provoked. The pre-eminent Soviet concern therefore is to contain China militarily as much as possible. In that light, Japan is seen as the only nation in the region with the capability not only to develop its own military capacity but also to assist in the development of Chinese military capability. A further expressed Soviet concern has been that Japanese involvement with China would inevitably lead to the involvement of the United States.[52] The Soviets are at least publicly divided over where to attribute the leading role in the development and maintenance of the China–Japan relationship. Two Soviet writers, Krupyanko and Petrov, argue that though Japan has economic reasons for seeking involvement with China, the *real* motive behind Japanese moves has been political. Petrov suggests

> The Japanese financial oligarchy thus directly ties in the economic relations with China with political aims and often shows readiness to forego immediate profit for the sake of the long-term tasks of separating China from the world socialist community. It aims at drawing it as deeply as possible into the world capitalist economy, confident that this will make it possible to bring pressure on the PRC's political line. Special emphasis is laid here on attempts to encourage the PRC's rapprochement with the United States within the framework of the Peking-Washington-Tokyo triangles.[53]

Krupyanko takes a similar view:

> An analysis of Japan's economic policy towards China during the 1970s and early 1980s shows that it is based above all on political, rather than commercial, considerations ... all actively involve China in the orbit of Western economic and political influence.[54]

We can contrast this position with that of another Soviet commentator who argues that

> The Peking leaders attach great importance to their ties with Japan and regard her as a partner who can play a significant role in the implementation of their plans of world domination ... China is trying to use the inter-governmental and other contacts with Japan to push her back on the dangerous track of military preparations ... and to steer Japan's policy towards anti-Sovietism.[55]

The Sino-Japanese treaty of 1978 is the most obvious benchmark by which to measure Soviet attitudes. Two statements can be used to illustrate Soviet *declaratory* views on the signing of the treaty. A broadcast by Radio Moscow on 10 August accused the Chinese of pressuring Japan but also stated that 'at the present time when the

Japanese delegation's attitude to the negotiations has come so close to that of the Chinese side, it would be useful for the Japanese to recall the Soviet Union's repeated warning that the conclusion of a treaty based on an anti-Sovietism would cause difficulties in the normal development of Soviet–Japanese relations. The Soviet Union will probably be compelled to revise its policy towards Japan.'[56]

A commentary in *Pravda* on 13 August suggested that

> many Japanese politicians, including some in the ruling LDP as well as the Japanese public and press, called on their government to take a cautious approach to the talks in Peking and not to give in to Chinese pressure . . . (however) by giving in to Peking's diktat and agreeing to sign the treaty on the latter's terms, Japan has placed itself in a position in which it may become an accessory to Chinese hegemonistic policy.[57]

Soviet media attacks upon the treaty and negotiations are surprisingly few in number and it is noticeable that these slackened-off in both tone and frequency as it became obvious that despite Soviet efforts both parties were going to proceed with the signing. In part this could be explained by Soviet recognition of a *fait accompli* but there is arguably more to it than that. Certain aspects of Soviet comment deserve attention:

1 In both the press and radio, comment was concentrated only in the few weeks preceding the actual signing and for a short while afterwards. Statements throughout the preceding year had only been sporadic.

2 The substantially critical attacks were confined to press and radio broadcasts; journal commentary was more constrained. We might expect this; however, a scanning of content of the relevant journals shows that no effort was made to make a significant issue out of the treaty either before or after its signing. The main Soviet journal on China and Japan, *Far Eastern Affairs*, seems to have devoted only a few articles to the treaty in the months prior to its signing, and none after. Nor was there any noticeable increase above normal levels in the journal's coverage of Japanese affairs.

3 Soviet comment is itself divided over which nation was the principal instigator of the treaty. On balance China was accused of 'dragging' Japan into negotiations.[58] Other commentators even accused the United States of being behind events.[59] Few openly attacked the Japanese government outright; often these accusations were made with the proviso that only 'certain circles' were responsible while other elements of

Japanese government and society were depicted as holding strong reservations on the desirability of this course of action.

4   A common thread to run through Soviet comment was that the Soviet government's response to the treaty would be based upon *future* Japanese behaviour. For example, as late as 24 August, Deputy Foreign Minister Firiubin is reported to have told the Japanese ambassador in Moscow that the Soviet Union 'would watch Japanese future policies and form its own conclusions as to whether it genuinely desired friendly relations with the USSR'.[60]

These Soviet statements cast doubt upon the thesis that they viewed the treaty as some sort of swing by the Japanese into some kind of Chinese alliance.

While publicly the Soviets were seen to be trying to dissuade Japan from participating in the treaty with China, their arguments were evidently not held with intensity in private. The immediacy of the military threat which featured so prominently in the public campaign was transferred in private to an emphasis upon the *potential* military consequences of Japanese–Chinese co-operation, indeed very much the long term potential. The suspicion held in more reasoned quarters was that Sino-Japanese co-operation, but more specifically military co-operation, would likely be kept within strict bounds, as has indeed proved the case since. Increasingly this has been stated in public also. 'To be sure, so far full-fledged military ties between Japan and China can be regarded as only a potentiality'; so wrote the Tokyo correspondent of *New Times* in 1982 in an article which touched upon the many problems besetting relations between Japan and China, particularly in the field of economics. (These stem from many of the constraints which we outlined above.) This writer concluded by stating that each of the signatories had adopted an attitude to solving its own problems 'at the expense of one's partner, to outwit and use one another in one's political game, mutual distrust and disrespect for one's obligations – such are the principles of relations between China and Japan at the present stage'.[61] The fact that the Soviets declared that their future policy towards Japan would be based upon future Japanese actions prompts the suspicion that they expected future developments to take this form.

Even Krupyanko qualifies his otherwise positive survey of relations by implicitly testifying to the existence of problems in the economic relationship which are indicative of wider political divergences. He points out that Japan's credit policy towards China is constantly bedevilled by a Chinese reversal of policy on overseas borrowing so

173

that China now seeks credits 'cautiously and as a subsidiary' to its own resources. According to him the Japanese government has purposely limited its co-operation in the development of the Chinese export base.[62]

Kimura cites a Soviet analyst as implying that part of the limitation on developments with China will result from conscious Japanese governmental decision; 'Japan prefers to keep an equidistance from China and from the USSR, without allowing any overt measure, which could do damage to her relations with the USSR. The developments in Sino-Japanese relations have thus their own objective limits.'[63]

We tried to show that gauging the Soviet position on Japanese relations with China purely from the rhetorical evidence would lead to an erroneous conclusion. In private, and in some cases from published work, it is clear that the Soviets are far more cautious in their estimation of the relationship. The Japan–United States relationship is the centre-piece of Soviet attention, and the stable situation on the Sino-Soviet border merely serves to reinforce that predisposition.

The Soviet Union, Japan and the United States

The following main points are distinctly seen now in the US administration's activity on the international scene, aimed at directing developments in Asia along a track that suits the interests of US imperialism. First, the US administration is out to maintain, even escalate, the presence of US armed forces, especially those with nuclear weapons, in Asian countries and adjoining seas and oceans. Second, it seeks closer political and military co-operation with imperialist Japan, the latter's total commitment to the global designs of US imperialism, to its confrontation with the Soviet Union and the other countries of the socialist community and the other members of the socialist community. Third, it is bent on forming a political and military alliance of the NATO model in Asia and the region of the Pacific ocean, which would unprotestingly serve the far-reaching expansionist plans of the US monopolies. Fourth, it is taking all possible steps to prevent China from reverting to good-neighbourly relations with the Soviet Union and other socialist countries ... Lastly, it has perfected the machinery of lies and slanders about the socialist countries, notably the Soviet Union, of frightening Asian peoples with talk of a 'threat' to them from their socialist neighbours.[64]

These points, quoted from an editorial in the main Soviet China journal, *Far Eastern Affairs*, in early 1984, summarise the basic Soviet view on American strategy in the Far East and Pacific.[65] The Soviets see their allegations as borne out by President Reagan's visit to Japan and South Korea in November 1983, when his prime purpose was seen to be expediting the two countries' war preparations and the speeding-up of a Washington–Tokyo–Seoul triple alliance. In connection with American overtures on the Far East, the Soviets voice the opinion that 'Japan is responding to Washington's calls for various sanctions against the USSR and other socialist countries. Moreover, Japanese leaders are endeavouring to play an active role in 'rallying' the West to the side of the United States and demanding, as Premier Nakasone has done at the Williamsburg summit meeting, that European capitalist powers should unreservedly support Reagan's adventurist policy.'[66]

Soviet interpretations of Japanese–American relations stress that 1978–80 has proved to be a turning point. The beginnings of changes can be traced back to the advent of the Ohira government. One of the foremost Japanese analysts of the Soviet Union concedes as much:

> To begin with, the Kremlin generally considered the foreign policy of the Ohira administration to be extraordinarily anti-Soviet ... even more important, Ohira was regarded as a more pro-Western, especially pro-United States-oriented leader than his predecessors. This belief was published by Mr. V. Kudryavstev in the May 27 issue of *Izvestiia* in these terms: 'No postwar government leader has formulated foreign policies with as much lack of independence and authority as Mr. Ohira'.[67]

The increasing pro-American orientation of Japan has progressed, according to the Soviets, through the period of office of the Suzuki government to its present high level of anti-Sovietism under Nakasone. Nakasone has been the subject of the most vitriolic Soviet attacks due to his pledges to increase military co-operation with the United States, his measures to facilitate American access to certain high technology more sophisticated than that presently utilised by them in missile guidance systems and his signing of the Williamsburg communiqué whereby he 'supported the NATO decision to deploy Pershing II and cruise missiles in Europe towards the end of 1983'.[68]

As we indicated in chapter 1 the Soviets are unsure who should be held primarily responsible for the trend of Japanese militarisation: the United States or Japan.

> Throughout almost the entire postwar period Japan has followed in the tracks of Washington's foreign policy. This became especially obvious at the start of the 1980s, when the American administration caused a dramatic increase in international tension and an intensification of the arms race. As the United States continued with this policy, it demanded from Japan an increase in its military might as

175

fast as possible, and more active co-operation with American strategy in Asia and the Pacific. American–Japanese relations reached their highest level in May 1981 when their relationship was officially declared to be an alliance. Behind this formulation was a desire on Washington's part to 'raise' the 'mutual security treaty' to a level of the North Atlantic pact, and thus impose alliance obligations on Japan similar to those of NATO countries. In 1982, the United States raised for the first time the suggestion that both nations' armed forces should co-operate in situations of 'special circumstances' outside Japanese territory in the Far East. This signalled that a new stage in American–Japanese military co-operation had been reached. Washington is also demanding that Japan fulfil its promise to patrol naval and air lines of communication in a radius of 1,700 kilometres from their shores . . . The Washington administration is constantly asking Japan to increase its military power and its defence budget . . . (actions by Weinberger and Congress) . . . are prime examples of interference in the country's internal affairs, which are designed to take it on a dangerous course with the most dire of consequences.[69]

The general thrust of Kuznetsov's comments is at odds with the emphasis of the article by Bunin cited earlier; Kuznetsov is clearly suggesting that Japan is conceding to American pressure. While he refers at a later stage (p. 102) to the 'Japanese ruling circles' also 'pursuing its own interests', this is almost a cursory reference in an argument which otherwise stresses the responsibility of the United States for guiding Japan in certain foreign policy directions.

As we also discussed in our conclusions on ideology and militarism, there is no doubt in Soviet opinion as to the end result of this Japanese course of action – rather that the distinction has been that in private the views held have been less intense and more cautious in appraising Japanese moves. However the division among the Soviets as to who (Japan or the United States) is the driving force behind the course of events, it has been argued, could have led the Soviets to be uncertain of the best counter-policy and to treat Japan as merely a subject of overall Soviet–US relations in north east Asia. This reasoning is the mainstay of those who argue that Soviet policy towards Japan is merely a by-product of Soviet policy on the United States and China. 'The Soviets simply do not have a clear, distinct positive policy towards Japan. Offers which they have made have really been spin-offs of Soviet policy towards the United States and/or towards China.'[70]

This argument cannot be substantiated. Soviet analysis of the Japan–United States relationship displays a more sophisticated framework than a simplistic dual 'independent or puppet' argument. Even if we were to accept the validity of the 'puppet' (and therefore, 'Soviet Japan policy is merely a spin-off of Soviet US policy') argument – this could only be accepted as such in relation to specific aspects of military policy, particularly the strategic nuclear. The Soviets have made very distinct economic and political approaches to Japan, and equally, Japan has pursued policies in these fields independently of the United States.

The United States has enormous interests in East Asia and the Pacific. Trade with the region has surpassed that of trade with Europe, and there is a wide range of treaty commitments, including the stationing of American troops. The Soviets are aware of this, and are also aware of the geographical relocation of United States' strength and commitment during the 1970s to north east Asia and the north west Pacific. Equally they are aware of the changes in policy emphasis initiated by the Reagan administration which according to one American analyst had criticised the 'zigzags, the inconsistency and general independability of previous administrations' and placed new emphasis on 'consistency and the need to demonstrate "loyalty" and "commitment" to US allies and friends at the top of its policy priorities'.[71]

The Soviets understand the 'selective commitment' strategy which the United States has been pursuing in East Asia since 1975. They are also aware of the inconsistencies and unresolved elements of that strategy which Carter, and subsequently Reagan, have tried to balance. On the one hand the United States has declared its renewed commitment to its allies, stressing the greater military emphasis in American policy, but on the other hand has often repeated its equally-held aim of desiring a greater division of labour between itself and its allies, in this case Japan. The Soviets claim that fundamentally this looks like 'decoupling' and a means of distancing the United States from Japan so that Japan can be used as a nuclear hostage.

> In deploying nuclear arms, including first strike weapons, at its base in Asia, the United States is reproducing the 'European option'. It is counting on a retaliatory strike being diffused and falling mainly on countries where the United States' nuclear weapons are deployed, while the United States itself escapes with minimal damage. Essentially Washington is trying to turn the Asian countries, on whose territory the United States has military establishments into 'hostages' of its policy, assigning them the dubious honour of becoming a theatre of military operations.[72]

In terms of regional security issues we can make a distinction between those which are primarily autonomous but affected by superpower relations, and those that are induced by superpower politics. North east Asian security falls into the latter category.

To be sure the main preoccupation of the Soviet Union with the United States is the strategic nuclear balance. The situation with regard to United States nuclear capability in East Asia and the Pacific has been particularly unfavourable to the Soviet Union. The proliferation of nuclear weapons and delivery systems (the deployment of nuclear capable F-16s, and air/sea launched cruise missiles) has complicated already probably difficult targeting requirements for Soviet planners, and made defence of the Far East more problematic. The defence of this region may for the Soviets constitute a worst-case nuclear scenario. The modernisation of Soviet nuclear forces in the Far East has been a part of their wider modernisation. But at whom is this process directed? V. Petrov, of the Sino-Soviet Institute at George Washington University, is of the opinion that, 'This action is geared to impressing US (and Chinese) eyes, and in this sense impressing Japan does not serve much purpose.'[73]

Is Japan therefore left-out of nuclear questions? While Japan obviously does not have the same degree of leverage with the United States over nuclear matters as the European allies, its leverage can nevertheless stem from the very fact that it is the indispensable ally of the United States in north east Asia. At an overall strategic level, Japan like the other allies effectively has to accept the arrangement worked-out by the superpowers, and its input into the final American–Soviet agreement may well be less than that of other allies. At this level, it is fair to state that the Soviets have not considered Japan as an object of policy. However at a theatre level this position is becoming less clear. In part this is due to the blurring of the boundaries between a 'strategic' and 'theatre' weapons system, but there are other reasons. V. P. Lukin, in an interview with the author cited above, argued that through the 1970s United States' doctrine in the Pacific had been consistent overall but had fluctuated in 'waves' – with Nixon in the early 1970s and with the second part of the Carter administration. He stated his belief that these 'waves' were indicative of the possibility to divorce specific theatre concerns from global concerns, and that the United States would have to accept (as it has done elsewhere in a European context) that there are East Asian regional peculiarities to security questions.

In the Japanese case the Soviets have begun to take regional nuclear security initiatives directed at Japan. Specifically, Lukin commented that the recent Soviet proposals on Confidence Building Measures (CBMs) were proof that the Soviet government recognised regional theatre peculiarities, and that behind the initiative was 'an assumption that Japan has some input to make into nuclear security processes in north east Asia'. The initiatives on CBMs therefore may foreshadow change in aspects of Soviet policy to make nuclear concerns a matter of bilateral relations with Japan.

CBMs of course also have applicability at the conventional level. Here the Soviets and the Japanese have more latitude in seeking a bilateral agreement, but it appears unlikely that Japan will do so, even in accord with the United States. Brezhnev stated in 1980 that the Soviets were interested in extending the CBM concept to naval matters also, and in 1982 particular reference to the suitability of the idea in a Japanese context was made by T. B. Guzhenko, head of the Soviet merchant fleet and Chairman of the USSR–Japan Friendship Society.[74] In a major speech at Vladivostok, given during his tour of Siberia and the Far East, Gorbachev also picked up on the theme of an increasing pace of naval militarisation and stressed the need for long term co-operative plans with Japan. To that end he proposed the idea of a conference à la Helsinki that would start talks on the reduction of fleets in the Pacific, especially nuclear armed ships. Moreover he suggested that restrictions be placed on the rivalry in the sphere of ASW weapons. A stage by stage 'reduction of armed forces and conventional armaments in Asia to limits of reasonable sufficiency' was his suggestion and that a 'switch be made to a practical plane on the discussion of CBMs and non-use of force in the region. A start could be made on the simpler measures, for instance measures for security of sea lanes in the Pacific, and for the prevention of international terrorism.'[75] Given the increasing stress within north east Asia on the military face of relations, the circumstances for negotiations into CBMs in the region could not be more appropriate. These proposals as applicable to the Pacific and Indian oceans were presented again by Gorbachev during his official visit to India in November 1986, but as of mid-1987 no progress had been made, despite more specific points having been added to the otherwise vague statements.

As far as economic or trade relations are concerned, the Soviets have indeed considered Japan a worthy subject of attention. In this sphere Japan has always been treated, and responded, as an independent nation. As detailed above, though trade may have been limited by ideological constraint and technical considerations, no significant limitation could be attributed to perception on the part of either party of bad relations with the other, or with third nations (United States or China). As we pointed out, for example, trade had already started to fall in absolute value before the sanctions over Afghanistan were implemented. Trading between the Soviet Union and Japan has its own dynamic and in fact set the tempo for overall conduct of relations.

The general problem for the Soviets in pursuing policies in East Asia is that the region lacks a focal point. It can be said that there is no one issue, or one nation which can act as a point of concentration. This is true even within the confines of north east Asia. A comparison with Soviet policy in Europe can help to illustrate the problem. Although Europe comprises numerous states this has not particularly hindered the Soviets from pursuing coherent policies with a 'Europe-wide' appeal. In Europe there has been a post-war tradition or 'shared experience', the development of European umbrella organisations such as the EEC and NATO, the focusing of mutual attention on the centrality of various aspects of the 'German question'. Even the various European communist parties have come to embrace many of the same aspirations, making the Soviet task of having to come to terms with 'Euro-Communism' that much more straightforward. The Soviets have to synthesise some sort of coherent policy *vis-à-vis* Japan out of dealing with the United States, China and Korea as well as Japan. The Soviet Union lacks significant diplomatic relations with South Korea, and in dealing with North Korea is involved in a clash with China and is, in South Korean eyes, vilified as a major sponsor of a nation viewed as the irreconcilable enemy. In these circumstances co-ordinating policy is especially problematic: in the short term the circumstances dictate contradictory actions, uncertainty in statements, and policy swings. These factors, we have suggested, have been the main contributory factors in commentators doubting the existence of a 'Soviet policy towards Japan'.

However these fluctuations are products of short term considerations. They are often reactions to particular stimuli or actions undertaken to achieve a specific immediate objective. Over the long term the evidence is that policymakers' actions are usually consistent with perceived goals; Soviet actions towards Japan have been no different.

If we assert that the Soviets do indeed have discernible policies and goals towards, or involving, Japan, we should distinguish between the long and short term. By not doing so we create a problem, through not identifying the difference in the nature of the goals and therefore not pointing out the limitations such a categorisation (long term/short term) imposes upon an ability to assess those goals and those actions declared to be in pursuit of them.

If for example we accept, for the sake of argument, that the neutralisation of Japan is a Soviet goal, then, assuming that a complete political volte face does not occur in Japan, this is patently a long term objective. It is then surely unrealistic to herald, as many commentators do, the 'failure' of the Soviets to achieve their objectives *vis-à vis* Japan or north east Asia. It is more credible to postulate that present trends indicate no progress towards certain objectives, but it would be premature to deduce failure from that.

A goal may be 'long term' for two principal reasons: because it is difficult, or because it is not important enough for much attention to be devoted to it. All the Soviet goals which involve Japan – neutralisation of Japan, 'containment' of China, limitation of the US role – can be encompassed by the first category, i.e. reasons of difficulty. Moreover, when the Soviets are accused of 'failing' to 'contain' China because, amongst other reasons, they have not been able to stop co-operation between Japan and China, we should ask: What is meant by 'containing' China? Unless we know (which we do not) specific Soviet aims, we cannot say definitely whether these aims are being achieved or not.

In the military dimension of Soviet–Japanese relations the goals speculated upon by analysts have been reinforced by the construction of likely scenarios which supposedly bestow credibility upon the objectives; i.e. scenarios which display a Soviet capability to invade or surprise Japan make the pursuit of a policy of coercion or neutralisation more believable. This line of reasoning neglects two points. First, even if the Soviet military in the Far East are preparing for a war this does not tell us what value their preparation has in the formation of policy towards Japan. Second, the recurrent problem with the search for, and demonstration of, scenarios is that it becomes an end in itself and detracts from the more important considerations of the political impact on Japan of the perception of power and from the factors which must be weighed if it is proposed to use that military power.

Centring the debate around the existence or not of a definable Soviet 'policy' runs the risk of distracting observers from the actual functioning of Soviet–Japanese relations on a day-to-day basis. Indeed, this has predominantly been the case expressed by both major Western schools of thought. Those who concede that the Soviets have a policy but that it has 'failed' suggest that in part it has occurred due to scant day-to-day contact. Those who have argued that the Soviets had no policy have also contended that this was due in part to a lack of contact on which to build.

It is noticeable that the Soviets and Japanese made steady progress from the mid-1950s (when they got off to a slow start) to the mid-1970s in normalising their relations. Since then contact between the two could be said to have levelled-off but has fluctuated recently, picking-up under new Gorbachev initiatives which included the visit of Shevardnadze to Japan, 15–19 January 1986, and the visit of the Japanese Foreign Minister Abe to the Soviet Union, 29–31 May 1986 – but levelling-off in a 'deterioration' of relations caused by the Toshiba technology transfer scandal of June–July 1987.[76]

Appraisal of the contacts between the two nations since the mid-1950s illustrates a continuity that conflicts with the received wisdom. Much has been made of the supposed gulf between the two nations, exemplified by the record of official visits by high ranking leaders. In the last twenty years, Japanese foreign ministers have visited the Soviet Union on seven occasions; Gromyko had been to Tokyo on three occasions, the last being in 1976. Japanese prime ministers have visited the Soviet Union three times but no equivalent ranking Soviet official has ever visited Japan. Gorbachev has repeatedly expressed his willingness, and intention, to visit Japan. The Japanese have placed high hopes on his visit, now expected in 1988. In fact Japan and the Soviet Union had an agreement for the annual exchange of foreign ministers but this was discontinued. Is the state of official contact to be considered as an important measure of relations? State visits are primarily symbolic, and not necessarily a guide to the real state of relations between nations. If any dialogue or contact exists between countries it is usually maintained, and can be measured by, contacts at the lower working levels. It is businessmen, traders, bureaucrats, parliamentary or trade union delegations, cultural exchanges, sporting contacts, scientific co-operation, etc. which establish the tempo of relations and determine the real depth of contact. In this regard, Japan's position vis-à-vis the Soviet Union is not significantly different from many major European nations, but there are differences in both the degree and scale of the above in regard to Japan's contact with the Soviet Union.

While the large scale business contacts that caused trade to develop so rapidly in the 1970s are on the wane in absolute value terms, as we have indicated in our section on trade contacts, a newer emphasis is beginning to be placed on smaller scale agreements. This approach may become the dominant trend for the future of economic relations.

Between the end of 1971 and 1975, (not including fisheries agreements), the Soviets and Japanese concluded sixteen major bilateral agreements. The subjects covered ranged from aviation communication, scientific and technical co-operation, and exchange of official publications, to international sea and air transport. Since then both nations have continued to conclude bilateral agreements on new areas such as the exchange of scientific personnel and compensation for accidents at sea, as well as renewing previous agreements and concluding regular talks on fishing and whaling, without any of the trouble associated with the 1977 agreement (which will be discussed in appendix 1). Since 1983 the Soviets and Japanese have held annual disarmament talks which have been used as a forum for an exchange of views on a wider range of subjects; the 1983 talks included discussions on Kampuchea and Afghanistan, for example.[77]

In assessing Soviet policy towards Japan commentators have generally sought to derive a theory from an overemphasis on observation of the symbolic or the most obvious, and in so doing have confused a lack of empathy with a lack of contact. Both sides maintain a larger degree of contact than they are commonly given credit for. A study of the events associated with the imposition of martial law in Poland in 1981–2 can be illustrative of that. Despite the imposition of martial law, the Japanese and Soviets still went ahead with the signing of that year's fishery agreement, nor did the Japanese cancel the planned visit of their Deputy Foreign Minister to the Soviet Union. By February 1982, in the midst of the problems over Poland and with the Japanese celebration of the 'Northern Territories Day' on 7 February (about which the Soviets made no protest), both parties went ahead with the appointment of new ambassadors – the Soviets replacing D. Polianski, their long-standing ambassador in Tokyo, with V. Pavlov, a full member of the Central Committee. Even on the very day when Japan announced sanctions (far more modest than American and some European sanctions), it also announced the conclusion of a new agreement to sell the Soviets 500 pipe-laying tractors.[78]

The conduct of relations has continued uninterrupted despite the high publicity given to various disturbances, including the first Soviet expulsion order against Japanese diplomats since World War II. On 20 August 1987 the Soviets expelled the Japanese naval attaché in Moscow along with a Japanese businessman. Both were accused of espionage. Japan, in turn, expelled a Soviet trade representative accused of industrial espionage. (In June, four Soviet diplomats in Tokyo had returned home after Japanese authorities charged them with espionage activities.) The former expulsions were the last acts of an uneasy summer which had been characterised by mutual recriminations. Rather than exacerbate matters, the Soviets sought to portray these, and other incidents, as inspired by right-wing groups out to sabotage the otherwise satisfactory state of Soviet–Japanese relations.[79]

The closing comment made by the writer of the cited *Radio Liberty* paper on Poland is one which would serve well as a general guide for viewing Soviet relations with Japan overall: '[It is] if nothing else, a reminder that the Soviet–Japanese relationship – deterioration and sanctions notwithstanding – continues to be marked by nuances that caution against any simplified description or analysis'.

CONCLUSIONS

The completion of the research has effectively substantiated the beliefs which originally prompted investigation and which were outlined in the introduction: that Japan does not rank highly in Soviet literature or media comment; that some of the comment by Western analysts is misleading; and that Soviet relations with Japan are more complicated than the vast body of Western literature would have us believe.

The Soviet ideological interpretations of Japan and the role of ideology in the formation of Soviet policy towards Japan have received negligible attention from Western and Japanese analysts. The problem in investigating this subject, as shown, was compounded by the comparatively low attention paid to Japan by the Soviets themselves in their academic literature. Most of the Soviet writing concerned with ideology was oriented towards economic appraisals of Japan.

In the time-frame in which this study is based, ideology can be seen to have influenced policy not merely in its accepted form as a backcloth but more directly as an issue of domestic politicking. Ideological justification of the necessity and extent of trade with the West and Japan was a salient feature of Soviet internal politics during the 1970s and impinged openly upon the conduct of trading relations with Japan. Specifically this was tied to the debates over the implications for the Soviet polity and economy of the scientific and technical revolution. It is important to stress that this was not a debate over a reversal of Soviet policy on autarky but over the degree to which it would be reversed and for how long.

Brezhnev, as a proponent of 'ideologically orthodox' solutions in this debate, benefited from this stance in his clashes with elements of domestic opposition.

Thus Soviet approaches to Japan during the period in which our examination is focused were based on a belief in the swing in the correlation of forces in favour of the Soviet Union, particularly in the regional context in north east Asia. The most basic Soviet ideological view of Japan depicted it as a member of a capitalist bloc racked by continual contradictions between the growth rates of mutually dependent states and the necessity to co-ordinate economic policies on the one hand and the antagonism of state monopoly to the limitation and regulation of economics on the other. The particular dynamism of the Japanese economy was seen to be an especial point of friction between capitalist nations. However, despite these economic contradictions many Soviet commentators accept that the political necessity of other concerns is likely to limit the friction caused by economic clashes. The need to maintain the unity of the political–military bloc of imperialism is the most important example of such a concern.

Soviet comment on Japanese relations – either economic or political – with nations apart from its main industrialised partners is very limited. We demonstrated this with reference to Japanese involvement in the Middle East and Latin America, which is substantial in both cases. Japan's relations with Asian nations on the Pacific rim are depicted solely in terms of the classic Marxist–Leninist theses on exploitation of developing countries. The centre-piece of the Soviet ideological analysis has been Japan's relationship with ASEAN states and with the Pacific Community scheme which is viewed as a means to formalise Japan's trading hold over the developing nations of the Pacific.

The Soviet ideological views of Japan as a society appear similar to Western interpretations at a macro level. However at more specific levels the Soviets have a vision of a Japan quite different from that held by the West. For the Soviets Japan is a slowly changing, stable polity. But the Soviets see the forces at work within the polity in different terms from Western analyses; the status of the working classes is declining, the gap between the 'rich' and 'poor' is widening. While Western commentators see a 'working class' and a 'poor' they also see that their position has improved significantly since the 1960s. The Soviets deny this and seek to stress the continuing struggle of the working classes. It is doubtful whether the Soviets in practice can really believe in this ideological vision of the position of the Japanese working class.

A general point to emerge from our work is that while certain Soviets – academics, some policy 'advisors' – can produce useful and accurate comment on Japan, there remains much more which the Soviets could do to enhance their knowledge of, and quality of comment on, Japan.

Both sides have stressed the centrality of economic issues. The Soviet–Japanese trade relationship is of long standing and in recent years has revolved around the trading of energy-related materials: oil, coal, gas and timber development.

In constituing a main plank on which wider relations have been built, and a tool by which the Soviets have sought to pursue policy, trading relations should accordingly be viewed as an important object of attention for analysts. This importance should not be over-drawn however. Our close examination of economic ties has shown them to be more shallow and subject to variance than we might have expected to be the case judging by their financial value and high profile in academic literature and popular press. However this press coverage has been disproportionate to the actual role of economic contacts in policy, and the financial value of trade with Japan becomes less impressive when seen in the context of Soviet trade contacts with other leading capitalist nations. The claims of complementarity of the Soviet and Japanese economies proved to be largely mythical.

Militarily, the situation in north east Asia and the wider Pacific is more complex than the conventional literature depicts. It is true that there has been a growth in the overall Soviet naval presence in the region; but this has been exaggerated by manipulation of the methods of quantification employed by the West. This is not to argue that all of the misleading or divergent reports on Soviet naval strength are deliberately contrived falsehoods but that such compromises and contrasts are almost inevitable when intelligence estimates are formu-lated in a competitive bureaucratic environment. As Admiral Turner, former Director of the CIA, points out in a recent work, the US Navy 'has vested interests that may well bias its interpretation'.[1] (Nor are these problems confined to naval analysis of course.) Agencies con-cerned can present differing pictures of Soviet naval strength depend-ing on whether they choose to paint it in terms of absolute numbers, comparative percentages or ratios. Nor is it uncommon for agencies arbitrarily to change more specific methods of assessment, such as the CIA undertook in 1979 when it reduced the basic tonnage threshold at which Soviet warships were considered in the balance, thus enabling small Soviet ships to appear on an order of battle for the first time. It has been shown how the Japanese Defence Agency uses the term 'vessels' to categorise Soviet ship movements without specifying how many 'vessels' are actually *warships*. An increase in quality of Soviet forces in the region can be seen, but as we have shown their ability to undertake the various missions that they might be called upon to fulfil in the event of war must be in doubt. Even the defence of the Sea of Okhotsk bastion is not without its problems. While actions by Soviet forces, in particular the air force, can be viewed as unnecessarily provocative in many cases, the thesis which argues that the Soviets have pursued a deliberate policy of coercion *vis-à-vis* Japan must remain unproven from the evidence supplied in this investigation.

The Soviet estimations of Japanese force levels have been accurate by and large. However the implications of the uses (political or military) of Japanese military strength have been overdrawn. The Japanese Self Defence Forces have the capabilities of a defensively-oriented force and their ability to mount serious 'offensive' operations on the scale claimed by the Soviets is strictly limited by equipment shortages and weaknesses in logistical support, and not least by the prevailing political sentiment in Japan.

The study has sought to concentrate on the trends in relations rather than on specific incidents which have come to be regarded as legitimate indicators of the state of relations and thus, by inference, of Soviet policy. In this regard it has been shown that in many cases – the China treaty, the sanctions imposed after the Afghanistan invasion and the Polish events, the 1977 fishing negotiations, the problems over the northern islands, for example – the observable trend of relations conflicts with the impressions of antagonism and pessimism which have (in some cases, falsely) been derived from treatment of such specific incidents in isolation.

Japanese relations with the United States are a source of uncertainty for the Soviets as to whether Japan should be seen as a victim or accomplice of American imperialism in the Far East. In practice there is no indication that the Soviets have tried to exploit the division which they believe to exist between Japan and the United States. They view this relationship as enduring despite the frictions, and realistically see little prospect of being able to weaken it.

Japan's relationship with China has been the subject of more emotive and variable Soviet comment than has the relationship with the United States. This reflects the Soviet concern with trying to ameliorate or minimise Chinese actions detrimental to the Soviet Union and is in part connected to Soviet ideological competition with China for the support of Asian communist parties. Despite the often charged nature of Soviet comment, the Soviets have displayed an understanding of the limits to Japanese contact with China, due to self-limitation on the part of both China and Japan and to objective factors. This belief was given substance by the early years of the 1980s when Japanese contact with China had been mitigated by a change of political heart by the Chinese, a limited Chinese ability to absorb Japanese technology and to provide sufficient hard currency, and a feeling of dissatisfaction on the part of the Japanese with the progress and potential of the Chinese market.

The attempt to gauge mutual levels of 'understanding' was a worthwhile exercise to undertake but the conclusions which we can realistically draw from this type of study must be tenuous. Care must be shown in drawing firm conclusions when dealing with 'abstract' concepts. Overall, in terms of 'understanding', there seems to be a problem for both nations, as their abilities to seek wider comprehension have been curtailed by rigid perceptions of each other or have been confined to specific groups within policy circles (e.g. the Japan desk in the Soviet Ministry of Foreign Affairs or the Soviet desk of the Gaimusho) whose influence we cannot measure with certainty. So while there is undoubtedly scope for expansion in this area, each nation's approach is still governed by preconceptions which will prove hard to break.

The Japanese position as a capitalist economic giant ensures it a central place in Soviet ideological formulations, while that same economic strength gives it a role to play in Soviet foreign trading. Its geographical location and the military forces which are based on Japanese territory bestow on Japan an equally crucial significance for Soviet military strategy in the Pacific. Finally, the long history of Russian and Soviet contact, often hostile, with Japan guarantees that the Soviets have strong perceptions of the Japanese which continue to influence behaviour.

To what extent can these differing trends be drawn together to talk of a Soviet 'policy' towards Japan? Research has shown that there is certainly an identifiable pattern of 'relations' but it is possible for states to conduct relations not supported by, or part of, a 'policy'.

It is believed that the investigation illustrates that while the articulation of a Soviet national policy may have faltered on instances and that its pursuit may have been erratic, the Soviets do indeed have a clear vision of what they should strive for and realistically hope to achieve. They seem to have pursued these goals with a minimum of contradiction between the differing arms of policy: political, economic, military and ideological. For the present, the most the Soviets can realistically hope for is the continuation of the regional status quo in north east Asia. The economic aspect provides the basic mechanism for contact with Japan, and though it has faltered in recent years, it is still likely to exist in a meaningful way, supplemented by the growing political contacts. Due to their increased political activity, and certainly their military activity, the Soviets have built-upon the economic and have successfully established themselves as a nation with legitimate interests in East Asia. Soviet expectations of seeing minimal Japanese involvement with China have been met and this situation is unlikely to change unless the Soviets initiate drastic changes in the regional military order. The American–Japanese position the Soviets take as given.

Soviet academics have been the most openly divided over aspects of their analysis of Japanese matters. For the most part these differences have been over ideological questions – over which there is always a degree of debate and flexibility. Whether these differences between academics and commentators can be viewed as representative of similar differences in the higher echelons of Soviet policy-making it is impossible to say. In each case there has been a dominant view which has prevailed in the conduct of policy, and the pursuit of the long term goals *vis-à-vis* Japan of itself indicates that there must be some sort of lasting consensus among Soviet policymakers of Japan as to the desirability of these goals. In pursuit of these goals the economic and military have both had their part to play, either providing a wider backcloth to Soviet involvement in East Asia or in direct contact with Japan.

Whether the different arms of policy have been altogether successfully integrated in terms of goal pursuit is questionable. While the economic has provided a framework for continual contact and helped to legitimate the Soviet presence in East Asia, Soviet military actions, while probably not reducing the frequency of contact, have certainly endowed it with overtones of suspicion. Whether that suspicion has ramifications which limit the potential for further Soviet gains is for the future to show.

In assessing the policy of a global power we should never seek to isolate one of its regional policies from the wider global policies. All of the factors which have been considered operable in a Japanese or north east Asian context are open to fluctuation due to non-regional influences. Radical changes in the Soviet approach to the region and to Japan are unlikely; incrementalism is the order of day. While a series of incremental changes may produce a significant change over time, change by this process has the advantage of being more susceptible to guidance and control. Soviet–Japanese handling in particular of the military situation has demonstrated an awareness of the need to 'manage' important concerns.

While Soviet policy in the Pacific and north east Asia has lacked a focal point, Soviet commitment to the region is very real, and thus Japan has held a relatively high ranking in Soviet eyes through the 1970s and 1980s, even if in some circumstances this was somewhat lower than European nations. If the Soviets become less decisively Euro-centric that importance is likely to be assured. As much as any other factor it was the increased Soviet attention to East Asia and the Pacific in the 1960s and through the 1970s that of itself could be said to have encouraged the Soviets to come to terms with Japan. While, as has been demonstrated, there may be shortcomings to the Soviet approach, the Soviets have nevertheless increasingly tried to do just that.

THE SOVIET–JAPANESE FISHERIES QUESTION

In terms of the approaches taken to this work it is difficult to find a clear category in which to deal with Soviet–Japanese fishing. It is not a military question and does not fit neatly under the heading of trade and economic relations. For these reasons it has been decided to include a discussion of the fishery question in an appendix.

The Soviets and Japanese have been in dispute over fishing rights for a number of years. Within our time-frame the crucial years are the late 1970s, and in particular 1977, which we shall argue was a turning point in relations over fishing matters.

The conventional wisdom over the wide issue of Soviet–Japanese fishing disputes has been that the Soviets make 'tough demands' on the Japanese; that they arrest large numbers of Japanese boats; that they have single-mindedly sought to drive the Japanese from the fishing grounds of the north west Pacific; and that the effect of these measures has been to reduce Japanese revenue from fishing and cause significant unemployment in the Japanese fishing industry.[1] It is this author's contention that in those cases where evidence is available some of these claims cannot be substantiated. The Soviet Union and Japan are the world's two largest catchers of fish. Both therefore have much at stake and much to lose where fishing is concerned. For both the period 1976–7, which saw the widespread introduction of 200-mile economic exclusion zones at sea, was a turning point.

On 13 December 1976 the EEC 'bluntly' informed the Soviets that from January to March 1977 they would only be allowed to take 40% of their previous year's catch in EEC waters, and that should the Soviet Union accept reciprocal rights, i.e. allow the EEC to fish in the Soviet 200-mile zone, it would be allowed to catch only 60,000 tons that year (1977). The EEC established its 200-mile zone from 1 January 1977.[2] The widespread assertion of exclusive economic zones was not an advantage to the Soviet Union, which does most of its fishing in foreign waters; however, 'negotiated' rights allowed the Soviets to

192

take fish in EEC waters surplus to the capacity of the coastal states of the EEC. A Soviet agreement with Canada (May 1976) gave them access to the Canadian zone, but the Canadians reserved the right unilaterally to determine the permitted quotas and species that the Soviets could fish.

The Soviets announced on 10 December 1976 their intention to establish their own 200-mile zone, and on 24 February 1977 declared that it would come into effect on 1 March 1977. Despite worldwide action by states in the preceding year to establish such zones, Japan still greeted the Soviet announcement with 'amazement' and 'shock'. This was a strange response seeing that in January the LDP had already launched two bills in the Japanese Diet extending Japan's own territorial waters.

The point is that although attention has been drawn to the Soviet–Japanese case due to their geographical proximity and the complications that stem therefrom, other nations also inflicted 'tough demands' on Japan and on the Soviet Union. Japanese catches in American and Canadian waters were in 1975–6 three times larger than their catch in Soviet waters, and both the United States and Canada took strong measures to limit Japanese (and Soviet) catches. In 1981 the United States enacted the Blow Act, which contained a clause aimed at phasing-out the operation of non-American fishing vessels in the 200-mile zone and also included a provision to make drastic increases in the fishing fee. From 1979 to 1981 the fee charged by the United States for fishing in its waters more than doubled. The Japanese catch in United States' waters in 1979 totalled 1,090,000 tons which 'constituted the greater part of Japanese pelagic fishing operations'.[3]

Salmon fisheries have been a preoccupation of Soviet–Japanese negotiations due to the importance of salmon and to the need to preserve stocks; however the publicity given to this aspect of Japanese fishing has obscured the fact that most of Japanese salmon fishing takes place in the Northern Pacific, off the mouths of rivers in the United States and Canada. A Japanese journalist writing on this situation commented that

> In fact, during recent fishery negotiations with the United States and Canada, Japan was compelled to accept considerable restrictions on salmon fishing, both in and outside the 200 mile limit. At the same time, this country supported the principle, now internationally recognised, that salmon, an anadromous fish, belongs to those countries whose rivers they ascend to spawn. What this means is the Japanese can hardly fish for salmon in the Northern Pacific, even on the high seas, without the consent of the United States, Canada or Russia.[4]

In 1981 the Japanese catch quota for salmon in the Northern Pacific was set by the United States at 42,500 tons but the fee was raised: the salmon catch quota set by the Soviets in 1980 was 42,500 tons, and was subsequently maintained at that level for 1981 and 1982.[5] The amount of the Soviet fee is unknown.

Accusations against the Soviet Union of undue harassment or arrest of Japanese fishing boats are not borne out by the available statistics. By 1983 Japanese sources were claiming that the Soviets had arrested 1,200 Japanese fishing vessels and 8,500 crew since 1945.[6] In the first nine months of 1976 twenty-seven Japanese boats were arrested (in the same period of 1975 the figure was sixteen).[7] In comparison with the number of arrests made in national waters of EEC countries, an average figure of thirty Japanese vessels arrested annually in Soviet waters is not abnormal. In fact, given the *total* number of Japanese vessels authorised to operate in Soviet waters, the figure is negligible. Soviet figures detail that between 4,000 and 5,600 Japanese vessels are authorised to fish in Soviet waters annually.[8] The overwhelming majority (as is detailed below) of the Japanese fishing fleet is coastal – the main Japanese fishing vessel is a small boat crewed by three to five people – and it is for the most part these very small, coastal boats which have been arrested for fishing in the disputed waters around the Kurils.

Assertions in Japan that the reduction in fishery quotas has caused retrenchment in the fishing industry receive only qualified support from statements by the Japanese Ministry of Agriculture and Fisheries. On fishery production in the late 1970s it has this to say: 'Largely because of the restrictions imposed in the 200 mile fishery waters of the US, the Soviet Union and other countries, deepwater catches for Japan in 1977 decreased, while offshore and coastal catches increased. Overall, therefore Japan was able to maintain fishery production.'[9] While on the numbers of persons employed in the industry they stated the following: 'The number of persons displaced by reductions in the number of fishing vessels authorised to operate in the North Pacific ocean is estimated at 7,600. Subsequently, however more than 50% of them appear to have found jobs, but only about 20% of them are believed to be in secure jobs.'[10]

This does not tell the full story. The statistics must be qualified further by detailing certain peculiar structural characteristics of the Japanese fishing industry. In 1979 the industry employed 470,000 workers, of which a figure of 3,800 made unemployed represents slightly over 0.8% of the workforce. Of this total number employed, 360,000 were involved in coastal fishery (of the 210,000 fishery firms in Japan, 95% are engaged in coastal fishing).[11] In short, the industry is

Table 27 *Japanese fisheries statistics*

Production by type of fishery (thousand tons)			
	1975	1978	1979
Total production	10,545	10,888	10,590
Coastal	2,208	2,907	2,836
Offshore	4,468	5,559	5,488
Deepsea	3,168	2,134	2,035

Source: Japan Institute for International Affairs, *White Papers of Japan 1980–81*, (Tokyo, 1982), p. 135. The Ministry of Fisheries estimated the levels of the 1980 catches to be similar.

Size of Japanese fishing fleet	
1975	390,480 vessels
1979	423,820 vessels
1980	428,207 vessels
1981	424,207 vessels

Numbers of workers in fisheries (1,000s)			
	Total	Coastal fishing	Others
1975	369.5	–	–
1979	467.8	364.0	103.8
1980	457.4	359.6	97.8
1981	449.0	354.1	94.9

Dashes indicate information not available
Source: Japan Institute of International Affairs, *White Papers of Japan 1982–83*, (Tokyo, 1984), pp. 162–3. From this it can be seen that even the total losses of the offshore deepsea fleet in numbers of workers is nearly a match for those of the coastal fleet workforce. Consequently the proportional losses are much higher for the offshore workforce.

configured around an old-fashioned, labour intensive, coastal fishing fleet of very small boats. These boats are least affected by the introduction of 200-mile zones as it is the more modern and larger units which participate in the offshore and deepwater fishing, and which take 70% of the total Japanese catch. (See table 27.)

Hence it is the workers associated with these deepsea zonal catches who are hardest hit:

> The number of workers employed in coastal fishing stood at 360,000 and the rate of decrease was smaller than the former average. However, the number of these employed by deepwater fishing operators – large, medium and small-scale operators alike –

decreased 3.8% below the preceding year to 99,000 owing to the
reduced number of fishery vessels in the North Pacific.[12]

but the report continues to say that

> More than 80% of those employed in fishing are men and the number
> of younger men has been decreasing with the years, thereby increas-
> ing the ratio of older men.[13]

It is clear, then, that at least part of the reduction in workforce of the
fishing industry can be explained by what is in effect 'natural wastage'
and voluntary displacement on the part of younger men seeking better
employment.

It remains to ask whether the Soviets have utilised the fishing
question with Japan as a political issue. The idea that the Soviets have
used it as such, or as a tool of leverage against the Japanese, has
stemmed mostly from the impression created by the very acrimonious
1977 negotiations. However these negotiations were somewhat
unusual as the introduction of the 200-mile zones made new catch
quotas difficult to determine. These negotiations are therefore atypi-
cal, but the image of Soviet–Japanese discontent has remained,
although evidence of subsequent years shows that this is really a false
image.

The Soviets and Japanese also reach yearly agreement on whaling in
the Northern Pacific. Little is heard of this aspect of Soviet–Japanese
relations simply because negotiations have presented no particular
difficulty. The original agreement was signed in 1972 and is now
extended each year by the exchange of diplomatic notes. Fishing
negotiations are more complicated. It is not merely a matter of
establishing an overall quota and one price. Different quotas have to
be agreed upon for different species of fish, types of fish allowed to be
caught have to be agreed upon, the number of boats to be licensed
decided on, the amount of compensation fees assessed and the dates
of the season must be fixed. Also other questions such as co-operation
on preservation of stocks and exchange of scientific data and proposals
for joint private fishing must be settled.

In interviews with the author, one Japanese academic expressed the
opinion that the fisheries question was a 'non-issue'.[14] The most
obvious evidence in support of his contention can be seen from the fact
that while in 1977 fishing negotiations took ninety days, by 1978 this
had been reduced to sixty-five by 1979 it was down to nineteen and by
1980 to sixteen days, and throughout subsequent negotiations after
1977 none of the serious conflict that plagued those negotiations was
to occur again. In fact the fisheries question, if anything, far from

becoming a political issue, took the form of a straight business transaction. Jain also suggests as much by stating that by 1979 'the Soviets had decided the Japanese quota on the basis of the size of the fishing co-operative fee that the Japanese were willing to pay'.[15] Shkolnikova, in the work cited above, quotes the *Mainichi Shimbun* as saying 'There is perhaps, no other example of more stable fishing relations than those between Japan and the Soviet Union since fishing entered the era of the 200 mile zone.'[16]

Progress in this field is such that the Soviets and Japanese have established a bilateral fisheries commission which examines questions of cooperation in coastal fishing and the joint study of raw material resources in the northwest Pacific. The third, and most recent, session of the commission, which ended on 11 December 1986, determined the upcoming 1987 quotas as a matter of course. Minor frictions have inevitably arisen, most notably in 1986–7, when in response to continual licence infractions by Japanese boats it is reported the Soviets reduced the number of licences for the upcoming year.

This policy has effectively insulated the fishing question from politics. The negotiations have continued, unaffected, through the troubles over the China treat of 1978, and the sanctions over Afghanistan and over Poland and during the deterioration in relations caused by the ramifications of the Toshiba scandal and mutual espionage expulsions. Aspects of them have been used by the Soviets as signals to Japan. In some cases this has been of a positive nature, e.g. releasing arrested crews or reducing fines on Japanese boats,[17] though in a small number of cases the Soviets have used them to show displeasure, as for example in 1978. Japanese businessmen are of the opinion that the Soviet cancellation of the private joint venture (the actual overall negotiations were never threatened at any time) plans for fishing in the end of the 1978 season was a retaliation for the signing of the treaty with China.[18] In recent years the Soviets have been reviving an old proposal to allow their fishing vessels rights to call in to Japanese ports. The Japanese have resisted the idea and to date the Soviets have not pressed the issue.[19] Those issues apart the Soviets have made no attempt to link the fisheries negotiations to political events, nor used them as a means of leverage against the Japanese.

AREA AND POPULATION OF THE SOVIET FAR EAST

Administrative unit (Administrative Centre)	Area (in thousands of square miles)	Population 1985 (in thousands)
Kamchatka District, including Koryak National Area (Petropavlovsk-Kamchatskii)	182.4	435
Magadan District, including Chukchi National Area (Magadan)	463	542
Amur District (Blagoveshchensk)	140.4	1,041
Sakhalin District (Yuzhno-Sakhalinsk)	33.6	700
Maritime Territory (Vladivostok)	64	2,164
Khabarovsk Territory, including Jewish Autonomous District (Khabarovsk)	318.4	1,760
Yakutia (Yakutsk)	1,198.2	1,009
Total	2,400	7,651

Cities of the Soviet Far East (Population figures, as of 1984)

Vladivostok	559,500
Khabarovsk	568,000
Nakhodka	172,300
Birobidzhan	76,800
Blagoveshchensk	195,200
Komsomolsk-na-Amure	291,400
Magadan	150,800
Petropavlovsk-Kamchatskii	252,400
Yakutsk	203,000
Yuzho-Sakhalinsk	163,700

Sources: E. B. Kovrigin, 'The Soviet Far East', in J.J. Stephan and V.P. Chichkanov (eds.), Soviet–American Horizons on the Pacific, (Honolulu, University of Hawaii Press, 1986), pp. 1–16. See p. 3. V. G. Smoliak, 'Cities of the Soviet Far East', in Ibid, pp. 165–72. Tsentra'lnoe Statisticheskie Upravlenie SSR, Narodnoe Khoziaistvo SSSR v 1985g. (Moscow, 'Finansi i Statistika', 1986), pp. 11–17.

NOTES

PREFACE

1 For an indication of these trends in the literature see for example, K. Ogawa, 'Japanese–Soviet Economic Relations: Present Status and Future Prospects', in *Journal of Northeast Asian Studies*, 2:1 ((March 1983). D. Rees, 'Gorshkov's Strategy in the Far East', in *Pacific Community* (January 1978), 143–55. T. Robinson, 'Soviet Policy in East Asia', in *Problems of Communism*, 22 (November–December 1973), 32–50. The compilation of chapters in D. Zagoria (ed.), *Soviet Policy in East Asia* (New Haven, Council on Foreign Relations Inc., Yale University Press, 1982). S. Kirby, 'Siberia: Heartland and Framework', in *Asian Perspectives* 9:2, (Fall–Winter 1985) 274–94.

2 T. Robinson, 'Soviet Policy in East Asia', in *Problems of Communism*, 22 (November–December 1973); G. J. Sigur and Y. Kim (eds.), *Japanese and US Policy in Asia*, (New York, Praeger, 1982). A. S. Whiting, *Siberian Development and East Asia: Threat or Promise?* (Stanford, Stanford University Press, 1981).

3 See for example, D. Rees, 'Japan's Northern Territories', in *Asia Pacific Community* No. 7, (Winter 1980) 13–42. F. Langdon, 'Japanese–Soviet 200 mile Zone Confrontation', in *Pacific Community* (October 1977), 46–58. M. Leighton, 'Soviet Strategy Towards Northern Europe and Japan', in *Survey*, 27:118/119, (Autumn/Winter 1983) 112–51.

INTRODUCTION

1 B. Jelavich, *A Century of Russian Foreign Policy 1814–1914* (New York, Lippincott Co., 1964), p. 236.

2 See, for example, Iu. Kuznetsov, 'Kuda Tolkaiut Iaponiiu?' (Where is Japan Heading?), in *Kommunist*, 4 (March 1983), 98–109. V. Bunin, 'Nakasone's Military Policy' in *Far Eastern Affairs*, 2 (1984), 64–74.

3 Soviet ambassador Troyanovsky to Admiral Kato, 9 June 1932. As quoted in *Soviet Foreign Policy*, (Moscow, Progress Publishers, 1980), Vol. I, 1917–1945, p. 274.

4 Lt Gen. M. M. Kir'ian, 'Pobeda Na Dal'nem Vostoke' (Victory in the Far East), in *Voprosy Istorii*, 8 (1985) 21–34. Quotation p. 23.

5 See, G. Lensen, *The Russian Push Towards Japan* (Princeton, Princeton University Press, 1959), p. 466, and B. Jelavich, *A Century of Russian Foreign Policy 1814–1914* (New York, Lippincott Co., 1984), p. 236. For a collection

of essays on various historical Russian views of Japan and the East see, I. J. Lederer, *Russian Foreign Policy: Essays in Historical Perspective* (New Haven, Yale University Press, 1962).

6 In recent times the Far East's imports were more than twice the value of its exports. See, *Narodnoe Khoziaistvo SSSR v 1967g*, (Moscow, Izdatel'stvo 'Finansi i Statistika', 1968). In the 1930s there was a rough balance between the Far East's exports and imports but the situation had been much worse in earlier years. One Soviet writer based at the Institute of Economic Research in Khabarovsk has commented that 'The Far East had a chronic deficit in its foreign trade balance in the sixty years before 1917. From 1906 to 1915, imports exceeded exports from three to nineteen times. Exports accounted for 45 percent of total trade in 1905 but dropped to only 5 percent in 1915.' See N. L. Shlyk, 'The Soviet Far East and the International Economy' in J. J. Stephan and V. P. Chichkanov (eds.), *Soviet–American Horizons on The Pacific* (Honolulu, University of Hawaii Press, 1986), pp. 114–25. Quotation p. 115. See also the information presented by Shlyk in table 1. A major historical influence on the economic development of the Soviet Far East has been the levels of trade with adjacent territories, mainly China and Japan. They are important today in terms of future prospects for development; in the 1920s, for example, China and Japan were the Far East's main trading partners. See, Shlyk, 'The Soviet Far East and the International Economy' in Stephan and Chichkanov (eds.), *Soviet–American Horizons*, p. 117. For evidence of the scale of earlier economic co-operation see, B. N. Slavinskii, 'Russia and the Pacific to 1917' in Stephan and Chichkanov (eds.), *Soviet–American Horizons*, pp. 32–49. Also, P. Gatrell, *The Tsarist Economy* (London, Batsford, 1986).

7 J. J. Stephan, 'The USSR and The Defeat of Imperial Japan 1945', in *Soviet Studies in History*, 24:3 (Winter 1985/6), 4–5.

8 Kir'ian, *Voprosy Istorii*, 8 (1985), 23. See also, General of the Army, Professor S. P. Ivanov, 'Krakh Kvantunskoi Armii' (The Fall of the Kwantung Army), in *Novaia i Noveishaia Istoriia*, 5 (1985), 79–97.

1 SOVIET IDEOLOGY AND JAPAN

1 For example see, L. Labedz, 'Ideology and Soviet Foreign Policy' in *Prospects of Soviet Power in the 1980s*, Adelphi Paper 151 (London, International Institute for Strategic Studies, 1979), Part I, pp. 37–45. Also, V. V. Aspaturian, *Process and Power in Soviet Foreign Policy* (Boston, Little, Brown and Co., 1971), chapter 10.

2 L. Maksudov, *Ideological Struggle Today* (Moscow, Progress Publishers, 1983), p. 19.

3 *Current Digest of the Soviet Press*, 28:8, pp. 8, 13. Hereafter abbreviated to *CDSP*.

4 G. Shakhnazarov, 'Effective Factors of International Relations', in *International Affairs* (Moscow), (February 1977), 84–5.

5 A. Sergiyev, 'Leninism on the Correlation of Forces as a Factor of International Relations', in *International Affairs* (Moscow), (May 1975), 99–107. Quotations pp. 99, 100, 101, 103.

6 *Ibid.*, p. 79.
7 V. Nekrasov, 'Absurd but Dangerous Myth', in *Kommunist*, 12 (1979), 91–201. Quotation p. 104. Joint Publications Research Service (JPRS) (Arlington, Virgina) translation.
8 V. Kulish, 'Detente, International Relations and Military Might', in *Coexistence*, 4:2 (1976), 175–95.
9 Sergiyev, *International Affairs* (Moscow), (May 1975), 103, 101.
10 For a Marxist appraisal of Japan by a native English speaking scholar see, R. Steven, *Classes in Contemporary Japan* (Cambridge, Cambridge University Press, 1983). This is a very thorough work which deals with a class analysis of Japan and is replete with numerous tables on a wide range of subjects from for example, patterns of shareholding in companies to levels of employment to appraisals of class consciousness by workers.
11 As quoted in J. Lenczowski, *Soviet Perceptions of U.S. Foreign Policy* (Ithaca, Cornell University Press, 1982), p. 112.
12 Y. Pevzner, 'Uneven development of Capitalism' in V. Tsygankov (ed.), *Present Day Japan*, Oriental Studies in the USSR No. 7, (Moscow, USSR Academy of Sciences, 1983), pp. 41–66. Quotation p. 47.
13 M. Maksimova, 'Kapitalisticheskaia Integratsiia i Mirovoe Razvitie' (Capitalist Integration and World Development), in *Mirovaia Ekonomika i Mezhdunarodnie Otnoshenia* 4 (1978), 14–24. Quotation p. 17. Hereafter cited as *MEMO*.
14 *Ibid.*, p. 23.
15 R. Aliev, 'Iaponiia i Zapadnaia Evropa: Partnerstvo i Sopernichestvo' (Japan and Western Europe: Partnership and Rivalry), in *MEMO*, 9 (1981), 69–80. Quotation p. 71.
16 Yu. Stolyarov, 'Japan's Monetary Ambitions', in *Far Eastern Affairs*, 3 (1981), 65–75.
17 See, Y. Kovrigin, 'Japanese Economic "Aid" to Developing Countries', in *Far Eastern Affairs*, 1 (1982), 63–75. Kovrigin argues that these percentages are all much higher than the respective figures for the EEC and the United States.
18 *Ibid.*, p. 64.
19 This is also an opinion expressed by The Oriental Economist, *Japan Economic Yearbook 1980/81* (Hong Kong), p. 56. 'Despite these improvements Japanese economic assistances are widely believed to be far from satisfactory.'
20 I. V. Volkova, *Iaponiia i Afrika*, ('Mysl', Izdatel'stvo, Moscow, 1981).
21 S. Ignatushchenko, 'Economic Relations with Developing Countries' in V. Tsygankov (ed.), *Present Day Japan*, Oriental Studies in the USSR No. 7, (Moscow, USSR Academy of Sciences, 1983), pp. 85–100. Quotation p. 92.
22 Iu. Bandura, 'The Pacific Community – Brainchild of Imperialist Diplomacy', in *International Affairs* (Moscow), (June 1980), 63–70. Quotation p. 65.
23 R. Aliev, 'Politika Tokio v Aziatsko–Tikhookeanskom regione' (Tokyo politics in the Asia–Pacific region), in *MEMO*, 9 (1980), 25–36. Quotation p. 25.

24 See, F. Anin, 'ASEAN in the focus of Japanese diplomacy', in *International Affairs* (Moscow), (March 1982), 41–45.
25 *Ibid.*, p. 42.
26 See, N. N. Mil'gram, 'Militarizm v Iaponii' (Militarism in Japan), in *Narodi Azii i Afriki*, 3 (1972). Also *Iaponskii Militarizm – Voenno–Istoricheskoe Issledovanie* (Japanese Militarism – A Military–History Study), (Moscow, Izdatel'stvo, 'Nauka', 1972). Both these studies are historically based with little else in the way of content except prediction based on past events. As such they are fairly typical of the very few commentaries on Japanese militarism of the early 1970s. For a change in style and for a linking of Japanese militarism to more contemporary politics see, for example, M. Ukraintsev, 'Krakh Militariskoi Iaponii' (The Fall of Militarist Japan), in *Kommunist*, 13 (1975), 110–17. This is an historical feature which reviews the past (written on the thirtieth anniversary of the defeat of Japan) but ties in references to Chinese prompting behind contemporary Japanese military expansion. M. Ukraintsev is a pseudonym for M. S. Kapitsa, leading sinologist, formerly a Deputy Foreign Minister of the Soviet Union, and recently appointed Director of the Institute for Oriental Studies in Moscow.
27 D. Petrov, 'Militarism in Japan imperils peace in Asia' in Tsygankov (ed.), *Present Day Japan*, pp. 67–84. Quotation p. 67.
28 I. Latyshev, 'New Foreign Policy Concepts of the Japanese Ruling Circles', in *Asia Quarterly* (Brussels), 4 (1971), 359–71. Quotation p. 359.
29 *Ibid.*, pp. 361–2.
30 Quoted in S. Zinchuk, 'The Threat to Peace in the Pacific', in *New Times* (Moscow), 25 (1984), 18.
31 *Bolshaia Sovetskaia Entsiklopedia*, 3rd edn, Moscow p. 523.
32 I. Kovalenko, *Soviet Policy for Asian Peace and Security* (Moscow, Progress Publishers, 1979), p. 214. This is an English language edition of the earlier 1976 Russian version. Changes were made in the text for the English edition in line with new emphases of Soviet policy. This might be of interest as Kovalenko is one of the few key specialists on Japan.
33 'The 26th Congress of the CPSU and the Soviet Union's Struggle for Peace and Security in Asia', in *Far Eastern Affairs*, 3 (1981), 3–15. Quotation p. 9.
34 N. Kapchenko, 'Scientific Principles of Soviet Foreign Policy', in *International Affairs* (Moscow), 10 (1977), 81–91. Quotation p. 83.
35 Latyshev, *Asia Quarterly* (Brussels), 4, (1971) p. 361, pp. 370–1.
36 A. Makarov, 'Financial and Monopoly Capital and Japan's Political Mechanism', in *Far Eastern Affairs*, 3 (1982), 83–91.
37 While a large number of Soviet sources have been examined it has not been possible to examine every single major Soviet source, thus the author adds the reservation that judgement here is not definitive. The question of *amakudari* arose in conversation with J. A. A. Stockwin, who suggested that the Soviets might be hesitant to comment on it because it could be viewed as running counter to economic determinism.
38 A. Orefemov, 'Labour and Capital in Japan', in *Far Eastern Affairs*, 1 (1982), 98–105. Quotation p. 105.
39 Prof. B. Pospelov, 'Nationalism in the Service of Anti-communism' in Tsygankov (ed.), *Present Day Japan*, pp. 123–141. Quotation p. 127.

40 I. Tamghinsky, 'Japan in the Vice of Contradictions', in *Far Eastern Affairs*, 4 (1980), 105–17. Quotation p. 105.
41 Pospelov, 'Nationalism in the Service of Anti-communism' in Tsygankov (ed.), *Present Day Japan*, p. 126.
42 Kuznetsov, *Kommunist*, 4 (1983), 98–109. Quotation p. 98.
43 *Ibid.*, p. 99.
44 Iu. Stolyarov, 'A Skidding Locomotive', in *New Times*, 39 (1983), 24–6. Quotation p. 24.
45 For an account of the reasons for the split and the resultant mainstream JCP swing towards China, see, R. Swearingen, *The Soviet Union and Post–war Japan* (Stanford, California Hoover Institution Press, 1978), pp. 108–14.
46 L. Mlechin, 'The Japanse Communist Congress', in *New Times*, 10 (1980), 7.
47 I. Kovalenko, 'The Fight of the Communist Party of Japan Against Peking's Great Power Influence', in *Far Eastern Affairs*, 1 (1981), 14–27. Quotation p. 26.
48 I. Tamghinsky, 'Japan in the Vice of Contradictions', in *Far Eastern Affairs*, 1 (1980), 110.
49 N. Vladimirov, 'Japan Faces the 1980s', in *Far Eastern Affairs*, 1 (1980), 26–36. Quotation p. 29.
50 V. Khlynov, 'Japan's Growing Internal Political Struggle in the 1970s', in *Far Eastern Affairs*, 4 (1979), 119–32. Quotation p. 122.
51 See, Iu. Barsukov, 'Grazhdanskie Dvizhenie v Iaponii' (The People's Movement in Japan), in *MEMO*, 3 (1977), 56–63. These comments by Barsukov are echoed by the more recent writings of Kuznetsov and Tamghinsky. See below.
52 Kuznetsov, *Kommunist*, 4 (1983), 104. See also, I. Tamghinsky, 'The Women's Movement in Japan', in *Far Eastern Affairs*, 4 (1982), 55–66. Quotation p. 63.
53 It is not the author's intention here to suggest that moves to modify the constitution are merely a 'recent' phenomenon. It is a phenomenon which has recurred since its high point in the 1950s to the present day, thus it has been a target for Soviet criticism for thirty years.
54 Iu. Barsukov, 'Iaponiia i Latinskaia Amerika' (Japan and Latin America), in *MEMO*, 7 (1975), 116–19.
55 See, R. Judson Mitchell, *Ideology of a Superpower* (Stanford, California, Hoover Press, 1982). Also, T. Gustafson, *Reform in Soviet Politics* (New York, Cornell University Press, 1981).
56 G. Marchuk, 'Components of Scientific progress', in *Kommunist*, 13 (1978), 43–53, JPRS translation.
57 A. Ulyanov, 'Iaponskii Proletariat i Tekhnicheskii Progress' (The Japanese Proletariat and Technical Progress), in *MEMO*, 9 (1978), 149–50.
58 See, S. Ul'ianichev, 'Skol'ko v Iaponii Bezrabotnikh?' (How Many Unemployed Are There in Japan?') in *MEMO*, 12 (1983), 114–20.
59 See, Iu. Stolyarov and S. Ulianichev, 'Nauchno – Tekhnicheskaia Strategia Iaponii' (Japan's Scientific and Technical Strategy), in *MEMO*, 6 (1983), 48–58; V. Zaitsev, 'Japan's S and T Policy: Change of Priorities', in *MEMO*, 1 (1987), 40–51. (Foreign Broadcast Information Service (*FBIS*) translation.)
60 R. Laird, and E. P. Hoffman, 'The STR and Developed Socialism and Soviet

International Behaviour' in E. P. Hoffman and F. J. Fleron (eds.), *The Conduct of Soviet Foreign Policy* (New York, Hawthorne, 1980), pp. 386–405. Quotation p. 389.

61 B. Parrott, *Politics and Technology in the Soviet Union* (Cambridge, Mass., MIT Press, 1983), p. 6.

62 For the primacy of the military sector in budget allocations see, for example, G. W. Breslauer, *Khrushchev and Brezhnev as Leaders: Building Authority in Soviet Politics* (London, Allen and Unwin, 1982). Also, H. Gelman, *The Brezhnev Politburo and the Decline of Detente* (New York, Cornell University Press, 1984), chapter 3 and pp. 178–81.

63 Parrott, *Politics and Technology*, p. 260.

64 Press Office of the USSR Embassy, 'Mikhail Gorbachev's Stay in Dnepropetrovsk', *Soviet News Bulletin*, Soviet Embassy, Canberra.

65 V. V. Aspaturian, 'Soviet Global Power and the Correlation of Forces', in *Problems of Communism* (May–June 1980), 1–18. Quotation p. 9. The only clear 'definition' of the 'correlation of forces' is contained in, Ministerstvo Oboroni SSSR, *Sovetskaia Voennaia Entsiklopedia* (Soviet Military Encyclopedia), (Moscow, Izdatel'stvo, 'Voennoe', 1979), vol. VII, p. 445. This is a definition of the term as used in a purely military context.

66 It is accepted that there is superpower parity at the strategic nuclear level. In terms of theatre nuclear forces, especially in Europe, the Soviets are thought to have the edge. At a conventional level Soviet land forces in Europe are at least on a par with NATO forces (though many commentators argue they are the stronger) and in the Far East are probably superior to Chinese forces. The overall naval balance favours strongly the NATO powers, Japan and China. However the large number of Soviet submarines are a source of serious concern to NATO planners. While the Soviets have built up a power projection capability it is limited and still surpassed by the capabilities of the United States alone, not including the capabilities of other US allies.

67 As quoted in H. Adomeit, 'Capitalist contradictions and Soviet policy', in *Problems of Communism* 33 (May–June 1984), 7–18.

68 See, A. Utkin, 'Atlantizm' i Iaponiia' (Atlanticism and Japan), in *MEMO*, 6 (1976), 56–63 and Maksimova, *MEMO*, 4 (1978). For sources which stress division more see, Maksudov, *Ideological Struggle*, and Sergiyev, *International Affairs* (Moscow), (May 1975).

69 S. Ignatushchenko, 'Economic Relations with Developing Countries', in V. Tsygankov (ed.), *Present Day Japan*, Oriental Studies in the USSR No. 7, (Moscow, USSR Academy of Sciences, 1983), p. 87. Mineral fuels constituted 41.2% of the total import bill of Japan in 1979, an increase of 50% over 1978 although the actual quantity imported had increased by only 5.8%. See, The Oriental Economist, *Japan Economic Yearbook 1980/81*, (Hong Kong) pp. 36–8.

70 *Ibid.*, p. 58.

71 *Ibid.*, pp. 58–9.

72 K. Brutents, 'The Soviet Union and the Newly Industrialised Countries', in *International Affairs* (Moscow), 4 (1979), 3–14. Quotation p. 4.

73 As quoted in A. Sergiyev, 'Bourgeois Theories of Interdependence Serves

Neocolonialism', in *International Affairs* (Moscow), 11 (1976), 103–11. Quotation p. 110.

74 'Statement by Head of the USSR Delegation to 4th UNCTAD Session' in *Foreign Trade* (Moscow), 7 (1976), pp. 2–9. Quotation p. 9.

75 Bandura, 'The Sino-Japanese Alliance runs Counter to Peace Interests', *International Affairs* (Moscow), (August 1979), p. 69.

76 See *Soviet News*, 4 April 1978. (London, Press department of the Soviet Embassy.)

77 Latyshev, *Asia Quarterly* (Brussels), 4 (1971), p. 369.

78 See, R. Swearingen, *The Soviet Union and Post-War Japan*, pp. 76–9 for an examination of the San Francisco conference and Soviet terms.

79 For purposes of comparison, Soviet attacks on rumours of Japan acquiring a nuclear capability are of interest. In this case, presumably also acquiring nuclear weapons would be a contravention of Article 9; however this point is not the main pillar of Soviet argument, though it is used. The Soviets stress that it would be a violation of the self-declared three non-nuclear principles but more importantly that it would be violating the non-proliferation treaty which Japan signed in 1970 and ratified in 1976. 'Violation of the Constitution' is an argument seldom used seriously against the Japanese when nuclear matters are discussed. See, for example, *Pravda*, 31 March 1978. Also 'Japan Playing With Fire Over Nuclear Weapons' in *Soviet News*, 4 April 1978; I. Ivkov, *Japan: Heading For Militarisation* (Moscow, Novosti Press Agency, 1979).

80 I. Tamghinsky, 'Japan in the Vice of Contradictions', in *Far Eastern Affairs*, 4 (1980), 105–17. Quotation p. 117.

81 State Statistical Bureau, People's Republic of China, *Statistical Yearbook of China 1984*, (Hong Kong, Economic Information and Agency, 1984), p. 84. See appendix 2 for further details on Soviet population figures for 1983–6.

82 Interview with V. Khlynov at IMEMO, Moscow, September 1984.

83 *CDSP*, 34:12 (1982), 6.

84 See, for an emphasis of the Japan approaches, L. I. Brezhnev, 'Iaponskim Pisateliam – Avtoram Obrashcheniia s Prizivom Protive Iadernoi Voini' (To the Japanese Writers – Authors of a Letter Protesting Against Nuclear War), in *Kommunist*, 4 (March 1982), 20–1. He says, 'Apart from this the Soviet Union is prepared to conclude a special agreement with non-nuclear states. We see no obstacle to opening these discussions with Japan based on the proposals made at the 26th congress of the CPSU for establishing CBMs in the Far East, or on the basis of some other scheme acceptable to both parties.' (p. 21).

85 *FBIS: USSR Daily report*, 19 April 1983, p. 1.

86 I. I. Ivkov, (pseudonym of Kovalenko) 'The Lockheed Shadow over Japan', in *New Times*, 31 (1976), 24–5. Quotation p. 24. See also, S. Levchenko, 'Pre-election Scene', in *New Times*, 28 (1977), 22–3. He suggests that due to an ailing economy the monopolies have been forced to take reductions in their 'superprofits' and to have been reducing sharply their contributions to the LDP.

87 I. Kovalenko, 'The Struggle of the JCP for Democratic Reforms', in *Far Eastern Affairs* 2 (1980), 52–71. Quotation p. 62.

88 See, R. Godson and R. Schultz, *Dezinformatsia: Active Measures in Soviet Strategy* (New York, Pergamon, 1984). Quotation p. 178. For a far longer description of Levchenko's activities in Japan see, J. Barron, *KGB Today* (London, Coronet, 1985).

89 Lt Belenko defected with his Mig-25 jet in 1976. The Soviets demanded the aircraft's immediate return. However it was not handed back until American and Japanese experts had had the opportunity to examine it. The choice here of the term 'lobby' is one which the author is somewhat unhappy with. It is an unsatisfactory term in itself and in a political context it is always difficult to gauge the extent of any such group, its influence or its motivations. In the examples of the Mig-25 and Afghanistan incidents the interested parties may have been constituted by different individuals in each case. The Afghanistan affair and sanctions clearly has more of a business aspect to it. The members of any 'lobby' might presumably be mainly comprised of those Japanese 'associated' with Soviets, either indirectly through membership of organisations such as the USSR–Japan Friendship Society, or of those directly involved with Soviets such as Levchenko (e.g. socialist politician Shigeru Ito, ex-Minister Hirohide Ishiden, Takuji Yamane, editor in chief of the newspaper *Sankei*), and those who thought Japan had anything particular to gain from placating the Soviets. It would be overstating the case however, to suggest that the 'lobby' is a fixed feature of Japanese politics or that any members are/were prepared to 'go into bat' for the Soviet side on any or all occasions. Motivations are far more complex and the association of any such group relatively loose. Qualifying influence with any certainty is also an equally elusive objective. See, L. Bittman, *The KGB and Soviet Disinformation* (London, Pergamon, 1985), pp. 21, 78.

90 See, The Oriental Economist, *Japan Economic Yearbook 1980/81*, (Hong Kong), pp. 184–5, 172–5.

91 R. Buckley, *Japan Today* (Cambridge, Cambridge University Press, 1985). Quotation p. 119.

92 *Ibid.*

93 *Ibid.*, p. 88.

94 J. Halliday, 'Capitalism and Socialism in East Asia', in *New Left Review*, 124 (November–December 1980), 3–24. Quotation pp. 13–14.

95 E. F. Vogel, *Japan as Number One* (Cambridge, Mass., Harvard University Press, 1979). Quotation p. 22.

2 SOVIET–JAPANESE ECONOMIC RELATIONS

1 V. Spandaryan, 'Soviet–Japanese Trade Relations', in *Far Eastern Affairs*, 4 (1980), 88–94. Quotation p. 88.

2 R. Jain, *The USSR and Japan 1945–80* (Brighton, UK, Harvester Press, 1981).

3 K. Ogawa, 'Japanese–Soviet Economic Relations: Present Status and Future Prospects', in *Journal of North East Asian Studies*, 2: 1 (March 1983), 3–15. Quotation p. 5.

4 V. Spandaryan, 'A New Development in Soviet–Japanese Trade', in

Foreign Trade of the USSR (Ministry of Foreign Trade, Moscow) 12 (1977), 14–19. See p. 14.

5 See, 'Agreement on the Exchange of Goods and Payments Between the USSR and Japan From the Period 1981–85', in *Foreign Trade of the USSR* (Ministry of Foreign Trade, Moscow) 11 (1981), 52–4.

6 US Congress, Office of Technology Assessment, 'Japanese–Soviet Energy Relations', in *Technology and Soviet Energy Availability* (Washington DC), (1982), 325–48.

7 A 'territorial production complex' (TPK) is a form of regional economic organisation whereby interrelated and independent activities are located together in a specific territory. Various different enterprises jointly utilise the infrastructure, available labour pool, raw materials etc. The South Yakutia complex is the latest to be so designated.

8 Figure quoted from M. Guskin and N. Singur, 'Iuzhno–Iakutskii TPK', in *Planovoe Khoziaistvo*, 1 (1983) in L. Dienes, 'The Development of Siberia: Regional Priorities and Economic Strategy', Paper presented at Centre National de la Recherche Scientifique colloquium on *La Siberie: Colonisation, Developpement et Perspectives 1582–1982*, Paris (May 1983), p. 14.

9 See, 'Big Boost to Offshore Oil Search', in *Petroleum Economist* (April 1984), 145–7.

10 See, *USSR and the Third World* (1 September–15 December 1977), 101.

11 K. Suzuki and K. Yokowo, 'Japan's Trade Mission to Moscow, February 1983: What Did it Accomplish?', in *Japanese Economic Studies*, 12:1 (Fall 1983), 54–70. Quotation pp. 59–60.

12 See, Japan–Soviet Trade Association, *Nisso Boeki Handobukku 1983* (Japan–Soviet Trade Handbook), (Tokyo, 1983), p. 243.

13 V. Alexandrov, 'Siberia and the Soviet Far East in Soviet–Japanese Economic Relations', in *Far Eastern Affairs*, 2 (1982), 21–32. Quotation p. 29.

14 Yu. Tavrovsky, 'The Millionth Container', in *New Times* (Moscow), 40 (1982), 25–6. Quotation p. 25.

15 *Ibid.*

16 Figures quoted from R. S. Mathieson, *Japan's Role in Soviet Economic Growth* (New York, Praeger, 1979), pp. 108–9.

17 'USSR Energy Targets 3 – Gas', in *Soviet Analyst*, 10: 14 (July/August 1981).

18 US Congress, Office of Technology Assessment, 'Japanese–Soviet Energy Relations', in *Technology and Soviet Energy Availability* (Washington DC), (1982), 330.

19 V. P. Gruzinov, *The USSR's Management of Foreign Trade* (New York, Sharpe Inc., 1979), pp. 10–15.

20 M. Goldman, 'Will the Soviet Union be an Autarky in 1984?', in *International Security*, 3:4 (Spring 1979), 18–20.

21 See Congressional Research Service, Library of Congress, *The German Question Forty Years After Yalta*, 20 April 1985. Quotation p. CRS–41.

22 W. Turpin, *Soviet Foreign Trade* (Mass., Lexington Books, D.C. Heath and Co., 1977).

23 H. S. Gardner, *Soviet Foreign Trade – The Decision Process* (Boston, Mass., Kluwer-Nijhoff, 1983), p. ix.

24 Turpin, *Soviet Foreign Trade*, p. 6.

25 Gruzinov, *The USSR's Management*, chapter 1.
26 M. Goldman, *The Enigma of Soviet Petroleum*, (London, Allen and Unwin, 1980), p. 88.
27 *Ibid.*, p. 92.
28 The issues of autarky and preferential trading with fellow CMEA members rather than Japan can be well illustrated by the example of the construction of merchant shipping. Given the constant Soviet demand for new merchant shipping it would have been natural to turn to one of the world's leading producers of high quality shipping, i.e. Japan, to fill orders, all the more so if this could be used as a lever to promulgate further trade links. In fact nothing of the sort took place. The only orders which the Soviets placed with Japanese yards throughout the 1970s were in 1974–5 for two small woodchip carriers (23,606 dwt). The last Soviet order prior to that had been in 1966. In terms of a comparison, Finland in 1980–4 built for the Soviets 839,171 dwt. Between 1961 and 1980 the Japanese constructed marginally more (839,362 dwt). Over the last twenty years the Greeks have built larger tonnages for the Soviet Union than have the Japanese. (Greece built 140,000 dwt in 1982–3.) The mainstay of Soviet orders went to Eastern European yards, e.g. East Germany for stern trawlers and factory ships. Figures taken from, A. Greenway, *Soviet Merchant Ships* (Hampshire, UK, Mason Publishing, 1985).
29 See, for examples, *Ekonomicheskaia Gazeta*, 4 (January 1987), 3–4. 'Draft Law on State Enterprise Association' in *Pravda*, 8 February 1987.
30 *Ekonomicheskaia Gazeta*, 3 (January 1987), 6–7. *Pravda*, 22 May 1987.
31 K. Ogawa, 'Japanese-Soviet Economic Relations: Present Status and Future Prospects', in *Journal of North East Asian Studies*, 2:1 (March 1983), 4.
32 E. Hoffman and R. F. Laird, *The Politics of Economic Modernisation in the Soviet Union* (New York, Cornell University Press, 1982), pp. 88–90.
33 *Ibid.*, p. 84.
34 G. W. Breslauer, 'Reformism, Conservatism and Leadership Authority at the 26th Party Congress' in S. Bialer and T. Gustafson (eds.), *Russia at the Crossroads – The 26th Congress of the CPSU* (London, Allen and Unwin, 1982). Quotation p. 65.
35 *Ibid.*, pp. 65, 70, 71.
36 See, G. W. Breslauer, *Khrushchev and Brezhnev*, pp. 246–50.
37 P. Volten, *Brezhnev's Peace Programme: a Study of Soviet Domestic Political Process and Power* (Boulder, Colorado, Westview, 1982), pp. 115–16.
38 J. Dornberg, in his biography *Brezhnev* (London, Andre Deutsch, 1974), p. 29, levels the same accusation, e.g. Brezhnev 'is also a salesman. In talks with German industrialists he drew enticing pictures of limitless possibilities'. But he also notes that when urged to do business with small German firms he replied 'That's OK by me but only two or three firms. I won't have the whole world coming in.'
39 V. Spandaryan, 'A New Development in Soviet–Japanese Trade', in *Foreign Trade of the USSR* (Ministry of Foreign Trade, Moscow), 12 (1977), 14–19. Quotation p. 18.
40 See the comments made by Breslauer above for example, and E. Hoffman

and R. F. Laird, *The Politics of Economic Modernisation*, chapter 6, which provides an outline of the 'modernisers' and pp. 150–6. They comment on Brezhnev's 'penchant for incremental administrative changes rather than dramatic system reforms . . . without altering the essentials of planning, pricing and incentive structures' (p. 155).

41 Quoted in D. Dyker, 'Technological Progress and the Development of Siberia and the Far East', in *Radio Free Europe – Radio Liberty Research*, RL 443/82 (5 November 1982), 2.

42 Baikal–Amur Mainline. The second trans-Siberian railway. It runs from Ust-Kut on the Lena river to Komsomol'sk on the Amur with an outlet to the Pacific, and is 3,145 kilometres long. Construction on it began in 1973 and the line was declared completed in 1985.

43 D. Dyker, 'Planning in Siberia on the Wrong Track', in *Soviet Analyst*, 9:2 (23 January 1980), 5.

44 See, N. Bratchikov and G. Yastrebtsov, 'Facing the Ocean', in *Pravda*, 6 December, 1980, p. 2. Translation in *CDSP*, 33:49 (1981), 11.

45 L. Dienes, 'The Development of the Siberian Region: Economic Profiles, Income Flows and Strategies for Growth', in *Soviet Geography*, Review and Translation (April 1982) 205–44. Quotation p. 206.

46 Interviews conducted with L. Dienes at the Slavic Research Centre. Hokkaido University, while he was in residence as visiting fellow, August 1984.

47 US Congress, Office of Technology Assessment, 'Japanese–Soviet Energy Relations', in *Technology and Soviet Energy Availability* (Washington DC), (1982), 339.

48 *Tendentsii Ekonomicheskovo Razvitiia Sibiri 1961–75 gg.* (Trends in Siberian Economic Development 1961–75) (Moscow, 1979).

49 Dienes, *Soviet Geography* (April 1982), 209.

50 L. Dienes, 'The Development of Siberia: Regional Priorities and Economic Strategy', in *La Siberie: Colonisation, Developpement et Perspectives 1582–1982*, Centre National de la Recherche Scientifique, Paris (May 1983).

51 Reports in the Soviet press on construction in Siberia are literally legion. A few illustrations which detail the construction difficulties are, N. Bratchikov and G. Yastrebstov, 'Facing the Ocean', in *Pravda*, 6 December 1980. Translated in *CDSP*, 33:49 (1981), 11. Iu. Kuzmin, 'Long Kilometres', in *Pravda*, 14 July and 16 July 1977. Translated in *CDSP*, 19:28. 'Baikal–Amur Mainline: People, Experience, Problems' in *Kommunist*, 7 (May 1977), 47–56. JPRS translation. See also, *Radio Liberty Reports*, 'Working and Living Conditions of Baikal–Amur railroad builders' *Radio Free Europe – Radio Liberty Research*, RL 256/78 (16 November 1978), and 'Imported Pipe Fails to Reach Pipeline Builders' RL 194/77 (11 August 1977).

52 Writing on the same area one analyst states that 'building costs in Yakutsk today are three times higher than elsewhere in the Soviet Union. Modern buildings must be huddled together to permit water supply and plumbing. A metre of plumbing, water pipes, gas pipes and telephone lines protected by a concrete sheath 15 foot thick, costs about 1,000 roubles.' See, N. Ushakov, 'Yakutia – Frozen gem of the USSR', in *Soviet Analyst*, 7: 25 (21 December 1979), 5–7. Quotation p. 6.

53 Dienes, *Soviet Geography* (April 1982), 225.

54 See, P. Hanson, *Trade and Technology in Soviet–Western Relations* (New York, Columbia University Press, 1981), p. 81.

55 P. Hanson, 'Backlash Against Technology Imports' in *Radio Free Europe – Radio Liberty Research*, RL 453/81 (12 November 1981).

56 Quoted in R. Byrnes (ed.) *After Brezhnev* (Bloomington, Indiana University Press, 1983), p. 102.

57 Central Intelligence Agency, Office of Soviet Analysis, *Joint Economic Committee Briefing Paper – USSR: Economic Trends and Policy Developments*, Washington D.C., 14 September 1983. pp. 2–6 and Appendix B: Selected Economic Statistics.

58 *Socialisticheskaia Industriia*, 7 June 1982, p. 2. See also, BBC, *Summary of World Broadcasts*, SU/6653/A3/3, 19 February 1981. As a cause for the delays Soviet officials cited 'extremely severe weather conditions and a breakdown of Japanese-supplied mining equipment'.

59 D. Baldwin, 'Interdependence and Power: a Conceptual Analysis', in *International Organisation*, 34:4 (Autumn 1980), 471–506. Quotation p. 475.

60 T. Gustafson, *Selling the Russians the Rope? Soviet Technology Policy and the United States' Export Controls*, (Santa Monica, California, Rand Corporation, Rand Report, R–2649–ARPA, April 1981), p. 25.

61 BBC, *Summary of World Broadcasts*, SU/6712/A3/2, 1 May 1981.

62 See P. Hanson, *Trade and Technology*. This is a concept advocated by him of investment being channelled into 'new plant' or 'existing plant'. It is slightly different to Gustafson's two investment strategies but basically the same idea. See p. 66.

63 R. Campbell, *Soviet Technology Imports: The Gas Pipeline Case* (California Seminar on International Security and Foreign Policy, Paper 91, February 1981, p. 13.

64 Iu. Bandura, *Izvestiia* (28 June 1983), 4.

65 Mathieson, *Japan's Role*, p. 112.

66 *Ibid.*, p. 235.

67 Japan–Soviet Trade Association, *Nisso Boeki Handobukku 1984*, p. 243.

68 See, Tavrovsky, *New Times*, 40 (1982).

69 See, J. L. Scherer (ed.), *USSR Facts and Figures Annual* (Florida, Academic International Press, 1982) p. 327. N. Shylk, 'The Soviet Far East and the International Economy', in Stephan and Chichkanov (eds.), *Soviet–American Horizons*, claims that volume on the trans-Siberian 'land-bridge' increased seventy-five times between 1971 and 1982. However in 1982, shipments had declined by 12% in comparison to 1981. The opening of BAM reduces transit time to *c* 20 days. See p. 121.

70 Baldwin, *International Organisation*, 34:4, (Autumn 1980), 471–506. Quotation p. 438.

3 THE SOVIET MILITARY AND JAPAN

1 I am indebted to P. Dibb of the Strategic and Defence Studies Centre, Australian National University for the use of the term.

2 For example see, *Asian Security 1980* (Tokyo, Research Institute for Peace and Security, 1980), p. 45; 'Soviet Build-up Worries Japan', in *Soviet*

Analyst, 8:24 (6 December 1979); H. Kimura. *The Impact of the Soviet Military Build-up on Japan and Asia* (Paper presented for the Workshop on 'Reducing Nuclear Threats in Asia', part of the Security Conference on Asia and the Pacific, April 13–15, 1984 at San Diego, California).

3 Kimura, *The Impact of the Soviet Military Build-up*.

4 *Asian Security 1979* (Tokyo, Research Institute for Peace and Security, 1979), p. 29.

5 See, V. Suvorov, 'Strategic Command and Control: The Soviet Approach' in *International Defence Review*, 12 (1984), 1813–20. Radio Liberty Research, 'More Evidence that General Govorov Heads All Forces in Far East' *Radio Liberty Research Bulletin* RL 78/82 (17 February 1982).

6 J. Erickson, L. Hansen *et al.*, *Organising For War: The Soviet Military Establishment Viewed Through the Prism of The Military District* (College Station Paper 2), (Center for Strategic Technology, The Texas A & M University System, College Station, Texas, September 1983), p. 3.

7 In the Soviet organisational breakdown the Indian Ocean has an attached 'adjacent area', i.e. the Arabian Sea. The Pacific fleet is responsible for operations here also. 'TV' is the Soviet abbreviation for 'theatre of war', a larger scale concept than 'TVD'. A 'TV' is usually comprised of two or more 'TVDs'. 'GTVD' is a main theatre of military operations. The Sea of Japan is referred to by the Soviets as a 'zakritii' MTVD, i.e. an 'enclosed' maritime theatre of military operations. For basic definitions see Ministerstvo Oboroni SSSR, *Voennii Entsiklopedicheskii Slovar* (Moscow, Izdatel'stvo, 'Voennoe', 1983) p. 732.

8 B. Lambeth, 'On Thresholds in Soviet Military Thought', in *Washington Quarterly*, 7:2 (Spring 1984), 69–76. Quotation p. 71. For a good summary of the different schools of interpretation of Soviet military doctrine see, D. Hart, 'The Hermeneutics of Soviet Military Doctrine', in *Washington Quarterly*, 7:2 (Spring 1984), 77–88.

9 From a manuscript by W. Lee, 'Soviet nuclear targeting strategy' in D. Ball and J. Richelson (eds.), *Strategic Nuclear Targeting* (London, MacMillan, 1986). 'TVD' is the Soviet abbreviation for 'theatre of military operations'.

10 B. Lambeth, 'On Thresholds in Soviet Military Thought', in *Washington Quarterly* 7:2 (Spring 1984), 73.

11 B. Lambeth and G. Lewis, 'Economic Targeting in Nuclear War', in *Orbis* 27:1, (1983), 127–50. Quotations pp. 143, 144.

12 As quoted in *Strategic Review* (Winter 1982), p. 83, *Pravda*, 25 July 1981.

13 As quoted in *Strategic Review* (Summer 1984), p. 85.

14 See for example, *Tank and Tank Troops* (Moscow, Voenizdat, 1980). The book is written by various high ranking officers connected with the tank arm of the Soviet forces. They are talking of events which describe the performance of tanks in situations where nuclear weapons are utilised in a battlefield environment. Excerpts from this book can be found in *Strategic Review* (Winter 1982), pp. 87–90. A more recent work which implies that the Soviets should pursue the limited use of nuclear weapons is V. G. Reznichenko, *Taktika* (Tactics) (Moscow, Voenizdat, 1984). W. E. Odom, in 'Soviet Force Posture: Dilemmas and Directions', argues that the develop-ment of Soviet force structure and advances in technology have led them to

realise that a 'limited' nuclear battle is more feasible than they have ever publicly admitted. See *Problems of Communism*, 34, (July–August 1985), 1–14.

15 Marshal V. D. Sokolovskii, *Soviet Military Strategy*, ed. H. F. Scott, 3rd edn, (London, Macdonald and Jane's, 1975). Quotation pp. 284–5.

16 Admiral S. G. Gorshkov, *The Sea Power of the State* (translated by Naval Institute Press, Annapolis, Maryland), (New York, Pergamon Press, 1982). Quotation p. 221.

17 As quoted in *Strategic Review* (Fall 1981), p. 106. *Morskoi Sbornik*, No. 4 (April 1981).

18 Gorshkov, *Sea Power*, p. 222.

19 L. Dzirkals, *Soviet Perceptions of Security in East Asia: A Survey of Soviet Media Content* (Santa Monica, California, Rand Corporation, R–6038, November 1977), p. 3.

20 Quoted in *USSR and the Third World*, 7 November 1982 to 6 March 1983, p. 9. For other threats of retaliation see for example, N. Shashkolskii, 'Dangerous Mirages: Japan in US Naval Strategy', in *Krasnaia Zvezda*, 3 November 1983, p. 3. Translation in *FBIS: USSR Daily Report*, III, 8 November 1983, pp. C4–6.

21 D. Petrov, 'Japan's Place in US Asian Policy', in *International Affairs*, 10 (October 1978), 52–9. Quotation p. 53.

22 Dzirkals, *Soviet Perceptions*, pp. 36–7.

23 *FBIS: USSR Daily Report*, III, 2 June 1983, p. CC12.

24 See for example, A. Biryukov, 'Dangerous Role of Reagan's Visit', in *FBIS: USSR Daily Report*, III, 8 November 1983, pp. 3–4. V. Bunin, 'Nakasone's Military Policy', in *Far Eastern Affairs*, 2 (1984), 64–74. Also see chapter 1 of this work: section headed 'Soviet ideology and the remilitarisation of Japan'.

25 P. Keal, *Japanese Defence and Australian Interests* (Seminar paper presented in Department of International Relations, Australian National University, 26 September 1985), p. 30.

26 Comparisons made on figures provided by *The Military Balance* (yearly) 1970–85. International Institute for Strategic Studies, London. Also US Arms Control and Disarmament Agency, *Japan's Contribution to Military Stability in North East Asia*, prepared for the Subcommittee on East Asia and Pacific Affairs, Committee on Foreign Relations, US Senate (Washington DC, USGPO, 1980), pp. 30–8.

27 *Financial Review*, 22 October 1984.

28 As quoted in *Far Eastern Economic Review* 16 June 1983, p. 76.

29 Centre for Strategic Studies, *The Defense of Japan – An Alternative View from Tokyo* (Washington DC, Heritage Foundation, 7 August 1981), pp. 12–14.

30 US Arms Control and Disarmament Agency, *Japan's Contribution To Military Stability in North East Asia* prepared for the Subcommittee on East Asia and Pacific Affairs, Committee on Foreign Relations, US Senate, (Washington, DC, USGPO, 1980), pp. 38–9.

31 J. Moore (ed.), *Jane's Fighting Ships 1984–85* (London, Macdonald and Jane's).

32 N. D. Levin, *The Strategic Environment in East Asia and the US-Korean Security*

Relations in the 1980s (Santa Monica, California, Rand Corporation, Rand Note, N–1960 FF, March 1983).

33 We should note that, as pointed out above, theoretically the Soviets do not see the distinction in such terms for more so than in Western eyes the Soviets see the use of nuclear weapons as an integral part of any major warfighting situation.

34 US Department of Defence, *Soviet Military Power* (Washington DC, USGPO, April 1984), p. 79.

35 A. Whiting, *Siberian Development and East Asia: Threat or Promise?* (Stanford, Stanford University Press, 1981), p. 101.

36 *Ibid.*, p. 108.

37 I. Bellany, 'Sea Power and Soviet Submarine Forces', in *Survival*, 24:1 (January/February 1982), 2–8.

38 J. J. Tritten, *Soviet Naval Forces and Nuclear Warfare* (Boulder, Colorado, Westview Press, 1986). While it is politically and militarily (enchancing first strike threat) advantageous to deploy *Yankees* forward there are the drawbacks of losses likely to be suffered in transition to the Eastern Pacific and the question of whether it is worthwhile as the number of warheads added to Soviet strike capabilities by an increased deployment of *Yankees* is not significant in terms of overall numbers that can be launched by other classes (e.g. *Deltas* and *Typhoons*).

39 Tritten, *Soviet Naval Forces*, p. 155.

40 N. Rivkin, 'No Bastion For the Bear', in *Proceedings US Naval Institute*, 110/4/974 (April 1984), 37–43. Quotation p. 39. See also, J. S. Breemer, 'The Soviet Navy's SSBN Bastions: Evidence, Inference and Alternative scenarios', in *RUSI Journal*, 130:1 (March 1985), 18–26. For a good summary of the Western response to the development of bastions see J. Mearsheimer,, 'The Maritime Strategy and Deterrence in Europe', in *International Security*, 11:2 (Fall 1986, 1–36. Interestingly enough comment on the mechanics of implementing 'The Maritime Strategy', has concentrated almost exclusively on the role of Northern Europe with no details provided on Pacific operations. It would be misleading to view the Soviet 'bastion' strategy as operationally a 'defensive' concept. Bastions will not be passively defended but will be protected by offensive action carried-out far from the Soviet coast if necessary, the idea being not merely to protect Soviet fleet assets but also to protect the integrity of Soviet territory itself.

41 G. McCormick and M. Miller, 'American Seapower at Risk: Nuclear Weapons in Soviet Naval Planning', in *Orbis*, 25:2 (Summer 1981), 351–67. Quotation p. 357.

42 Tritten, *Soviet Naval Forces*, p. 101. See also pp. 99–101 and p. 159. Tritten argues that 'although according to open sources there is apparently no role for ballistic missiles to be used against naval forces at sea, the lack of such information is not such to make the analyst discount its very real possibility' (p. 159).

43 Though Soviet technology with regard to ASW and to quiet running lags behind Western technology it is generally accepted that it is a narrowing gap. See J. E. Moore and R. Compton-Hall, *Submarine Warfare* (London, Michael Joseph, 1986), pp. 139–53.

44 See, M. Vego, 'Submarine Surveillance Soviet Style', in *Jane's Defence Weekly*, 28 July 1984, pp. 117–21. For an overview of Soviet submarine operations and tactics see the appropriate chapters in Moore and Compton-Hall, *Submarine Warfare*. Soviet SSGN can obviously resort to attacking shipping (of all sorts) with torpedoes but this necessitates closing with the target and weighing the dangers attendant in that. C3I disruption is a potentially serious problem for both sides and could equally affect Allied abilities to hunt down Soviet submarines, but here its importance for us is in affecting Soviet abilities for attack – the crucial point is the likelihood of shipping surviving regardless of whether Soviet submarines are sunk or not.

45 R. Betts, 'Washington, Tokyo and North East Asian Security: A Survey', in *Journal of Strategic Studies*, 6:4, (December 1983), 5–30. Quotation p. 22.

46 J. J. Tritten, *Declaratory Policy For The Strategic Employment of the Soviet Navy* (Santa Monica, California, Rand Corporation, Rand Paper, P-7005, September 1984), pp. 137–8.

47 A note on scenarios would be in order at this point. In considering operations, planners have to proceed on the basis of situations most likely to occur, rather than those least likely. They should, however, be aware of the less expected contingencies. This has been the approach taken throughout this section with regard to scenarios. There are two major 'what-if' scenarios to be considered, the outcome of which would affect the direction of conventional war: what-if the Soviet air force launches pre-emptive strikes against Air Self Defence Force/US Air Force (ASDF/USAF) airbases, and what-if the American carriers are destroyed or immobilised early-on in any conflict? While willing to accept that they are possibilities – with dire consequences – the author is not convinced that they are achievable. It is unlikely that a Soviet air attack on the *scale* necessary to gain the desired result of neutralising the ASDF/USAF could achieve the surprise necessary. Destruction of American carriers is more open to question. Chance has a greater role to play in this case; as there is only one target that is the focus of any attack, the Soviets might only have to be 'lucky' once to achieve their objective. The assumption underlying the arguments in this section has been that the formidable defensive capabilities of American carrier battle groups minimise any such Soviet opportunities.

48 Conversation with Mr Mackintosh, Oxford, June 1986.

49 See for example, S. M. Meyer, *Soviet Defence Decisionmaking*, Arms Control and International Security Working Paper No. 33 (Centre for International and Strategic Affairs, University of California, Los Angeles, January 1982). A. Alexander, *Decisionmaking in Soviet Weapons Procurement* Adelphi paper 148 (London, International Institute for Strategic Studies, 1978). K. F. Spielman, *Analysing Soviet Strategic Weapons Decisions* (Boulder, Westview, Colorado, 1978).

50 H. Bull, 'Sea Power and Political Influence' in J. Alford, *Sea Power and Influence: Old Issues and New Challenges*, Adelphi Library 2, (London, International Institute for Strategic Studies, 1980), pp. 3–12.

51 See references in note 2 for example. Kimura 'agrees with the observation

prevalent even among many non-Soviet watchers that the Soviet military build-up in East Asia appears to be counterproductive'. (p. 1). M. Leighton, 'Soviet Strategy Towards Northern Europe and Japan', in *Survey*, 27 (Autumn/Winter 1983) 112–51, talks of 'patterns of Soviet coercion against northern Europe and Japan' (p. 112). 'Japan ... has experienced Soviet Military provocations that are evidently intended both for gaining political leverage and conducting dry runs for wartime operations' (p. 133).

52 S. Kaplan, *The Diplomacy of Power* (Washington, Brookings Institute, 1981), p. 13.

53 *Ibid.*, pp. 13–15.

54 Ibid., p. 17.

55 S. Eto, 'Japanese Perceptions of National Threats' in C. E. Morrison, *Threats to Security in East Asia-Pacific*, (Mass., Lexington Books, D. C. Heath and Co., 1983), pp. 53–64. Quotation p. 57.

56 *Ibid.*, p. 58.

57 Y. C. Kim and G. Sigur (eds.), *Japan and US Policy in Asia* (New York, Praeger, 1982), p. 17.

58 *Ibid.*, p. 20.

59 *Kyodo*, 3 April 1982. Quoted in *USSR and the Third World* (London, Central Asian Research Centre, 7 March to 6 July 1982, p. 48.

60 On commenting on the increasing number of scrambles it says that 'The reason the number of scrambles is increasing these days is that flights of Soviet aircraft to Vietnam have been constantly scheduled, thus, the number is increasing in the West and southwestern airspace of Japan, and the Soviet flight activities over the Japan sea have been extended closer to Japan'. Defence Agency, Tokyo, *Defence of Japan 1983* (Tokyo, 1983), p. 155.

61 For a greater description of these flights – codenamed 'Cobra Ball' and 'Rivet Joint' – see, Seymour Hersh, *The Target Is Destroyed*, (New York, Random House, 1986). In an interview between Hersh and Marshall P. S. Kirsanov, former Soviet Air Defence Commander in the Far East, Kirsanov claimed that his men who track such flights view them as 'routine' and unless something 'unusual' occurs the Soviets do not bother to scramble jets to intercept. See also, the article based on 'The Target Is Destroyed' in *Atlantic Monthly* (September 1986), 47–69.

62 R. Horiguchi, 'Hokkaido – Japan's Front Line', in *Pacific Defence Reporter* (August 1984) 24–7. Quotation p. 27. A *Kyodo* report of 16 March 1978 stated that two Soviet missile destroyers sighted passing through the Tsugaru channel on March 15 were 'the first passage of the channel by Soviet warships since August 1971'. See *USSR and Third World*, 1 February to 30 June 1978, p. 29. If true, this is quite a striking statement. However the author has not been able to obtain confirmation of it from other sources.

63 *Jane's Defence Weekly*, 18 May 1985, p. 833, and 18 July 1987.

64 For an example of both see, *USSR and Third World*, 7 July to 6 November 1981, p. 77.

65 *USSR and Third World*, 15 December 1977 to 13 January 1978, p. 4.

66 As quoted in *USSR and Third World*, 1 February to 30 June 1978, p. 29.

67 *Financial Times*, 26 January 1983.

4 SOVIET POLICY AND JAPAN

1 The focus of the discussion concerns Soviet 'policy' rather than 'relations'. Providing a lexical definition of 'policy' tends to lead in an abstract circular pattern involving the relationship between a 'strategy' and a 'policy'. Therefore the proposed definition of policy utilised herein is an operative – ends/means – one. Foreign policy here is being viewed as that area of government responsibility for promoting the national interest involving political, economic and military means. It involves the formation of desired outcomes and means of achieving them within those terms of reference. It expresses the aims of government in terms considered to be more or less capable of fulfilment.

2 C. Chapman, R. Drifte, and H. Gow, *Japan's Quest for Comprehensive Security: Defence, Diplomacy, Dependence* (London, F. Pinter, 1983). Quotation p. 81.

3 Quoted in N. Akao, *Japan's Economic Security* (London, Royal Institute of International Affairs, 1983), p. 7.

4 Statements made by Ohira at the Japan Press Club, January 22 1980. Quoted in H. Kimura, 'The Impact of the Afghanistan Invasion on Japan–Soviet Relations' in R. Kanet (ed.), *Soviet Foreign Policy and East–West Relations* (New York, Pergamon Press, 1982), pp. 144–65. Quotation p. 149.

5 *Ibid.*, p. 149.

6 *Ibid.*, pp. 147–8.

7 J. A. A. Stockwin, *Japan: Divided Politics in a Growth Economy* (London, Weidenfeld and Nicolson, 1975).

8 D. C. Hellmann, *Japanese Foreign Policy and Domestic Politics: The Peace Agreement with the Soviet Union* (Berkeley, University of California, 1969). Quotation p. 14, p. 18.

9 J. A. A. Stockwin, 'Politics in Japan', in *Current Affairs Bulletin*, (Sydney University), 59:2 (July 1982), 22–30. Quotation p. 27.

10 S. Kimura, 'The Role of the Diet in Foreign Policy and Defence' in F. Valeo and C. Morrison, (eds.) *The Japanese Diet and the US Congress* (Boulder, Colorado, Westview, 1983), pp. 99–114. Quotation p. 105.

11 'Keidanren' is the Federation of Economic Organisations. 'Keiretsu' the big-business corporations.

12 C. Higashi, *Japanese Trade Policy Formulation* (New York, Praeger, 1983), p. 42.

13 R. Godson and R. Shultz, *Dezinformatsia: Active Measures in Soviet Strategy* (New York, Pergamon, 1984). Quotation p. 179.

14 B. Gordon and L. Vasey, 'Security in East Asia and the Pacific' in C. E. Morrison, *Threats to Security in East Asia and the Pacific* (Mass., Lexington Books, D. C. Heath and Co., 1983). Quotation p. 37.

15 V. Zagladin, 'A Step Closer to Each Other?', in *New Times*, 47 (1984), 18–20. Quotation p. 18.

16 Yu. Tavrovsky, 'Grey Jeeps from the Past', in *New Times* 15 (1983), 12–13.

17 V. Dalnev, 'Impediments to Soviet–Japanese Relations', in *International Affairs*, (Moscow), (February 1981), 49–53. Quotation p. 49.

18 K. Kimura argues that 'it is almost impossible for anyone to pinpoint the

major policy orientation of the Suzuki administration towards the Soviet Union . . . because . . . (it) has been marked by ambiguities, inconsistencies, zigzagging and even mysteries'. See 'Recent Japanese–Soviet Relations: From Clouded To "Somewhat Crystal"' in *Journal of North East Asian Studies* (Winter 1982), 3–22. Quotation p. 4. For more details of the inconsistencies see the upcoming section on 'The Soviet Union, Japan and the United States' which shows how Japanese contact with the Soviets continued despite the public rhetoric.

19 S. Verbitsky, 'Japan's Policy Towards the Soviet Union', in *Present Day Japan*, Social Sciences Today Editorial Board (Moscow, USSR Academy of Sciences, 1983). pp. 100–22. Quotations pp. 103–5.

20 As of 1 December 1984 main party strengths were – House of Representatives (511 seats total): LDP – 264; JSP – 111; JCP – 27; Komeito – 59. House of Councillors (252 seats total): LDP – 138; JSP – 43; JCP – 14; Komeito – 27.

21 J. A. A. Stockwin, *Japan: Divided Politics*, p. 125.

22 Interview with Sarkisov, Institute of Oriental studies, Moscow, September 1984.

23 For 'insider' views of the Soviet international research institutes and the relationship with Party and government see, N. Beloff, 'A Defector's Story', in *Atlantic Monthly* (November 1980), 42–9 and A. N. Shevchenko, *Breaking with Moscow* (London, Jonathan Cape, 1985).

24 A. Orfemov, 'Labour and Capital in Japan', in *Far Eastern Affairs*, 1 (1982), 98.

25 See, L. Schapiro, 'The International Department of the CPSU: Key to Soviet Policy', in *International Journal* (Winter 1976–7), 41–55. Also, R. W. Kitrinos, 'International Department of the CPSU', in *Problems of Communism*, 33 (September–October 1984), 47–75.

26 Conversations with H. Kimura, Slavic Research Centre, Hokkaido University. Some reports indicate that Kovalenko was actually the commandant of a camp for Japanese POWs.

27 See, L. Dzirkals, T. Gustafson and A. Johnson, *The Media and Intra-Elite Communication in the USSR* (Santa Monica, California, Rand Corporation, Rand Paper R–2869, September 1982). A more recent study lists three members of the Japan Sector of the International Deparatment. A. Senatorov (Head); V. Kuznetzov (responsible for JCP affairs); V. Saplin (JSP affairs). See, W. Spaulding, 'Shifts in CPSU ID', in *Problems of Communism* (July–August 1986), 80–6.

28 V. Zagladin, 'A Step Closer to Each Other', in *New Times*, 47 (1984), 18–20. Quotation p. 18.

29 Congressional Research Service, Library of Congress, *Soviet Negotiating Behaviour: Emerging New Context for US Diplomacy*, (Committee on Foreign Affairs, Document No. 96–238, 1979). Quotation p. 505.

30 See for example, C. Jonsson, *Soviet Bargaining Behaviour* (New York, Columbia University Press, 1979), pp. 45–8. Also, Congressional Research Service, *Soviet Diplomacy and Negotiating Behaviour*, pp. 493–502. This sets out a list of basic Soviet attributes or tactics. Soviets have an 'aggressive sense of realism . . . are competent negotiators but always unpleasant, mostly unpleasant . . . (they) do not compromise willingly'. (p. 501).

31 Higashi, *Japanese Trade Policy Formulation*. Quotation p. 4.
32 R. C. Christopher, *The Japanese Mind: the Goliath Explained* (New York, Linden Press, Simon and Schuster, 1983). Quotation p. 178.
33 For contents of each text see, Y. Tagano, 'The Treaty of Peace and Friendship of 1978 Between Japan and the People's Republic of China', in *Japanese Annual of International Law*, 23 (1979–80), 1–16. The qualifying clause is in Article 4 of the 1978 Treaty, which states that the treaty will not affect the position of either signatory as far as its relations with a third country is concerned.
34 V. Dalnev, *International Affairs* (Moscow), (February 1981), 49–53. Quotation. p. 51.
35 H. Kimura, 'Soviet Foreign Policy Towards Japan Since the Conclusion of the Japan–China Peace Treaty', in *Slavic Studies* (Hokkaido University), 26 (1980), 31–55. Quotation p. 32.
36 P. Dibb, *The Soviet Union's Security Outlook*. A paper presented for the conference on 'Asian Perspectives on International Security', 11–14 April 1983, Strategic and Defence Studies Centre, Australian National University, Canberra.
37 See V. P. Lukin, 'Tikhookeanskii Region i Protessi Razriadki Mezhdunarodnoi Napriazhenosti' ('The Pacific and Processes of Detente and International Tension'), in *SShA: Problemi Tikhovo Okeana: Mezhdunarodno – Politicheskie Aspekti* (Moscow, Mezhdunarodnie Otnosheniia, 1979).
38 See, V. G. Leshke, *Iapono – Amerikanski Soiuz: Itogi Trekh Desiatiletii* (The Japanese – American Alliance: the Thirty Year Mark) (Moscow, 'Nauka', 1983). The section, for example, which begins p. 97.
39 While Nakasone has taken Japan closer to the United States than his predecessors the gulf between statement and deed has remained. The 'commitment' to the defence of the 1,000 mile naval zone of communication is the most outstanding example. Nakasone also made comments at the same time (January 1983) about Japan's armed forces being able to defend Japan's airspace, and control the straits surrounding Japan. The Self Defence Force is still in no position to do either unsupported by American forces and is a long way from achieving either goal.
40 *Jane's Defence Weekly*, 11 August 1984, p. 178.
41 *Jane's Defence Weekly*, 31 August 1985, p. 397. On increasing co-operation with the US the Japanese record is mixed. There has been an increase in Japanese participation in exercises with the US, e.g. the 12–20 September 1984 joint naval exercise (90 ships, 125 aircraft, 22,000 Japanese) but US success at gaining access to next generation dual technologies has been limited. The record of sharing knowledge of technologies which have a military application has been to date limited. By November 1985 the US was still requesting that Japan invoke legislation to control the export of technology to the USSR as a precondition of Japanese involvement in the Strategic Defence Initiative. See *Jane's Defence Weekly*, 23 November 1985, p. 1121.
42 See for example, R. Menon, 'The Soviet Union in East Asia', in *Current History* (October 1983), 313–17, 339–43. J. R. Kelly, Deputy Assistant Secretary of Defence, East Asia and Pacific Affairs, *Statement to the House Foreign Affairs Subcommittee on Asian and Pacific Affairs*, 19 October 1983.

43 Y. Lugovskoi. 'The United States and Asia – The Withdrawal That Didn't Take Place', in *Soviet News*, 6 March 1979, p. 76.
44 The *Guardian*, 9 December 1986. See also F. Evgeniev, 'Fresh Winds over Oceania', in *Izvestiia*, 7 August 1986. The Soviet fishing agreement with Kiribati fell-through at the end of 1986. The Soviets were disappointed by the low catches and sought to renegotiate the agreement for a lower fee and involving fewer boats. No agreement to date has been reached on this with Kiribati and the Soviets have effectively withdrawn.
45 See, P. Dibb, *Soviet Capabilities, Interests and Strategies in East Asia in the 1980s* Strategic and Defence Studies Working Paper No. 45 February 1982, Australian National University, Canberra. *Soviet Military Power 1984* published by the US Department of Defence gives the Soviets a stockpile of material in the East that would support operations for two months. See p. 79.
46 P. Langer, 'Soviet Military Power in Asia' in D. Zagoria, *Soviet Policy in East Asia*, (New Haven, Council on Foreign Relations Inc., Yale University Press, 1982), pp. 255–82. Quotation 256.
47 D. Zagoria, 'The Soviet Union's Eastern Problem' in M. Weinstein (ed.), *North East Asian Security After Vietnam* (Urbana, Univ. of Illinois Press, 1982), pp. 72–94. Quotation p. 72.
48 It could be argued, from a Soviet viewpoint, that a weakened United States would be a worthwhile trade for a strengthened China. The obvious problem with this would lie in achieving the balance between weakening the US and strengthening the Chinese.
49 R. Menon, 'The Soviet Union in East Asia', in *Current History* (October 1983) 313–17, 339–43. Quotation p. 313.
50 J. Ha, 'Moscow's Policy Towards Japan', in *Problems of Communism*, 26 (September–October 1977), 61–72. Quotation p. 62.
51 This involved the burning of a Chinese flag at a trade fair by some Japanese. The issue escalated and relations were effectively severed.
52 See for example, V. Andreyev, 'The Partnership between Peking and Imperialism: A Threat to Peace and Independence', in *International Affairs* (Moscow), (November 1980) 68–78. He writes 'In May–June 1980, a Chinese delegation headed by Premier Hua Guo-feng made an official visit to Japan ... to prepare the ground for a military and political alliance between the US, Japan and China' (p. 72). See also Bandura, *International Affairs* (Moscow), (August 1979), 70–7, especially p. 76 for Chinese proposal of joint US/Japan/PRC action.
53 D. V. Petrov, 'Japanese–Chinese relations: Problems and Trends', in *Far Eastern Affairs*, 1 (1985), 25–34. Quotation p. 28.
54 M. Krupyanko, 'Japan's Economic Ties with China', in *Far Eastern Affairs*, 2 (1985), 52–9. Quotation p.58.
55 V. Andreyev, 'The Partnership Between Peking and Imperialism a Threat To Peace and Independence', in *International Affairs* (Moscow), (November 1980), 68–78. Quotation p. 73.
56 BBC, *Summary of World Broadcasts*, SU/5887/A3–2, 10 August 1978.
57 M. Demchenko, 'In Defiance of the Interests of Peace and Detente', in *Pravda*, 13 August 1978, p. 5. Also translated in *CDSP*, 30:32, (1978), 4.

58 See, Gromyko's view that China was 'foisting' a treaty on Japan. BBC, *Summary of World Broadcasts*, SU/5709/A3/1, 10 January 1978.
59 See for example, Petrov, *International Affairs* (Moscow), 10 (October 1978), 52–9. He cites Secretary of Defence, Brzezinski as an 'instigator and mediator' of the treaty negotiations (p. 58).
60 *USSR and the Third World* 1 July to 31 December 1978, p. 73.
61 Yu. Tavrovsky, 'Ten Years of Mirages', in *New Times*, 24 (1982), 26–7.
62 Krupyanko, *Far Eastern Affairs*, 2 (1985), 52–3.
63 Quoted in Kimura, *Slavic Studies* (Hokkaido University), 26 (1980), 31–55. Quotation p. 39.
64 Editorial, *Far Eastern Affairs*, 2 (1984), 19–29. Quotation p. 20.
65 For more detailed views see S. L. Tikhvinskii, *Mezhdunarodnie Problemi Azii 80-kh Godov* (International Problems of Asia in the 1980s) (Moscow, Izdatel'stvo 'Mezhdunarodnie Otnosheniia', 1983). Pp. 145–50 deal with Japan's Asia policies and pp. 81–5 with the Asian policies of the Reagan administration; pp. 138–44 deal with the US and China under the heading of '*sotrudnichestvo i protivorechiia*' ('co-operation and contradictions'). For a full exposition of the US-Chinese relationship as seen by two Soviet analysts see, A. A. Nagornii and A. B. Parkanskii, *S. Sh. A i Kitai: Ekonomicheskie i Nauchno-Tekhnicheskie Aspekti Kitaiskoi Politiki Vashingtona* (USA and China: Economic and Scientific-Technological Aspects of Washington's China Policy) (Moscow, Izdatel'stvo 'Nauka', 1982). This is a detailed treatment of the process of normalisation of relations between the US and China and deals in depth with trade and the ties in scientific and technical collaboration. In it they deal with many of the problems and 'objective limitations' which hinder a full development of relations. These are in numerous instances the same problems which place limits on Chinese-Japanese collaboration. Amongst others that 'there are those in Peking who do not agree with the tendencies of the US approach. Firstly, the Chinese leadership wish to limit the tempo of economic and scientific connections ... Secondly, military-bureaucratic circles at a high level in China do not wish to lose control of their lever over the leadership of the political and economic administration of the country ... thirdly, Peking's economic experiments have not strengthened, but weakened internal political stability ... there are different levels of internal Chinese economic development' (pp. 204–5).
66 *Ibid.*, p. 25.
67 H. Kimura, 'Japanese–Soviet Relations From Afghanistan to Suzuki', in *Slavic Studies* (Hokkaido University), 25 (1981), 55–80. Quotation pp. 73–4.
68 V. Bunin, 'Nakasone's Military Policy', in *Far Eastern Affairs*, 2 (1984), 64–74. Quotation p. 73.
69 Kuznetsov, *Kommunist*, 4 (March 1983), 98–109. Quotation pp. 100–1.
70 B. Dmytryshyn, as quoted in Kimura, *Slavic Studies* (Hokkaido University), 26 (1980), 31–55. Quotation p. 32.
71 N. D. Levin, *In Search of a Strategy: the Reagan Administration and Security in North East Asia* (Santa Monica, California, Rand Corporation, Rand Paper, P–6801, August 1982). Quotation p. 3.
72 N. Nikolayev, 'Asia: Washington's Imperial Ambitions', in *Izvestiia*, 10 June 1983. *FBIS translation: USSR Daily Report*, 13 June 1983, pp. C2–C4.

73 Interview with Petrov, Washington DC, October 1984.
74 See, T. B. Guzhenko, 'Soviet-Japanese Relations', in *Far Eastern Affairs*, 3 (1982).
75 *TASS*, 28 July 1986.
76 E. g. Geidar Aliyev's meeting with a visiting Japanese delegation on 12 October 1984; the significance attached to Gorbachev's major tours of Siberia and the Far East, 4–6 September 1985, 24–31 July 1986. Also Gorbachev's personal meeting with a JSP delegation, 25 September 1985. Demichev's meeting with Nakasone, 13 September 1985. More attention than usual was also paid to Japan and China at the 27th Congress. For an account of the Shevardnadze and Abe visits see, P. Berton, 'Soviet–Japanese Relations: Perceptions, Goals, Interactions', in *Asian Survey*, 26: 12 (December 1986), 1259–83. 'Winds of Change Hit Foreign Ministry', *Radio Free Europe – Radio Liberty Research*, RL 274/86 (16 July 1986). For an account of the Toshiba affair see, *Financial Times*, 30 June 1987; *Asahi Shimbun*, 16 May 1987, p. 1; *Nihon Keizai*, 16 May 1987, p. 3.
77 *FBIS: USSR Daily Report*, III, 18 July 1982, p. C.1.
78 'Soviet-Japanese Relations Since the Imposition of Martial Law in Poland', *Radio Free Europe – Radio Liberty Research*, RL 89/82 (24 February 1982).
79 See, for example, *Pravda*, 20 August 1987 and 10 June 1987. On 5 August 1987, *Pravda* carried an item detailing how the crews of two Soviet fishing vessels, the *Maiskaye* and *Sarychevsk*, were maltreated by a crowd of about 1,000 Japanese who subjected them to a barrage of anti-Soviet abuse while the ships had docked on a pre-arranged two day visit. The commentary described these actions as 'stage-managed' by 'ultra-right hoodlums' out to 'darken good-neighbourly relations between the two countries'.

CONCLUSIONS

1 Admiral S. Turner, *Secrecy and Democracy*, (London, Sidgwick and Jackson, 1985), p. 236. The book is a general treatise on the problems of intelligence analysis. For a more detailed treatment see, J. Prados, *The Soviet Estimate: US Intelligence Analysis and Soviet Strategic Forces* (New Jersey, Princeton University Press, 1986). For a breakdown of the US intelligence community and an overview of the factors and influences involved in analysis, see, L. Freedman, *US Intelligence and The Soviet Strategic Threat*, 2nd edn, (London, Macmillan, 1986), pp. 8–61. ('The Intelligence Community' and 'The Estimating Process'.)

APPENDIX 1

1 See, for example, F. Langdon, 'Japan–Soviet 200 Mile Zone Confrontation', in *Pacific Community* (October 1977), 46–58. *The Australian*, 27 May 1983.
2 *Soviet Analyst*, 5:25 (23 December, 1976).
3 The Oriental Economist, *Japan Economic Yearbook 1981/2*, (Hong Kong), p. 53.
4 *Japan Times*, 13 April 1978.

5 See, BBC, *Summary of World Broadcasts*, SU/6702/A3/3, 17 April 1981. Also T. Shkolnikova, 'Co-operation in Fisheries' in *New Times*, 19 (1982), 8–9.
6 *The Australian*, 27 May 1983.
7 *USSR and the Third World*, 12 September to 31 December 1976, p. 207.
8 *Izvestiia*, 8 July 1983. Translated in *FBIS: USSR Daily Report*, III, 11 July 1983, p. C.2. 'Hunting Poachers' in *Moscow News*, 40 (1987), 4.
9 Japan Institute of International Affairs (ed.), *White Papers of Japan 1978–79* (Tokyo), p. 108.
10 *Ibid.*, p. 116.
11 Japan Institute of International Affairs (ed.), *White Papers of Japan 1980–81* (Tokyo), pp. 138–9.
12 Japan Institute of International Affairs (ed.), *White Papers of Japan 1979–80*, (Tokyo), p. 116.
13 *Ibid.*
14 Conversations with H. Kimura, Slavic Research Centre, Hokkaido University. August 1984.
15 Jain, *Soviet Union and Japan.*
16 T. Shkolnikova, 'Co-operation in Fisheries', in *New Times*, 19 (1982), 8.
17 See BBC, *Summary of World Broadcasts*, SU/5959/A3/3, 3 November 1978.
18 BBC, *Summary of World Broadcasts*, SU/5980/A3/1, 3 September 1978.
19 *FBIS: USSR Daily Report*, 22 July 1983.

SELECT BIBLIOGRAPHY

Only those sources which were of particular use have been cited in this bibliography. Many of the articles in both English and Russian were repetitive; the most informative and representative are listed below. No page numbers have been given as full citations have been supplied in the notes.

RUSSIAN LANGUAGE PUBLICATIONS

Books and monographs

Akademiia Nauk SSSR, *Ezhegodnik 'Iaponiia'*, Moscow 'Nauka'

Berezin, V. N., *Kurs na dobrososedstvo i sotrudnichestvo i evo protivniki: iz istorii normalizatsii otnosheniia SSSR s poslevoennoi Iaponiei* Moscow, Izdatel'stvo 'Mezhdunarodnie Otnosheniia', 1977

Bolshaia Sovetskaia Entsiklopedia, 3rd edn, Moscow

Eidus, Kh.T *SSSR i Iaponiia: Vneshneipoliticheskie Otnosheniia Posle Vtoroi Mirovoi Voini* Moscow, Izdatel'stvo 'Nauka' 1964

Iaponskii Militarizm – Voenno-Istoricheskoe Issledovanie, Moscow, Izdatel'stvo 'Nauka', 1972

Istoriia 20-letnei Iapono-Sovetskoi Pribrezhnoi Torgovli 1964–1984, Aiast-Sotobo, Tokyo, Japan Association for Trade with the Soviet Union, 1984

Krustskikh, A. V., *Amerikanskaia Politika 'Partnerstva' v Vostochno-Aziatskom Regione*, Moscow, Izdatel'stvo 'Mezdhunarodnie Otnosheniia', 1980

Leshke, V. G. *Iapono-Amerikanski Soiuz: Itogi Trekh Desiatiletii*, Moscow, Izdatel'stvo 'Nauka', 1983

Lukin, V. P. (ed.) *SShA i Problemi Tikhovo Okeana: Mezhdunarodno-Politicheskie Aspekti* Moscow, 'Mezhdunarodnie Otnosheniia', 1979

Ministerstvo Oboroni SSSR, *Voenni Entsiklopedicheskii Slovar'*, Moscow, Izdatel'stvo, 'Voennoe' 1983

Sovetskaia Voennaia Entsiklopediia, Moscow, Izdatel'stvo, 'Voennoe' 1979

Voenno-Morskoi Flot, *Atlas Okeanov: Tikhii Okean*, Moscow, Glavnoe Upravlenie Navigatsii i Okeanografii, 1974

Ministerstvo Vneshnei Torgovli, *Vneshniaia Torgovlia SSSR*, Moscow, Izdatel'stvo 'Finansi i statistika'

Nagornii A. A. and A. B. Parkanskii, *S.Sh.A. i Kitai: Ekonomicheskie i Nauchno-Tekhnicheskie Aspecti Kitaiskoi Politiki Vashingtona* Moscow, Izdatel'stvo 'Nauka', 1982

Petrov, D. V., *Iaponiia v mirovoi politike* Izdatel'stvo 'Mezhdunarodnie Otnosheniia', Moscow, 1973

Stolyarov, Iu and Iu S. Pevzner (eds.), *SSSR-Iaponiia: Problemi Torgovno-Ekonomicheskikh Otnoshenii*, Moscow, Izdatel'stvo 'Mezhdunarodnie Otnosheniia', 1984

Tikhvinskii, S. L., *Mezhdunarodnie Problemi Azii 80-kh godov* Moscow, Mezhdunarodnie Otnosheniia', 1983

Vneshniaia Politika SSSR: Sbornik Dokumentov, 1972–83 (yearly), Moscow, Ministerstvo Inostrannikh Del SSSR

Volkova, I. V., *Iaponiia i Afrika* Moscow, Izdatel'stvo 'Mysl', 1981

Articles

Aliev, R., 'Iaponiia i Zapadnaia Evropa: Partnerstvo i Sopernichestvo', *MEMO*, 9, (1981)

'Politika Tokio v Aziatsko-Tikhookeanskom Regione', *MEMO*, 9 (1980)

Barsukov, Iu., 'Grazhdanskie Dvizheniia v Iaponii', *MEMO*, 3 (1977)

'Iaponiia i Latinskaia Amerika', *MEMO*, 7 (1975)

Baskakova, M., 'Gosudarstvenni Sektor v Ekonomike Iaponii', *MEMO*, 9 (1984)

'Osobennosti Nauchno-Tekhnicheskoi Politiki Iaponii', *MEMO*, 2 (1980)

Ivanov, Professor S. P. General of the Army, 'Krakh Kvantunskoi Armii', *Novaia i Noveishaia Istoriia*, 5 (1985)

Karagina, T. and V. Khlynov, 'Politika Gosudarstva v Oblasti Truda i Trudovikh Otnoshenii v Iaponii' in *MEMO*, 1 (1983)

Kir'ian, Lt Gen. M. M., 'Pobeda Na Dal'nem Vostoke', *Voprosi Istorii*, 8 (1985)

Kuznetsov, Iu., 'Kuda Tolkaiut Iaponiiu?', *Kommunist*, 4, (March 1983)

Lukin, V. P. and A. Parkanskii, '"Tikho-Okeanskoe Soobshchestvo": Proekti i Real "nost"', *MEMO*, 3 (1981)

Maksimova, M., 'Kapitalisticheskaia Integratsiia i Mirovoe Razvitie', *MEMO* 4 (1978)

Mil'gram, N.N., 'Militarizm v Iaponii', *Narodi Azii i Afriki*, 3 (1972)

Okumura, K., 'Predprinimatel'skie Gruppi v Iaponii', *MEMO*, 4 (1984)

Petrov, D. V., 'Iaponiia v Sovremennom Mire', *MEMO* 12 (1980)

Shakhnazarov, G., 'K probleme Sootnosheniia Sil v Mire', *Kommunist*, 3 (1974)

Stolyarov, Iu. and S. Ul'ianichev, 'Nauchno – Tekhnicheskaia Strategia Iaponii', *MEMO*, 6 (1983)

Tsvetov, V., 'Iaponiia: Vneshnepoliticheskaia Doktrina Na 70 Godi', in *Novi Mir*, 12 (December 1974)

Ukrainstev, M., 'Krakh militariskoi Iaponii', *Kommunist*, 13 (1975)

Ul'ianichev, S., 'Skol'ko v Iaponii Bezrabotnikh?', *MEMO*, 12 (1983)

Ulyanov, A., 'Iaponskii Proletariat i Tekhnicheskii Progress', *MEMO*, 9 (1978)

Utkin, A., 'Atlantizm' i Iaponii', *MEMO*, 6 (1976)

Zanegin, B., 'Aziatskaia Bezopasnost': Dva Podkhoda' *Aziia i Afrika Sevodniia* (March 1978)

Journals

Aziia i Afrika Sevodniia

Kommunist

Kommunist Vooruzhennikh Sil

Mirovaia Ekonomika i Mezhdunarodnie Otnosheniia (MEMO)
Narodi Azii i Afriki
Novaia i Noveishaia Istoriia
Novi Mir
Socialisticheskaia Industriia
SShA – Ekonomika, Politika, Ideologiia

ENGLISH LANGUAGE PUBLICATIONS

Books and monographs

Akao, N., *Japan's Economic Security*, London, Royal Institute of International Affairs, 1983

Asian Security 1979, Tokyo, Research Institute for Peace and Security, 1980

Asian Security 1980, Tokyo, Research Institute for Peace and Security, 1981

Asian Security 1981, Tokyo, Research Institute for Peace and Security, 1982

Barron, J., *KGB Today*, London, Coronet, 1985

Breslauer, G. W., *Khrushchev and Brezhnev as Leaders: Building Authority in Soviet Politics*, London, Allen and Unwin, 1982

Byrnes R. F., (ed.), *After Brezhnev*, Bloomington, Indiana University Press, 1983

Campbell, R., *Soviet Technology Imports: The Gas Pipeline Case*, California Seminar on International Security and Foreign Policy, Paper No. 91, February 1981

Central Intelligence Agency, Office of Soviet Analysis, *Joint Economic Committee Briefing paper – USSR: Economic Trends and Policy Developments*, Washington DC, 14 September 1983

Centre for Strategic Studies, *The Defense of Japan – An Alternative View from Tokyo*, Washington DC, Heritage Foundation, 1981

Chapman, J. W. M., R. Drifte and H. Gow, *Japan's Quest for Comprehensive Security, Defence, Diplomacy, Dependence*, London, F. Pinter, 1983

Collective authors, *Capitalism, Socialism and the Scientific and Technical Revolution* Moscow, Progress Publishers, 1983

Committee on Armed Services, US Congress, *Hearing Before the Committee on Armed Services United States Senate*, Part 6 – Sea Power and Force Projection, Washington DC, USGPO, March 1982

Committee on Foreign Affairs, US House of Representatives Subcommittee on Asian and Pacific Affairs, *The Soviet Role in Asia*, 21 July 1983 Washington DC, USGPO, 1983

Congressional Research Service, Library of Congress, Washington DC, *Soviet Negotiating Behaviour: Emerging New Context for US Diplomacy*, Committee on Foreign Affairs, Document No. 96–238, 1979

Defence Agency, Tokyo, *Defence of Japan 1976–1984* (Yearly), Tokyo

Dibb, P., *The Soviet Union's Security Outlook*, Paper presented for the conference on 'Asian Perspectives on International Security', 11–14 April 1983, Strategic and Defence Studies Centre, Australian National University, Canberra

Dienes, L. and T. Shabad, *The Soviet Energy System: Resource Use and Policies*, Washington D.C., Winstons and Sons, 1979

Directorate of Intelligence, CIA, *International Energy Statistical Review*, GI IESR 82–007, 27 July 1982

Dornberg, J., *Brezhnev*, London, Andre Deutsch, 1974

Dyker, D., *The Process of Investment in the Soviet Union*, Cambridge, Cambridge University Press, 1983

Dzirkals, L., *Soviet Perceptions of Security in East Asia: A Survey of Soviet Media Content*, Santa Monica, California, Rand Corporation, R-6038, November 1977

Economist Intelligence Unit, *Quarterly Economic Review USSR*, London Economist

Erickson, J., *The Road to Stalingrad*, London, Weidenfeld and Nicolson, 1975

Evan, O., *The Mezhdunarodniki*, Israel, Turtledove Publishing, 1979

Food and Agricultural Organisation, *Yearbook of Fishery Statistics*, Vol. 49, 1979, Rome, FAO, 1981

Freedman, L., *US Intelligence and the Soviet Strategic Threat*, 2nd edn, London, Macmillan, 1986

Gardner, H. S., *Soviet Foreign Trade – The Decision Process*, Boston, Mass., Kluwer-Nijhoff, 1983

Gelman, H., *The Brezhnev Politburo and the Decline of Detente*, New York, Cornell University Press, 1984

    The Soviet Far East Buildup and Soviet Risk-Taking Against China, Santa Monica, California, Rand Corporation, Rand Paper R–2943–AF, August 1982

Godson, R. and R. Schultz, *Dezinformatsia: Active Measures in Soviet Strategy*, New York, Pergamon Press, 1984

Goldman, M., *The Enigma of Soviet Petroleum*, London, Allen and Unwin, 1980

Gorshkov, S. G., *The Sea Power of the State*, Annapolis, Maryland, Naval Institute Press, 1982

Gottemoeller R. E., and P. F. Langer, *Foreign Area Studies in the USSR*, Santa Monica, California, Rand Corporation, Rand Report R–2967–RC

Greenway, A., *Soviet Merchant Ships*, Hampshire, UK, Mason Publishing, 1985

Gruzinov, V. P., *The USSR's Management of Foreign Trade*, New York, Sharpe Inc., 1979

Gustafson, T., *Reform in Soviet Politics*, New York, Cornell University Press, 1981

    Selling the Russians the Rope? Soviet Technology Policy and the United States' Export Controls, Santa Monica, California, Rand Corporation, Rand Report R–2649–ARPA, April 1981

Hanson, P., *Trade and Technology in Soviet–Western Relations*, New York, Columbia University Press, 1981

Hellmann, D. C., *Japanese Foreign Policy and Domestic Politics: The Peace Agreement with the Soviet Union*, Berkeley, University of California, 1969

Higashi, C. *Japanese Trade Policy Formation*, New York, Praeger, 1983

Hoffman, E. P. and R. F. Laird, *The Politics of Economic Modernisation in the Soviet Union*, New York, Cornell University Press, 1982

International Institute for Strategic Studies, *The Military Balance*, London, I.I.S.S., 1976–86

Ivkov, I., *Japan: Heading for Militarisation*, Moscow, Novosti Press Agency, 1979

Jain, R., *The USSR and Japan 1945–80*, Brighton, UK, Harvester Press, 1981

Japan External Trade Organisation, *White Papers on International Trade*, Summary Yearbooks, Tokyo

Japan Institute of International Affairs (ed.), *White Papers of Japan 1979–80*, Tokyo, 1981

White Papers of Japan 1980–81, Tokyo, 1982

Japanese Centre for Strategic Studies, *The Defense of Japan: An Alternative View from Tokyo*, Tokyo, August 1981

Jonsson, C., *Soviet Bargaining Behaviour*, New York, Columbia University Press, 1979

Kaplan, S., *The Diplomacy of Power*, Washington DC, Brookings Institute, 1981

Kim, Y.C. and G. Sigur (eds), *Japan and US Policy in Asia* New York, Praeger, 1982

Kimura, H., *The Impact of the Soviet Military Build-up on Japan and Asia*, Paper presented at the workshop on 'Reducing Nuclear Threats in Asia', part of the Security Conference on Asia and the Pacific on 13–15 April 1984 at San Diego, California

Koropeckyj I.S. and G. S. Schroder (eds.), *Economics of Soviet Regions*, New York, Praeger, 1981

Kovalenko, I. *Soviet Policy for Asian Peace and Security*, Moscow, Progress Publishers, 1979

Kubalkova V. and A. Cruickshank, *Marxism-Leninism and the Theory of International Relations*, London, Routledge and Kegan Paul, 1980

Leebaert D. (ed.), *Soviet Military Thinking*, London, Allen and Unwin, 1981

Lenczowski, J., *Soviet Perceptions of US Foreign Policy*, Ithaca, Cornell University Press, 1982

Lensen, G. A., *Russia's Eastward Expansion*, New Jersey, Prentice Hall, 1964

The Russian Push Toward Japan, Princeton, Princeton University Press, 1959

Levin, N. D., *The Strategic Environment in East Asia and the US-Korean Security Relations in the 1980s*, Santa Monica, California, Rand Corporation, Rand Note N–1960 FF, March 1983

In Search of a Strategy: The Reagan Administration and Security in North East Asia, Santa Monica, California, Rand Corporation, Rand Paper P–6801, August 1982

Maksudov, L., *Ideological Struggle Today*, Moscow, Progress Publishers, 1983

Marwah, O. and J. Pollack, *Military Power and Policy in Asian States: China, India and Japan*, Boulder, Colorado, Westview Press, 1980

Mathieson, R., *Japan's Role in Soviet Economic Growth*, New York, Praeger, 1979

Mitchell, R. J., *Ideology of a Superpower*, Stanford, California, Hoover Press, 1982

Moore, J. (ed.), *Jane's Fighting Ships 1984–85*, London, MacDonald and Jane's, 1986

Moore, J. and R. Compton-Hall, *Submarine Warfare*, London, Michael Joseph, 1986

Morrison C. E. and F. Valeo (eds.), *The Japanese Diet and the US Congress*, Boulder, Colorado, Westview, 1983

Threats to Security in East Asia-Pacific, Mass., Lexington Books, D. C. Heath and Co., 1983

Organisation of Economic Co-operation and Development, *Review of Fisheries in OECD Member Countries 1981*, Paris, OECD, 1982

Parrott, B., *Politics and Technology in The Soviet Union*, Cambridge, Mass., MIT Press, 1983

Polmar, N., *Guide to the Soviet Navy*, 3rd edn, Annapolis, Maryland, Naval Institute Press, 1983

Prados, J., *The Soviet Estimate: US Intelligence Analysis and Soviet Strategic Forces*, New Jersey, Princeton University Press, 1986

Scherer, J. L., (ed.), *USSR Facts and Figures Annual*, Florida, Academic International Press, 1979, 1980, 1982

Sokolovskii, V. D., *Soviet Military Strategy*, ed. H. F. Scott, 3rd edn, London, MacDonald and Jane's, 1975

Stephan, J. J., *The Kuril Islands: Russo–Japanese Frontier in the Pacific*, Oxford, Clarendon Press, 1974

Stephan, J. J. and V. P. Chichkanov, (eds.), *Soviet–American Horizons on the Pacific*, Honolulu, University of Hawaii Press, 1986

Stern, J. P., *Soviet Natural Gas Development to 1990*, Mass., Lexington Books, D. C. Heath and Co., 1980

Stockwin, J. A. A., *Japan: Divided Politics in a Growth Economy*, London, Weidenfeld and Nicolson, 1975

Swearingen, R., *The Soviet Union and Post-War Japan*, California, Hoover Press, Stanford, 1978

Thomas, R. G. C., *The Great Power Triangle and Asian Security*, Mass., Lexington Books, D. C. Heath and Co., 1983

Tritten, J. J., *Soviet Naval Forces and Nuclear Warfare*, Boulder, Colorado, Westview Press, 1986

    Declaratory Policy For The Strategic Employment of The Soviet Navy, Santa Monica, California, Rand Corporation, Rand Paper P–7005, September 1984

    Soviet Navy Data Base: 1982–3, Santa Monica, California, Rand Corporation, Rand Paper P–6859, April 1983

Tsygankov, V., (ed.), *Present Day Japan*, Oriental Studies in the USSR No. 7, Moscow, USSR Academy of Sciences, 1983

Turpin, W., *Soviet Foreign Trade*, Mass., Lexington Books, D. C. Heath and Co., 1977

US Arms Control and Disarmament Agency, *Japan's Contribution to Military Stability in North East Asia*, Prepared for the Subcommittee on East Asian and Pacific Affairs, Committee on Foreign Relations, US Senate, Washington DC, USGPO, 1980

US Department of Defence, *Soviet Military Power*, Washington DC, USGPO, 1983, 1984, 1985

Vernon, G. D., (ed.), *Soviet Perceptions of War and Peace*, Washington DC, National Defense University Press, 1981

Volten, P., *Brezhnev's Peace Programme: A Study of Soviet Domestic Political Process and Power*, Boulder, Colorado, Westview Press, 1982

Watson, B. M., *Red Navy at Sea: Soviet Naval Operations on the High Seas 1956–80*, Boulder, Colorado, Westview Press, 1982

Watson, B. M. and S. Watson, *The Soviet Navy: Strengths and Liabilities*, Boulder, Colorado, Westview Press, 1986

Weinstein, M., (ed.), *North East Asian Security after Vietnam*, Urbana, University of Illinois Press, 1982

Japan's Postwar Defense Policy 1947–68, New York, Columbia University Press, 1971

Whiting, A. S., *Siberian Development and East Asia: Threat or Promise?*, Stanford, Stanford University Press, 1981

Wilson, D., *The Demand for Energy in the Soviet Union*, London, Croom Helm, 1983

Zagoria, D., *Soviet Policy in East Asia*, New Haven, Council on Foreign Relations Inc., Yale University Press, 1982

Articles

Agafanov, V. and R. Khasbulatov, 'Ideological Interpretations of the Scientific and Technical Revolution', *Kommunist*, 12 (1978). JPRS translation

'Agreement on the Exchange of Goods and Payments Between the USSR and Japan From the Period 1981–85', *Foreign Trade of the USSR*, 11 (1981)

Alexandrov, V., 'Siberia and the Soviet Far East in Soviet-Japanese Relations', *Far Eastern Affairs*, 2 (1982)

'Siberia and the Far East on the Eve of the 26th Congress', *Far Eastern Affairs*, 4 (1980)

'Baikal–Amur Mainline: People, Experience, Problems', *Kommunist*, 7 (1977). JPRS translation

Baldwin, D., 'Interdependence and Power: A Conceptual Analysis', *International Organisation*, 34:4 (Autumn 1980)

Bandura, Iu., 'The Sino–Japanese Alliance Runs Counter to Peace Interests', *International Affairs* (Moscow), (August 1979)

Bellany, I., 'Sea Power and Soviet Submarine Forces', *Survival*, 24:1 (January–February 1982)

Berton, P., 'The Soviet–Japanese Communist Parties: Policies, Tactics and Negotiating Behaviour', *Studies in Comparative Communism*, 15:3 (Autumn 1982)

Betts, R., 'Washington, Tokyo and North East Asian Security: A Survey', *Journal of Strategic Studies*, 6:4 (December 1983)

Breemer, J. S., 'The Soviet Navy's SSBN Bastions: Evidence, Inference and Alternative Scenarios', *RUSI Journal*, 130:1 (March 1985)

Brezhnev, L., 'CPSU Secretary Leonid Brezhnev's Answers To Questions Put By Asahi Editor Shoryu Hata', *New Times*, 24 (1977)

Brutents, K., 'The Soviet Union and the Newly Industrialised Countries', *International Affairs* (Moscow), 4 (1979)

Bulai, I., 'The Shady Aims of the Pacific Community' in *International Affairs* (Moscow), January 1983

Bull, H., 'Sea Power and Political Influence', J. Alford, *Sea Power and Influence: Old Issues and New Challenges*, London, Adelphi Library 2, International Institute for Strategic Studies (1980)

Clawson, C. H., 'The Wartime Role of Soviet SSBN's – Round Two', *Proceedings US Naval Institute*, 106/3/925 (March 1980)

Connolly, V., 'The Territorial Production Complex in Siberia and the Far East', *Radio Free Europe – Radio Liberty Research*, RL 339/76, 6 July 1976

Dalnev, V., 'Impediments to Soviet–Japanese Relations', *International Affairs* (Moscow), (February 1981)

Dienes, L., 'Soviet–Japanese Economic Relations: Have They Begun to Fade?', *Soviet Geography*, Review and Translation (September 1985)

'The Development of Siberia: Regional Priorities and Economic Strategy in *La Siberie: Colonisation, Developpement et Perspectives 1582–1982*, Paris, Centre National de La Recherche Scientifique, (May 1983)

'The development of the Siberian Region: Economic Profiles, Income Flows and Strategies for Growth', *Soviet Geography*, Review and Translation (April 1982)

Dyker, D., 'Planning in Siberia on the Wrong Track', *Soviet Analyst*, 9:2 (23 January 1980)

Ha, J., 'Moscow's Policy toward Japan', *Problems of Communism*, 26 (September–October 1977)

Hanson, P., 'Backlash against technology imports', *Radio Free Europe – Radio Liberty Research*, RL 453/81, 12 November 1981

'Western Technology in the Soviet economy', *Problems of Communism*, 27 (November–December 1978)

Horiguchi, R., 'Hokkaido – Japan's Front Line', *Pacific Defence Reporter* (August 1984)

Khlynov, V., 'Japan's Growing Internal Political Struggle in the 1970's, *Far Eastern Affairs*, 4 (1979)

Kimura, H., 'Soviet Foreign Policy Towards Japan Since the Conclusion of the Japan-China Peace Treaty', *Slavic Studies* (Hokkaido University), 26 (1980)

Kitrinos, R., 'International Department of the CPSU' in *Problems of Communism*, 33 (September–October 1984)

Krupyanko, M., 'Japan's Economic Ties with China', *Far Eastern Affairs*, 2 (1985)

Kubalkova, V. and A. Cruickshank, 'Marxist Perspectives and the Study of International Relations', *Review of International Studies*, 7:1 (January 1981)

Kulish, V., 'Detente, International Relations and Military Might', in *Coexistence*, 4:2 (1976)

Lambeth, B. S. and G. Lewis, 'Economic Targeting in Nuclear War', *Orbis*, 27:1 (Spring 1983)

Latyshev, I., 'New Foreign Policy Concepts of the Japanese Ruling Circles', *Asia Quarterly* (Brussels), 4 (1971)

Radio Liberty, 'More Evidence that General Govorov Heads All Forces in Far East', *Radio Free Europe – Radio Liberty Research*, RL 78/82, 17 February 1982

McCormick, G. and M. Miller, 'American Seapower at Risk: Nuclear Weapons in Soviet Naval Planning', *Orbis* 25:2 (Summer 1981)

Mitchell, R. J., 'The New Brezhnev Doctrine', *World Politics*, 30:3 (April 1978)

Nekrasov, V., 'Absurd But Dangerous Myth', *Kommunist* 12 (1979). JPRS translation

Petrov, D. V., 'Japanese–Chinese Relations: Problems and Trends', *Far Eastern Affairs*, 1 (1985)

'Japan's Place in US Asian Policy', *International Affairs* (Moscow), 10 (October 1978)

Rivkin, N., 'No Bastion for the Bear', *Proceedings US Naval Institute*, 110/4/974 (April 1984)

Schapiro, L., 'The International Department of the CPSU: Key to Soviet Foreign Policy', *International Journal* (Winter 1976–7)

Sergiyev, A., 'Leninism on the Correlation of Forces as a Factor of International Relations', *International Affairs* (Moscow), (May 1975)

Shakhnazarov, G., 'Effective Factors of International Relations', in *International Affairs* (Moscow), (February 1977)

Shipov, Y., 'Japan's Bedevilled Economy', in *Far Eastern Affairs*, 3 (1979)

Smith, G. B., 'Recent Trends in Japanese–Soviet Trade', *Problems of Communism*, 36:1 (January–February 1987)

Stephan, J. J., 'The USSR and the Defeat of Imperial Japan, 1945', *Soviet Studies in History*, 24:3 (Winter 1985/86)

Stockwin, J. A. A., 'Politics in Japan', *Current Affairs Bulletin*, 59:2 (July 1982)

Suzuki, K. and Yokowo, K., 'Japan's Trade Mission to Moscow, February 1983: What Did It Accomplish?', *Japanese Economic Studies* 12:1 (Fall 1983)

Tagano, Y., 'The Treaty of Peace and Friendship of 1978 Between Japan and the People's Republic of China', *Japanese Annual of International Law 23* (1979–80)

Tavrovsky, Y., 'Barbed Wire – Bound Okinawa', *New Times*, 27 (1983)
'Visiting Fishermen in Hokkaido', *New Times*, 4 (1982)
'Ten Years of Mirages', *New Times*, 4 (1982)
'The Millionth Container', *New Times*, 40 (1982)

Teague, E., 'Japanese and Soviet Communist Parties Exchange Polemics', *Radio Free Europe – Radio Liberty Research*, RL 335/81, 26 August 1981

Tolkunov, L., 'Japan Today', *New Times*,, 31 (1980)

Vosnesenskaia, N. 'Participation by Soviet Foreign Trade Organisations in Joint Companies', *Soviet Law and Government*, 17 (Fall 1977)

Westwood, J. T., 'Soviet Naval Theater Forces: Their Strategy and Employment' in Jones, D. R., *Soviet Armed Forces Review Annual 1984–85*, Gulf Breeze, Florida, Academic International Press, 1986

Zaitsev, V., 'Japan's Scientific and Technology Policy: Change of Priorities', *MEMO*, 1 (1987), *FBIS* translation

Journals
Air Force Magazine
Asian Aviation
Asian Defence Journal
Coexistence
Current Affairs Bulletin
Current Digest of the Soviet Press (*CDSP*)
Current News
Defense Electronics
Far Eastern Affairs
Far Eastern Economic Review
Foreign Broadcast Information Service (*FBIS*): *USSR Daily Report*
Foreign Trade of the USSR
International Affairs (Moscow)

International Defence Review
International Organisation
Jane's Defence Weekly
Japanese Annual of International Law
Japanese Economic Studies
Journal of North East Asian Studies
Journal of Strategic Studies
Orbis
Pacific Defence Reporter
Petroleum Economist
Problems of Communism
Problems of Economics
Proceedings US Naval Institute
Radio Free Europe – Radio Liberty Research
Royal United Services Institute Journal (RUSI Journal)
Slavic Studies
Soviet Analyst
Soviet Geography
Soviet Law and Government
Summary of World Broadcasts (BBC)
Survival
USSR and the Third World
World Politics

INDEX

For EU product safety concerns, contact us at Calle de José Abascal, 56–1°,
28003 Madrid, Spain or eugpsr@cambridge.org.

 www.ingramcontent.com/pod-product-compliance
Ingram Content Group UK Ltd.
Pitfield, Milton Keynes, MK11 3LW, UK
UKHW010040140625
459647UK00012BA/1502